Consolidated Financial Sta
A Step-by-step Approach

2nd Edition

Consolidated Financial Statements:
A Step-by-step Approach

2nd Edition

Paul Mahony
and
Niall MacLochlainn

Chartered
Accountants
Ireland

Published in 2013 by
Chartered Accountants Ireland
Chartered Accountants House
47–49 Pearse Street
Dublin 2
www.charteredaccountants.ie

ISBN: 978-1-908199-47-8

Typeset by Datapage
Printed by CPI Group (UK) Ltd, Croydon, CR0 4YY

Contents

Preface

The preparation and the presentation of consolidated financial statements have long been a cause of difficulty for students preparing for examinations in accountancy, both those of the accountancy bodies, such as Chartered Accountants Ireland, as well as those studying for third-level qualifications involving financial or corporate reporting.

With over 30 years' experience as lecturers in corporate reporting, we set out to write a step-by-step guide that would remove the mystery from 'consolidation'. We wanted to design a user-friendly text for students and lecturers alike.

This textbook covers:
1. The regulatory, legal and economic requirements for consolidated financial statements.
2. The preparation and presentation of a consolidated statement of financial position (SoFP) incorporating a subsidiary, an associate, a joint venture and a trade (simple) investment and including 'complications', such as intragroup balances, unrealised profits on intragroup transactions and intragroup dividends (IASs 1 and 28 and IFRSs 3, 10, 11 and 12).
3. The preparation and presentation of a consolidated statement of profit or loss and other comprehensive income (SPLOCI) and a consolidated statement of changes in equity (SoCIE), again incorporating a subsidiary, an associate, a joint venture and a trade (simple) investment, and including 'complications' (IASs 1 and 28 and IFRSs 3, 10, 11 and 12).
4. IFRS 3 *Business Combinations*, which has as its objective "to improve the relevance, reliability and comparability of the information that a reporting entity provides in its financial statements about a business combination and its effects".
5. The treatment of a foreign operation in consolidated financial statements (IAS 21).
6. The preparation and presentation of a consolidated statement of cash flows (IAS 7).
7. The disposal of a subsidiary or shares in a subsidiary by a parent (IFRS 10).

We believe that the approach in this book is unique in that, for every example and question involving the preparation of a consolidated SoFP, workings are presented using both:
• the traditional **T account method**; and
• the **columnar method**, which is now used by many lecturers.

As stated in the text, both methods result in identical consolidated statements of financial position.

We would like to express our thanks to Barry Smith for his suggestions and professional advice.

We have always advised students to study alternative texts as another author's approach and focus can only assist the learning process. In this regard, we can confidently refer you to the relevant chapters of *International Financial Accounting and Reporting* (4th Edition) by Ciaran Connolly (Chartered Accountants Ireland, 2013).

When you have finished studying *Consolidated Financial Statements: A Step-by-step Approach* (2nd Edition), we are confident that you will be more than adequately prepared to sit your examinations in 'consolidation' and that we will have realised our goal of making the subject more approachable and understandable.

(*Note:* this text adopts the principles and practices of the relevant IAS/IFRS extant at the time of writing.)

Paul Mahony, FCA, FCPA, MBS

Niall MacLochlainn, B.Comm, FCA

Abbreviations

The following abbreviations are used throughout this text in order to help with presentation and clarity:

A Ltd	associate
Bal. Fig.	balancing figure
IAS	international accounting standard(s)
IFRS	international financial reporting standard (s)
Jnl.	journal entry
JV	joint venture
S Ltd	subsidiary/subsidiary company
SoCIE	statement of changes in equity
SoCF	statement of cash flows
SoFP	statement of financial position
SPLOCI	statement of profit or loss and other comprehensive income
SPLOCI – OCI	statement of profit or loss and other comprehensive income – other comprehensive income section
SPLOCI – P/L	statement of profit or loss and other comprehensive income – profit or loss section
NCI	non-controlling interests
OCI	other comprehensive income
P Ltd	parent/parent company
Post-acq.	post-acquisition
TCI	total comprehensive income
y/e	year ended

Chapter 1

Why Consolidate Financial Statements?

LEARNING OBJECTIVES

After reading this chapter you should be able to:
- explain why entities engage in business combinations;
- identify the legal and regulatory requirements to prepare consolidated financial statements; and
- demonstrate an understanding of the need for consolidated financial statements.

Introduction

Terms such as 'takeovers', 'acquisitions', 'mergers' and 'amalgamations' have traditionally been used to describe situations where two or more businesses come together. The term '**business combinations**' is now the most appropriate term to summarise all the above.

A business combination is deemed to occur where the assets acquired and the liabilities assumed constitute a business. If the assets acquired are not a business, the transaction is deemed to be an asset acquisition (IFRS 3 *Business Combinations*).

Business combinations occur for many reasons such as synergies, economies of scale, taxation advantages, risk diversification, increased efficiencies, elimination of competition, etc., and can be achieved by two usual methods:

1. **Acquisition of Net Assets** This is where *all* of the **assets** of the acquired entity are purchased and its **liabilities** assumed, i.e. the net assets are acquired (a national supermarket chain might use this method, for example, to acquire a local franchise in order to increase market share);
2. **Acquisition of Shares** This is where the **shares** of the acquired entity are purchased.

These two methods are quite different in substance and therefore give rise to **different accounting treatments** (post-acquisition) in the financial statements of the acquiring entity.

Now, let us take two entities, Apple Ltd and Banana Ltd, to illustrate the alternative approaches to business combinations.

Method 1: Acquisition of Net Assets

Apple Ltd can carry out the acquisition of Banana Ltd with one of two approaches:

(a) Apple Ltd acquires the net assets of Banana Ltd. Banana Ltd goes out of existence and subsequently the statement of financial position of Apple Ltd contains the combined net assets of both entities.

(b) A new entity Banap Ltd could be formed to acquire the net assets of both Apple Ltd and Banana Ltd. In this case, both of the previous entities would be liquidated and the statement of financial position of Banap Ltd would then show the combined net assets.

> *Key Note:* The significant feature of the above examples is that a group is *not* formed in either case and, therefore, the requirement to prepare consolidated financial statements does *not* arise.

Method 2: Acquisition of Shares

Apple Ltd could acquire the share capital of Banana using one of two approaches:

(a) Apple Ltd could acquire all the issued share capital of Banana Ltd. Apple Ltd would now be a *parent* and Banana Ltd its *subsidiary*. Both entities would continue to exist and would prepare their individual financial statements after the business combination.

(b) A new entity Banap Ltd could be formed to acquire all the issued share capital of both Apple Ltd and Banana Ltd. After the acquisition there would be three entities in existence: Banap Ltd would be the parent; and both Apple Ltd and Banana Ltd would be its subsidiaries.

> *Key Note:* Each of these examples gives rise to the formation of a **group**, as the parent now owns all of the share capital of the subsidiaries and controls their activities. **There is now both a legal and regulatory requirement, as well as an economic need, to prepare consolidated financial statements.**

IFRS 3 *Business Combinations*

IFRS 3 *Business Combinations* defines a '**business**' as "an integrated set of activities and assets that is capable of being conducted and managed for the purpose of providing a return in the form of dividends, lower costs or other economic benefits directly to investors or other owners, members or participants."

A '**business combination**' is defined as "a transaction or other event in which an acquirer obtains control of one or more businesses."

A business consists of inputs, e.g. non-current assets, intellectual property, employees, etc., and processes applied to those inputs, e.g. strategic management processes, operational processes, etc., that have an ability to create outputs that can generally be either sold or exchanged and provide a return. The nature of the elements of a business varies by industry and by the structure of an entity's operations. An established business may have many different types of inputs, processes and outputs, while a new business often has few inputs and processes and only one or two outputs. Though nearly all businesses have liabilities, this need not necessarily be the case.

IFRS 3 (the subject of **Chapter 3**) determines that all business combinations within its scope should be accounted for using the **acquisition method**, which looks at a business combination from the perspective of the acquirer. Fair values are a key aspect of the acquisition method of accounting. The standard also deals with the calculation and treatment of goodwill.

Definition of a 'Group'

IFRS 10 *Consolidated Financial Statements* defines a **group** as "a parent and its subsidiaries" (Appendix A).

Requirements to Prepare Consolidated Financial Statements

Both international accounting standards (IFRS) and EU company law require the presentation of consolidated financial statements when a group exists. As stated above, a **group** is deemed to exist where a parent acquires one or more subsidiaries.

The International Accounting Standards Framework

IFRS 10 *Consolidated Financial Statements* states the following (at para 4):
1. an entity that is a parent shall present consolidated financial statements; *and*
2. consolidated financial statements must include all subsidiaries of the parent.

Note, however, that IFRS 10, paragraph 4(a), permits **exemptions** from this requirement *principally* when:
 (a) the parent is itself a wholly-owned subsidiary;
 (b) the parent's debt or equity instruments are not traded in a public market;
 (c) the parent did not file nor is in the process of filing its financial statements with a securities commission or other regulatory organisation for the purpose of issuing any class of instruments in the public market;
 (d) the ultimate or any intermediate parent produces consolidated financial statements available for public use that comply with IFRS; and
 (e) the parent is an investment entity which measures all its subsidiaries at fair value through profit or loss.

The Legal Framework

In addition to preparing their own financial statements, parent undertakings are required to prepare consolidated group accounts and to lay them before their annual general meetings (AGMs) at the same time as their individual financial statements.

In Ireland, the requirement to prepare group accounts (i.e. consolidated financial statements) is contained in regulation 5 of the European Communities (Companies: Group Accounts) Regulations 1992 (S.I. No. 201 of 1992) (the 'GAR 1992'), which states that:

> "At the end of its financial year a parent undertaking shall prepare group accounts in accordance with these Regulations and such accounts shall be laid before the annual general meeting at the same time as the undertaking's annual accounts are so laid."

Note, however, **exemption** from this requirement is contained in regulation 7 of the GAR 1992 where the parent is a private company and certain financial and size constraints are not exceeded.

The Economic Need to Prepare Consolidated Financial Statements

Even if there were no legal or regulatory requirements to prepare group financial statements, business and economic needs would demand them. In essence, both the international accountancy standards and EU law recognise these needs. This is because the financial statements of a parent alone would not give a complete account of the parent's economic activities or financial position as its statement of financial position merely reflects the cost of its investment in the subsidiary. The various users of a parent's financial statements (particularly the shareholders) would require further information about, for example, the:

- financial results for the period in question;
- financial position at the reporting date;
- cash flows for the period; and
- changes in financial position;

of the group as a whole.

Consolidated financial statements provide such information because they contain information about the results and financial position of a group **as if it were a single entity**.

Key Note: The concept behind the phrase '**as if it were a single entity**' is extremely important, as you will realise when you study **Chapters 4** and **5**.

In this chapter, we have identified the statutory and regulatory requirements for the presentation of consolidated financial statements as well as the economic and business needs for these.

Once an investing entity acquires an interest, i.e. makes an investment, in another entity, this will bring about accounting requirements. In the next chapter, we will discuss the different levels of influence that an investor can achieve and the consequential accounting treatment appropriate to each type of investment.

SUMMARY

- Business combinations can be achieved either by one entity acquiring the net assets of another or by acquiring the shares of the acquired entity.
- If a parent acquires a subsidiary, a *group* is formed.
- The formation of a group brings accounting responsibilities both under IFRS and EU law to present consolidated financial statements.
- The requirements to present consolidated financial statements are in essence recognising the economic needs of the shareholders and other stakeholders of the parent to receive information about the parent's investment in a subsidiary or subsidiaries.

QUESTIONS

Question 1.1

Describe the usual ways in which a business combination can be achieved.

Solution

A business combination can be achieved by either:
(a) the investing entity acquiring the net assets of another entity; or
(b) the investing entity acquiring the shares of another entity.

Question 1.2

When is a group formed?

Solution

A group is formed when a parent acquires a subsidiary or subsidiaries.

Question 1.3

Explain the IFRS and EU law consequences of the formation of a group.

Solution

IFRS 10 and EU law both require a parent with a subsidiary or subsidiaries to prepare and present consolidated financial statements. All subsidiaries must be consolidated under the requirements of IFRS 10.

Question 1.4

Explain the need for consolidated financial statements.

Solution

The need for consolidated financial statements arises from the fact that financial statements of the parent alone would not give an adequate account of its economic activities or financial position. Consolidated financial statements are prepared so as to present the results and financial position of a group as if it were a single entity.

Chapter 2

Accounting for Investments

LEARNING OBJECTIVES

After reading this chapter you should be able to:
- Understand four differing degrees of influence that an investor can get over the relevant activities and policies of an investee.
- Set out the required accounting treatment for each degree of influence.

Introduction

This chapter will provide you with the first crucial steps on the road to understanding and applying the principles and techniques for the preparation of consolidated financial statements. Indeed, this chapter is a roadmap for the rest of this book.

> **Beware!** When sitting examinations in financial accounting and corporate reporting, you must be able to clearly identify the nature of the relationship between the investor and the investee in order to be able to apply the correct international financial reporting standard. If you cannot do this, you will lose a significant amount of the marks allocated to the question.

When an investing entity decides to purchase an investment in another entity using the acquisition of shares method (see **Chapter 1**), the relationship between the investor and investee determines:
(a) the level of influence that the investor can exercise over the policies of the investee; and
(b) the accounting treatment which applies to the investment under international financial reporting standards (IFRS), in the financial statements of the investor.

Investments in other entities can give rise to influence over the **relevant activities and financial policies** of the investee, ranging from control to limited influence.

The proportion of voting shares purchased in another entity is frequently the principal determining factor in the amount of influence the investor may have. The 'operating and financial policies' of an entity usually include the following:

- dividend policy (of course, this will be crucial for the investor to control);
- raising of finance;
- strategic direction;
- approval of business plans and budgets;
- approving capital expenditure.

In this chapter, we will examine **four differing degrees of influence** recognised by IFRS that an investor could acquire in another entity and the relevant accounting treatment in each case.

The size of the holding acquired by an investor in an investee is usually the determining factor in the application of IFRS. However, there are other factors which must also be considered. There are four important types of investees:
1. Subsidiary
2. Associate
3. Joint Venture
4. Trade (or Simple) Investment

These are summarised as follows:

1. Subsidiary

ACCOUNTING STANDARDS: IFRS 10 *Consolidated Financial Statements*
IFRS 3 *Business Combinations*

KEYWORD: 'Control'

Definition of a 'Subsidiary'

IFRS 10 *Consolidated Financial Statements* defines a subsidiary as "an entity that is controlled by another entity".

'Control'

An investor **controls** an investee when the investor is exposed, or has rights, to variable returns from its involvement with the investee and has the ability to affect those returns through its power over the investee.

To determine whether it controls an investee an investor shall assess whether it has the following:
(a) **Power** over the investee. The investor must have existing rights that give it the current ability to direct the relevant activities. Examples of relevant activities are:
  - selling and purchasing of goods and services;
  - managing financial assets;
  - selecting, acquiring or disposing of assets;

- research and development;
- obtaining funding.

Power arises from rights. An investor must have existing rights that give a current ability to direct the relevant rights. Examples of rights include: voting rights or potential voting rights, i.e. rights to obtain voting rights of an investee, such as those arising from convertible instruments or options, including forward contracts. Potential rights are only considered when they are substantive, i.e. the holder must have the practical ability to exercise the rights.

(b) **Exposure or rights to variable returns** from its involvement with the investee. Variable returns are returns that are not fixed and have the potential to vary as a result of the performance of the investee. Examples of returns are:
- dividends, other distributions of economic benefits, e.g. interest from debt securities issued by the investee;
- remuneration from servicing an investee's assets or liabilities, fees and exposure to loss from providing credit or liquidity support;
- returns that are not available to other interest holders.

(c) **The ability to use its power** over the investee to affect the amount of the investor's returns. An investor with decision-making rights must determine whether it is a principal or agent. An investor that is an agent does not control an investee when it exercises decision-making rights delegated to it.

Key Note:
1. **Straightforward cases** In many instances decision-making is dictated by **voting rights**. In these cases the entity that holds a majority (over 50%) of the voting rights controls the investee;
2. **Other instances** The evidence of control is not immediately clear, e.g. where the investor holds less than a majority of voting rights, where there are potential rights or in the case of structured entities. **Structured entities** are defined in IFRS 12 as "entities that are so designed so that voting or similar rights are not the dominant factor in deciding who controls an entity, such as when any voting rights relate to administrative tasks only and the relevant activities are directed by means of contractual arrangements."

In any non-standard case, the three criteria above must be applied to establish whether control exists. The following questions must be addressed:
- Is there power over the investee?
- Is there exposure or rights to variable returns from its involvement with the investee?
- Is there the ability to use power over the investee to affect the amount of the investor's return?

Examples of Different Levels of Investment

EXAMPLE 2.1:
Where Park Ltd acquires more than 50% of the voting rights of an Entity (Stop Ltd) and decision-making is dictated by voting rights

On 1 July 2013, Park Ltd acquired 240,000 of the ordinary shares of Stop Ltd. At that date Stop Ltd had 300,000 ordinary shares in issue. Park Ltd has acquired an 80% holding.

Park Ltd (the parent), acquires a *subsidiary* (Stop Ltd) because it has acquired more than **50%** of the voting shares and decision-making is dictated by voting rights. A group has been formed. Park Ltd has **control** over the operating and financial policies of Stop Ltd so as to obtain benefits from its activities. Significantly, this includes control over the dividend policy of Stop Ltd.

EXAMPLE 2.2:
Where Pepper Ltd acquires 50% of the voting rights of an Entity (Salt Ltd)

Pepper Ltd acquired **50%** of the ordinary shares of Salt Ltd on 1 March 2013. Salt Ltd has 10 directors, five of whom are appointed by Pepper Ltd, one of whom is always chairman with a casting vote. Pepper Ltd has **control over the board of directors and therefore over the policies of Salt Ltd**. Salt Ltd is a *subsidiary* of Pepper Ltd.

EXAMPLE 2.3:
Where Patch Ltd acquires a dominant percentage of voting rights in an Entity (Stitch Ltd) but which is less than a majority.

Patch Ltd acquired 48% of the voting rights of Stitch Ltd. The remaining voting rights are held by thousands of shareholders, none of whom own more than 1% of the voting rights. None of the shareholders has any arrangements to consult any of the others or make collective decisions. **The major investor concludes that it has a sufficiently dominant voting interest to give it control.**

EXAMPLE 2.4:
Where Pop Ltd is a major shareholder in Shop Ltd but is not in a position to direct the relevant activities.

Pop Ltd owns 35% of the voting rights of Shop Ltd. Three other shareholders each own 5% of the voting rights of Shop Ltd while the remaining shares are held by numerous shareholders, none of whom hold more than 1% of the voting rights.

None of the shareholders has arrangements with any of the others or make collective decisions. A majority of votes cast is necessary concerning decisions about the relevant activities while 75% of the voting rights of Shop Ltd have been cast at recent relevant shareholders' meetings. **The active participation of the other shareholders at recent shareholders' meetings indicates that Pop Ltd would not have the practical ability to direct the relevant activities and therefore does not control Shop Ltd.**

Accounting Treatment for Subsidiaries

A subsidiary is accounted for using **full consolidation** (see **Chapter 4**, "The Consolidated Statement of Financial Position" (SoFP) and **Chapter 8**, "The Statement of Profit or Loss and Other Comprehensive Income and Statement of Change in Equity" (SPLOCI and SoCIE), where full consolidation is comprehensively demonstrated). Full consolidation is a method of accounting that produces a statement of financial position (SoFP) similar to the SoFP that would be produced if the parent had acquired the net assets of the subsidiary rather than a majority of its voting shares (as discussed as '**Method 1**' in **Chapter 1**) Under full consolidation, each asset, liability, income and expense of a subsidiary is consolidated with those of the parent.

2. Associate

ACCOUNTING STANDARD: IAS 28 *Investments in Associates and Joint Ventures*

KEYWORDS: 'Significant Influence'

Definition of Associate

IAS 28 *Investments in Associates and Joint Ventures* defines an **associate** as an "entity over which the investor has **significant influence**."

Definition of Significant Influence

Significant influence is the "power to participate in the financial and operating policy decisions of the investee but is **not** control or joint control of those policies".

If an entity holds directly or indirectly (e.g. through subsidiaries) 20% or more of the voting power of the investee, it is presumed that the entity has significant influence, unless this presumption can be rebutted. Conversely, less than 20% of the voting power does not give significant influence, unless such influence can be clearly demonstrated. The existence of significant influence by an investor is best evidenced by representation on the board of directors of the investee.

EXAMPLE 2.5:
Where Pear Ltd acquires between 20% and 50% of the voting power of an entity (Apple Ltd)

On 1 January 2013 Pear Ltd acquired 80,000 of the 200,000 ordinary shares in issue by Apple Ltd. Pear Ltd has now acquired an *associate* (because it has purchased between 20% and 50% of the voting shares). The leverage is reduced from control in the case of a subsidiary (see **Subsidiary** above) to **significant influence** over an associate, meaning the power **to participate** in the operating and financial policies (including dividend policy) of Apple, but not to control them.

Accounting Treatment for Associates

An associate is accounted for in consolidated financial statements using the **equity method** (see **Chapter 6** (SoFP) and **Chapter 8** (SPLOCI/SoCIE). Under this method the investment in an associate is initially recorded at cost and adjusted thereafter by the post-acquisition change in the investor's share of the net assets of the investee. The investor's profit or loss includes its share of the associate's profit or loss, and the investor's other comprehensive income includes its share of the associate's other comprehensive income.

Note: an investor without a subsidiary would still have to use equity accounting for an investment in an associate.

3. Joint Venture

ACCOUNTING STANDARDS: IAS 28 *INVESTMENTS IN ASSOCIATES* AND *JOINT VENTURES*
IFRS 11 *JOINT ARRANGEMENTS*

KEYWORDS: 'Joint Control'

Definition of Joint Venture

IAS 28 *Investments in Associates and Joint Ventures* defines a **joint venture** as "a joint arrangement whereby the parties that have joint control of the arrangement have rights to the net assets of the arrangement" (para 3).

Definition of 'Joint Control'

Joint control "is the contractually agreed sharing of control of an arrangement, which exists only when decisions about the relevant activities require the unanimous consent of the parties sharing control" (para 3).

EXAMPLE 2.6: ACQUISITION OF AN INTEREST IN A JOINT VENTURE
where an investor Paint Ltd acquires an interest in another entity so
that Paint Ltd and another venturer jointly control that entity

On 1 March 2013 Paint Ltd and Cement Ltd, entities that are not related, acquire 50%
each of the ordinary shares of Grass Ltd and will jointly control the arrangement.

Accounting Treatment for Joint Ventures

A joint venture is accounted for in consolidated financial statements using **the equity method
(as in the case of an associate)** (see **Chapter 7** (SoFP) **and Chapter 8** (SPLOCI/SoCIE).

Note: an investor without a subsidiary would still have to use equity accounting for an investment in a joint venture.

4. Trade (or Simple) Investment

Definition of Trade (or Simple) Investment

A trade (or simple) investment arises where an investor acquires less than 20% of the
voting rights of the investee and the investment cannot be deemed to give rise to significant influence.

ACCOUNTING STANDARD: IFRS 9 *Financial Instruments*
IAS 39 *Financial Instruments Recognition and Measurement*[1]

KEYWORDS: 'Little or No Influence'

EXAMPLE 2.7: ACQUISITION OF A TRADE INVESTMENT
where Pot Ltd acquires less than 20% of the shares of an entity, Kettle Ltd

On 1 May 2013 Pot Ltd acquired 15% of the ordinary shares of Kettle Ltd as part of
its investment strategy.

This is termed a *trade* (or *simple*) investment, which probably gives Pot Ltd **little or
no influence** over the operating and financial policies of the investee Kettle Ltd.

Accounting Treatment for Trade Investments

The investment is recorded at **fair value**. Such an investment is the subject of IAS 39/
IFRS 9, details of which are outside the scope of this text. However, it is important to

---

[1] See Chapter 25, "Financial Instruments" of *International Financial Accounting and Reporting*
by Ciaran Connolly (4th Edition, Chartered Accountants Ireland, 2013) ('**Connolly**').

note that the investment is carried to the consolidated SoFP. Any dividends received, as well as gains and losses on changes to fair value, will be recognised in the consolidated SPLOCI – P/L.

Note: some trade investments will be designated on acquisition as "not held for trading". In such cases, gains and losses on changes to fair value will be taken directly to OCI.

IFRS 12 Disclosure of Interests in Other Entities

Because of the different accounting treatments for the various degrees of influence attained, the investor must disclose the significant judgements and assumptions it has made in determining that the investee is:
- a subsidiary;
- an associate;
- a joint venture/joint operation; and
- a trade investment.

This information should enable the users to understand for example:
(a) the composition of the group;
(b) the effect of non-controlling interests;
(c) the effect of an acquisition or disposal of an investee during the reporting period.

Where there are joint arrangements or associates the investor must set out the contractual arrangements with other investors, and the nature, extent and financial effects.

Conclusion

The contents of this chapter enable you to differentiate between:
1. investments in subsidiaries
2. investments in associates
3. investments in joint ventures; and
4. trade investments.

You should now be able to relate each type of investment to the appropriate international financial reporting standard and the correct accounting treatment. **Chapters 4 to 9** will comprehensively explain how to consolidate a parent, a subsidiary, an associate and a joint venture, as well as how to account for a trade investment.

Recommended Reading

The authors advise students to read alternative texts, as the opinions and methods of others can only help to develop a greater understanding of all topics. To this end and in the context of this chapter, it is recommended that you also read Chapter 26, "Business Combinations and Consolidated Financial Statements", of *International Financial Accounting and Reporting* (4th Edition) by Ciaran Connolly.

SUMMARY

An investor acquires:

1. A **subsidiary**, if the parent gains control over its relevant activities. The parent can **control** the operating and financial policies of the subsidiary. **Full consolidation** is the required accounting treatment for a subsidiary in consolidated financial statements.
2. An **associate**, if between 20% and 50% of the voting shares are purchased (unless rebutted). In this case, the investor can exercise **significant influence** over the policies of the investee and the investment is accounted for in consolidated financial statements using the **equity method**.
3. A **joint venture**, if the investor and another entity jointly control a joint arrangement and have rights to the net assets of the arrangement. Jointly controlled entities are accounted for using **the equity method**.
4. A **trade** or **simple investment**, if less than 20% of the voting shares of the investee are purchased (unless significant influence can be proven). The investment is accounted for under IAS 39/IFRS 9. The investor accounts for dividends received/receivable from the investee. The investor must also account for movements in the fair value of the investment.

QUESTIONS

Question 2.1

The following is the summarised statement of financial position of Red Ltd as at 31 August 2013:

	€000
Sundry net assets	5,700
Ordinary share capital (€1)	2,000
Share premium	1,000
Retained earnings	2,700
	5,700

Requirement:

1. Explain the relationship between Black Ltd and Red Ltd in each of the following cases:
   (a) Black Ltd acquires 800,000 of the ordinary shares of Red Ltd.
   (b) Black Ltd acquires 1,500,000 of the ordinary shares of Red Ltd and decision-making is dictated by voting rights.
   (c) Black Ltd acquires 200,000 of the ordinary shares of Red Ltd.
   (d) Black Ltd and Cloud Ltd each acquire 1,000,000 of the ordinary shares of Red Ltd and will exercise joint control over the arrangement.

2. Give both:
   (a) The level of influence which Black Ltd can exercise over the relevant activities and policies of Red Ltd as a consequence of each of the four investments in question 1; and
   (b) the accounting treatment for each investment.

Solution

1. (a) Black Ltd acquired a 40% holding in the ordinary shares of Red Ltd (800,000/2,000,000), therefore, Red Ltd is an associate of Black Ltd.
   (b) Black Ltd acquired 1,500,000/2,000,000 or 75% of the voting shares of Red Ltd and decision-making is dictated by voting rights. Red Ltd would be a subsidiary of Black Ltd.
   (c) This investment would be regarded as a simple or trade investment as Black Ltd acquired 10% of the ordinary shares of Red Ltd.
   (d) Red Ltd would be a joint venture of Black Ltd and Cloud Ltd.

2. (a)
   (i)   Black Ltd would be able to exercise **significant influence** over the policies of Red Ltd.
   (ii) Black Ltd could **control** the policies of Red Ltd.
   (iii) Black Ltd would have **little or no influence** over the policies of Red Ltd.
   (iv) Black Ltd and Cloud Ltd could exercise **joint control** over the arrangement.

   (b)
   (i)   The equity method.
   (ii) Full consolidation.
   (iii) Account for the investment under IFRS 9/IAS 39, i.e. dividends received/receivable and also movements in fair value.
   (iv) The equity method.

Chapter 3

IFRS 3 *Business Combinations*

LEARNING OBJECTIVES

After reading this chapter you should be able to:
- give the appropriate accounting treatment for business combinations and explain how this accounting treatment is applied;
- explain how the component parts of the purchase consideration should be valued;
- give guidance on which assets and liabilities of the subsidiary should be recognised in the consolidated statement of financial position and how they should be valued;
- demonstrate an understanding of how goodwill is calculated and discuss a gain from a bargain purchase; and
- explain how goodwill can be attributable to non-controlling interests.

Introduction

IFRS 3 *Business Combinations* could be aptly called the 'Umbrella Standard' for the preparation of consolidated financial statements of a parent and a subsidiary. IFRS 3 states that a transaction or other event is a business combination if the assets acquired and the liabilities assumed constitute a business. If the assets acquired are not a business, the reporting entity must account for the transaction or other event as an asset acquisition.

IFRS 3 defines a business combination as a transaction or other event in which an acquirer obtains control over one or more businesses. An acquirer might gain control of an acquiree in many ways such as:
- transferring cash, cash equivalents or other assets;
- incurring liabilities;
- issuing equity interests;
- providing more than one type of consideration.

IFRS 3 includes the method for calculating goodwill or a gain from a bargain purchase and contains the principles for valuing each component part used in the calculation. The standard informs us how to:
- value the investment in a subsidiary;
- value the net assets of the subsidiary at the date of acquisition;
- identify which net assets should be included in the calculation;
- measure the non-controlling interests in the net assets of a subsidiary at the date of acquisition.

The objective of IFRS 3 is to improve the relevance, reliability and comparability of the information that a reporting entity provides in its financial statements about business combinations and their effects.

IFRS 3 details how the acquirer:

1. recognises and measures in its financial statements *the identifiable assets* acquired, the liabilities assumed and any *non-controlling interests* in the *acquiree;*
2. recognises and measures any *goodwill* acquired or a *gain from a bargain purchase;*
3. determines the information to be disclosed to enable the users of its financial statements to evaluate the nature and financial effects of a business combination.

Accounting Treatment for Business Combinations (the Acquisition Method)

IFRS 3 states that all business combinations shall be accounted for using the acquisition method.

There are five steps involved in applying the acquisition method (IFRS 3, para 5):

Step 1 Identify the acquirer
Step 2 Determine the acquisition date
Step 3 Ascertain the identifiable assets and liabilities of the entity being acquired, and determine how these assets and liabilities are to be measured
Step 4 Determine the non-controlling interests in the subsidiary and the attributable valuation
Step 5 Calculate the amount of goodwill or gain from a bargain purchase.

Step 1: Identify the Acquirer

The acquirer is the entity that obtains control over the other combining entity. An investor controls an investee when the investor is exposed, or has rights, to variable returns from its involvement with the investee and has the ability to affect those returns through its powers over the investee. In **Chapter 2** it was explained that control is normally achieved when a parent acquires more than half of the voting power of a subsidiary. However, control can also exist, under IFRS 10 *Consolidated Financial Statements,* where an acquirer owns less than 50% of the voting power of an entity but other conditions are met which give the acquirer control over the acquiree.

Step 2: Determine the Acquisition Date

The acquisition date is the date on which the acquirer gets **control** over the subsidiary. This is generally the date on which the acquirer legally transfers the consideration, acquires the assets and assumes the liabilities of the acquiree.

Step 3: Assets Acquired and Liabilities Assumed: Recognition and Measurement

The acquirer must recognise the identifiable assets acquired and the liabilities assumed at the acquisition date. To qualify for recognition, the identifiable assets acquired and liabilities assumed must meet the definitions of assets and liabilities in the International Accounting Standards Board's (IASB) *Conceptual Framework for Financial Reporting 2010*[1] i.e.:

Asset   A resource controlled by an entity as a result of past events and from which future economic benefits are expected to flow to the entity.

Liability A present obligation of the entity arising from past events, the settlement of which is expected to result in an outflow from the entity of economic benefits.

Recognising Contingent Liabilities The acquirer should recognise, as of the date of acquisition, any contingent liability assumed in a business combination if it is a present obligation that arises from past events and its fair value can be measured reliably.

Valuing the Assets Acquired and Liabilities Assumed The identifiable assets acquired and all liabilities assumed should be measured at their **fair values,** i.e. the price that would be received to sell an asset or paid to transfer a liability in an orderly transaction between market participants at the measurement date (IFRS 13).

Step 4: Non-controlling Interests (NCI)

Definition: 'non-controlling interests' is "equity in a subsidiary not attributable, directly or indirectly, to a parent" (IFRS 10 *Consolidated Financial Statements*, Appendix A).

Non-controlling interests at the date of acquisition were traditionally measured as follows:

Net assets (share capital plus reserves) of subsidiary × Non-controlling interests %

Note: Share Capital and Reserves of S Ltd = Net Assets of S Ltd, which are valued at fair value.

This could be called the 'Proportion of Net Assets Method'.

IFRS 3 also permits the **non-controlling interests** in the net assets of the subsidiary at the date of acquisition to be valued at fair value, which would impact on the value of goodwill and NCI, and which is dealt with later in this chapter.

This could be called the 'Fair Value Method'.

Purchase Consideration The amount of the purchase consideration is a major component in the calculation of goodwill. The valuation of the purchase consideration may not always be self-evident or straightforward as a purchase consideration can have many components, e.g. an issue of shares, a cash payment, a transfer of an asset, deferred consideration and contingent consideration. There is, however, one over-riding principle: all elements of the purchase consideration should be valued at fair value as at the date of acquisition, e.g.:
- shares issued – valued at **market value;**
- cash paid – valued at the **actual** amount;
- deferred consideration – valued at the **present value** of the future payment.

---

[1] For a complete discussion of the *Conceptual Framework for Financial Reporting*, see **Connolly**, Chapter 1, "Framework for Financial Reporting".

EXAMPLE 3.1: CALCULATION OF PURCHASE CONSIDERATION

Pat Plc acquired 90% of the ordinary shares of Susan Ltd on 1 September 2012 for the following consideration:
(a) the issue of two million €1 ordinary shares at market value €1.80;
(b) an immediate cash payment of €200,000; and
(c) a cash payment of €500,000, three years after the date of the acquisition.

Pat Plc can borrow funds at 10%.

Journal entry to record the purchase consideration in the financial statements of Pat Plc:

		€000	€000
Dr.	Investment in Susan Ltd	4,175	
Cr.	Ordinary shares		2,000
Cr.	Share premium (€0.80 × 2 million)		1,600
Cr.	Cash		200
Cr.	Deferred consideration		375

The deferred consideration is recorded at present value, at a discount factor of 0.751 (as per generally available present value tables).

The total deferred consideration discount of €125,000 (500 – 375) is unwound over three years and accounted for in the consolidated financial statements in the year ended 31 August 2013 as follows:

		€000	€000
Dr.	Finance costs (SPLOCI – P/L)	37.5	
Cr.	Deferred consideration		37.5
	(€375,000 × 10%)		

Contingent Consideration Contingent consideration is defined as an obligation of the acquirer to transfer additional assets to the former owners of the acquiree as part of the exchange for control of the acquiree if specified future events occur or conditions are met.

If the purchase consideration contains an element of contingent consideration, this must be valued at fair value at the date of acquisition. If the amount of contingent consideration changes as the result of a post-acquisition event, e.g. meeting a profit target, accounting for the changed consideration depends on whether the additional consideration is equity or cash/other asset. Equity instruments are not re-measured: if the additional amount is cash/other asset it is recognised in profit or loss.

If the fair value changes because of new information relating to events at the acquisition date, the cost of acquisition must be re-measured. (See **Examples 3.2(A)** and **3.2(B)**.)

EXAMPLE 3.2(A): PAYMENT IN CASH

Assume that in acquiring Susan Ltd above, Pat Plc had agreed to pay a further €360,000 in cash at the end of five years provided that the cumulative profits of Susan Ltd exceed €4 million. When the probabilities of reaching the target are evaluated the **fair value of the contingent consideration** at the date of acquisition is calculated at €100,000. At the end of Year 1 (31 August 2013), the probability of reaching the target has improved and the fair value is now estimated at €120,000. The additional €20,000 is expensed to profit or loss. This evaluation is carried out at the end of each reporting period and any change to the fair value is taken to profit or loss.

JOURNAL ENTRY in Consolidated Accounts

Dr. SPLOCI – P/L	€20,000	
Cr. Contingent consideration		€20,000

EXAMPLE 3.2(B): PAYMENT IN FIXED NUMBER OF SHARES

Assume that Pat Plc had agreed to give a further 200,000 shares (fair value of €360,000 at acquisition date) at the end of five years provided that the cumulative profits of Susan Ltd exceed €4 million. When the probabilities of reaching the target are evaluated the **fair value of the contingent consideration** at the date of acquisition is calculated at €100,000. The contingent consideration is classed as equity and is not re-measured each year.

Acquisition Costs Incremental costs of acquisition, such as general administration costs, any professional fees, cost of the acquisition department, etc., cannot be included as part of the acquisition costs. All such costs must be expensed to profit or loss as incurred.

Step 5: Calculating Goodwill or a Gain from a Bargain Purchase

Definition of Goodwill An asset representing the future economic benefits arising from other assets acquired in a business combination that are not individually identified and separately recognised.

IFRS 3 defines situations where:
1. the consideration paid (at fair value) plus the value of the non-controlling interests exceeds the net assets (capital plus reserves) acquired, at fair value, as **goodwill**

   and

2. the consideration paid (at fair value) plus the value of the non-controlling interests is less than the net assets acquired (at fair value) as **a gain from a bargain purchase**.

EXAMPLE 3.3: CALCULATION OF GOODWILL

Shrub Ltd
STATEMENT OF FINANCIAL POSITION
as at 31 August 2013

	€000
Property, plant and equipment	4,600
Current assets	2,200
Total assets	6,800
Equity and liabilities	
Equity	
Ordinary shares €1	2,500
Retained earnings	2,600
Total equity	5,100
Current liabilities	1,700
Total equity and liabilities	6,800

Scenario 1:
Petal Plc acquires 80% of the ordinary shares of Shrub Ltd on 31 August 2013 at a cost of €4.8 million. The fair values of the assets and liabilities of Shrub Ltd are the same as their carrying values except for property, plant and equipment, the fair value of which is €5 million.
Non-controlling interests are valued at their proportion of the net assets of Shrub Ltd at acquisition date. (This applies to both Scenarios 1 and 2.)

Scenario 2:
Petal Plc acquires 80% of the ordinary shares of Shrub Ltd at a cost of €3,780,000. The carrying values of all the assets and liabilities of Shrub Ltd are the same as their book values.

Solution – Scenario 1

JOURNAL ENTRY

		€000	€000
1. Dr.	PPE	400	
Cr.	Goodwill		400

Increase in Shrub Ltd PPE to fair value

Goodwill

Debit		Credit	
Investment in Shrub Ltd	4,800	Journal 1 Revaluation	400
NCI (5,500 × 20%)	1,100	Ordinary shares	2,500
		Retained earnings	2,600
			5,500
		Goodwill (SoFP)	400
	5,900		5,900

Non-controlling Interests

Debit		Credit	
SoFP	1,100	Goodwill	1,100

Any impairment of goodwill would not affect the value of the NCI as no goodwill has been attributed to their interests.

WORKINGS (Columnar Method)

	€000	€000
Goodwill (*W1*)		
Investment in Shrub		4,800
NCI at acquisition date (20% × 5,500)		1,100
		5,900
Net assets of Shrub at acquisition date:		
Ordinary shares	2,500	
Retained earnings	2,600	
Revaluation surplus	400	5,500
Goodwill at acquisition date		400
NCI (*W2*)		
Value at acquisition date (*W1*)		1,000

Solution – Scenario 2

Goodwill

Debit		Credit	
Investment in Shrub Ltd	3,780	Ordinary shares	2,500
NCI (20% × 5,100)	1,020	Retained earnings	2,600
Ret. earnings Petal – gain from a bargain purchase	300		
	5,100		5,100

Non-controlling Interests

Debit		Credit	
SoFP	1,020	Goodwill	1,020
	1,020		1,020

WORKINGS (Columnar Method)

Goodwill (W1)

	€000	€000
Investment in Shrub		3,780
NCI at acquisition date (20% × 5,100)		1,020
		4,800
Net assets of Shrub at acquisition date:		
Ordinary shares	2,500	
Retained earnings	2,600	5,100
Retained earnings Petal (gain from bargain purchase)		300
Non-controlling interests (W2)		
Value at acquisition date		1,020

Gain from a Bargain Purchase Before recognising a gain from a bargain purchase, the acquirer must:
(a) **re-assess** whether it has correctly identified all the assets acquired and all the liabilities assumed;
(b) **review** the measurement of the purchase consideration; and
(c) **re-assess** the fair values attributed to the assets acquired and the liabilities assumed.

A bargain purchase might happen, for example, in a business combination that is a forced sale in which the seller is acting under compulsion.

Treatment of a Gain from a Bargain Purchase If the gain remains after steps (a), (b) and (c) above have been carried out, the acquirer should take the gain to profit or loss at the date of acquisition:

JOURNAL ENTRY (FOR SoFP)
    Dr. Goodwill
    Cr. Retained Earnings of P Ltd

Non-controlling Interests and Goodwill Traditionally, goodwill on consolidation was only attributable to the parent company's investment, i.e. if the fair value of the purchase consideration exceeded the group's share of the net assets of the subsidiary at fair value. No goodwill was attributable to the non-controlling interests.

IFRS 3 permits the non-controlling interests in the net assets of subsidiary at the date of acquisition to be measured in two ways:
1. **The 'Traditional Method'** – non-controlling interests at the date of acquisition are measured as follows (this can be titled the Proportion of Net Assets method):

Net assets of subsidiary (at fair value) × Non-controlling Interests %

> ### Or

2. **The Fair Value Method** i.e. the non-controlling interests are measured at fair value. For example, an independent consultant could be employed to determine the fair value of the non-controlling interests at acquisition date.

See **Example 3.4** for the application of both methods.

EXAMPLE 3.4: VALUATION OF NON-CONTROLLING INTERESTS

Recalling **Example 3.3** above, Shrub Ltd (Scenario 1), the non-controlling interest at the date of acquisition was valued using the **proportion of net assets method:**

Non-controlling Interests			
Debit		**Credit**	
SoFP	1,100	Goodwill	1,100
	1,100		1,100

This could alternatively be stated as follows:	**€000**	**€000**
Net assets		
At acquisition date		5,100
Revaluation surplus		400
		5,500
NCI × 20%		1,100

Non-controlling Interests measured under 'The Fair Value Method'

Assume that the directors of Petal Plc engaged an independent consultant who determined that the fair value of the 20% non-controlling interest in Shrub Ltd was €1.2 million at the date of acquisition.

Solution

JOURNAL ENTRIES

		€000	**€000**
1. Dr.	PPE	400	
Cr.	Goodwill		400

Increase in value of Shrub Ltd's property, plant and equipment to fair value

WORKINGS (Columnar Method)

Goodwill (W1)

	Total	Petal	NCI
	€000	€000	€000
Investment in Shrub	4,800	4,800	
Fair value of NCI at acquisition date	1,200		1,200
	6,000	4,800	1200
Net assets of Shrub at acquisition date:			
Ordinary shares	2,500		
Retained earnings	2,600		
Revaluation surplus	400		
	(5,500)	(4,400)	(1,100)
SoFP – goodwill at acquisition date	500	400	100

Note: Any impairment in the above goodwill would be apportioned 80% against group profits and 20% against NCI.

	€000	€000
Non-controlling Interests (W2)		
Fair value at acquisition date (See W1)		1,200

WORKINGS (T Account Method)

Goodwill

Debit		Credit	
Investment in S	4,800	Ordinary shares S	2,500
NCI at fair value	1,200	Retained earnings S	2,600
		Revaluation surplus S	400
		SoFP: Goodwill	500
	6,000		6,000

Non-controlling Interests

Debit		Credit	
		Goodwill: fair value at	
SoFP	1,200	acquisition date	1,200

Conclusion

Having studied this chapter, you should now be able to appreciate how each figure in the calculation of goodwill was valued. Non-controlling interests at acquisition date can be measured using either (a) the proportion of net assets method or (b) the fair value method.

SUMMARY

1. The acquisition method is the only method permitted by IFRS 3 to account for business combinations, i.e. where an acquirer gains control over a subsidiary.
2. All elements of the purchase consideration must be recorded at fair value in the financial statements of the acquirer.
3. The assets and liabilities of a subsidiary must be revalued to fair value for consolidation purposes as at the date of acquisition.
4. The acquirer should recognise, as of the date of acquisition, a contingent liability assumed in a business combination if it is a present obligation that arises from past events and its fair value can be measured reliably.
5. Goodwill arises if the fair value of the consideration to acquire a subsidiary **plus** the value attributed to the non-controlling interests at acquisition date exceeds the fair value of the net assets (capital and reserves) of the subsidiary.
6. A gain from a bargain purchase arises if the fair value of the subsidiary's net assets at acquisition date exceeds the fair value of the purchase consideration plus the value attributed to the non-controlling interests.
7. Traditionally goodwill was only attributable to the acquirer's investment but IFRS 3 permits goodwill to be attributed to the non-controlling interests. This can arise where a fair value is attributed to the non-controlling interests at the acquisition date and this amount is greater than their share of the net assets of the subsidiary at fair value.

QUESTIONS

Question 3.1

What is the recognised method for accounting for business combinations in accordance with IFRS 3?

Solution

The acquisition method should be used to account for business combinations.

Question 3.2

Explain the term 'deferred consideration' and how it is measured as part of a purchase consideration.

Solution

Deferred consideration refers to a known amount payable at a future date. Deferred consideration should be recorded at the present value of the future payment. The discount is unwound in the consolidated financial statements over the period of deferral.

Question 3.3

What is contingent consideration? How is it measured?

Solution

Contingent consideration is an obligation of the acquirer to transfer additional assets to the former owners of the acquiree as part of the exchange for control of the acquiree if specified future events occur or conditions are met. Contingent consideration is measured at fair value as at the date of acquisition.

Question 3.4

Pete Ltd acquired an 80% interest in Sharon Ltd at the following cost:
(a) the issue of 500,000 ordinary €1 shares when the market value of each share was €2.
(b) a cash payment of €300,000 two years later. Pete Ltd can borrow funds at 8%.
(c) a cash payment of €350,000 after three years if Sharon Ltd produces total profits of €280,000 over that period. When the probabilities of reaching the target are evaluated the **fair value** at the date of acquisition is calculated at €120,000.

Requirement Show the entry to record the purchase consideration in the financial statements of Pete Ltd at the date of acquisition.

Solution

Present value of deferred consideration:
    €300,000 × 100/108 × 100/108 = say €257,000

JOURNAL ENTRY

	€	€
Dr. Investment in Sharon	1,377,000	
Cr. Ordinary shares		500,000

Cr. Share premium (500,000 × €1)   500,000
Cr. Non-current liabilities (257,000 + 120,000)   377,000

Question 3.5

Explain how goodwill can be attributed to the non-controlling interests.

Solution

This can occur where a **fair value** is attributed to the non-controlling interests at acquisition date which is **greater** than the NCI share of the **net assets** of the subsidiary (at fair value) at the same date.

> *Note:* the following questions, Questions 3.6 and 3.7, are review-type questions. These questions afford an opportunity to calculate goodwill using (a) the **proportion of net assets method** and (b) **the fair value method** of measuring non-controlling interests at acquisition date and to record a purchase consideration in accordance with IFRS 3.
>
> Each solution contains:
> 1. Journal entries
> 2. The T account method workings
> 3. The columnar method workings

Question 3.6

The following are the statements of financial position of Pilot Plc and its subsidiary Steward Ltd as at 30 September 2013:

	Pilot Plc €000	Steward Ltd €000
Assets		
Non-current assets		
Property, plant and equipment	16,560	13,240
Investment in Steward Ltd	8,300	
Current assets	4,970	3,950
Total assets	**29,830**	**17,190**
Equity and liabilities		
Equity		
Ordinary share capital (€0.50)	10,000	6,000
Retained earnings	15,840	8,030
Total equity	25,840	14,030
Current liabilities	3,990	3,160
Total equity and liabilities	**29,830**	**17,190**

Notes to the Statements of Financial Position:
1. Pilot Plc acquired 9,000,000 ordinary shares (75%) in Steward Ltd on 1 October 2012 when the retained earnings of Steward Ltd were €4,800,000.
2. The non-controlling interests in the net assets of Steward Ltd at the date of acquisition were independently valued at €2,800,000.
3. Goodwill was impaired in the amount of €40,000 for the year ended 30 September 2013.

Requirement:
(a) Calculate the goodwill on acquisition of Steward Ltd. and show the relevant journal entries.
(b) Account for the impairment of €40,000
(c) Calculate the goodwill **on acquisition** of Steward Ltd if the non-controlling interests at the date of acquisition was based on their share of the subsidiary's net assets.

Solution to Question 3.6(a) and 3.6(b)

WORKINGS (Columnar Method)

*(W1) Goodwill using the **Fair Value Method** for the non-controlling interests*

	Total €000	Pilot €000	NCI €000	Jnl.
Investment in Steward	8,300	8,300		1
Fair value of NCI at acquisition date	2,800		2,800	2
	11,100	8,300	2,800	
Net assets of Steward at acquisition date				
Ordinary shares	6,000			3
Retained earnings	4,800			4
	(10,800)	(8,100)	(2,700)	
Goodwill on acquisition	300	200	100	
Impairment (75: 25)	(40)	(30)	(10)	5
SoFP	260	170	90	

JOURNAL ENTRIES (Common to both the T account and the Columnar methods)

	€000	€000
1. Dr. Goodwill	8,300	
Cr. Investment in Steward		8,300
Investment in Steward		
2. Dr. Goodwill	2,800	
Cr. NCI		2,800

Fair value of NCI at acquisition date

3. Dr. Ordinary shares   6,000
   Cr. Goodwill   6,000
   Ordinary shares Steward at acq. date

4. Dr. Retained earnings Steward   4,800
   Cr. Goodwill   4,800
   Retained earnings at acq. date

5. Dr. Retained earnings Pilot   30
   Dr. NCI   10
   Cr. Goodwill   40
   Impairment of goodwill

WORKINGS (T Account Method)

Goodwill

Debit		Credit	
Investment in S (Jnl. 1)	8,300	Ordinary shares (Jnl. 3)	6,000
NCI at fair value (Jnl. 2)	2,800	Retained earnings (Jnl. 4)	4,800
		Impairment (Jnl. 5)	40
		Goodwill (SoFP)	260
	11,100		11,100

The goodwill on acquisition of €300,000 (W1) has been reduced by the impairment amounting to €40,000.

Solution 3.6(c)

NCI at acquisition date is based on their **share of the net assets of Steward**.

WORKINGS (Columnar Method)

(W1) Goodwill

	€000	€000
Investment in Steward		8,300
NCI 25% (6,000 + 4,800)		2,700
		11,000
Net assets of Steward Ltd at acquisition date:		
Ordinary shares	6,000	
Retained earnings	4,800	(10,800)
Goodwill		200

WORKINGS (T Account Method)

Goodwill

Debit		Credit	
Investment in S	8,300	Ordinary shares	6,000
NCI (25% × 10,800)	2,700	Retained earnings	4,800
		Goodwill (SoFP)	200
	11,000		11,000

Question 3.7

Polish Ltd acquired 60% of the ordinary shares of Shine Ltd on 1 September 2013 when the issued share capital of Shine Ltd was €3 million and its retained earnings €1 million. The consideration is as follows:
(a) the issue of one million ordinary €1 shares in Polish Ltd at market value €2.20;
(b) a cash payment of €400,000 on 1 September 2015.

Polish Ltd can borrow funds at 10%.

The non-controlling interests in the net assets of Shine Ltd as at 1 September 2013 is valued at €1,650,000.

Requirement:
(a) Show the journal entry to record the purchase consideration in the financial statements of Polish Ltd at 1 September 2013.
(b) Calculate the following as at 1 September 2013:
  (i) Goodwill
  (ii) Non-controlling interests

Solution to Question 3.7(a)

Journal Entry to Record Purchase Consideration:

		€000	€000
Dr.	Investment in Shine Ltd	2,530	
Cr.	Ordinary shares		1,000
Cr.	Share premium (1m x €1.20)		1,200
Cr.	Non-current liabilities (deferred consideration)		330

Deferred Consideration:
€400,000 × 100/110 × 100/110 say €330,000

Solution to Question 3.7(b)

WORKINGS (Columnar Method)

	Polish €000	Shine €000	NCI €000	Jnl.
Goodwill (W1)				
Investment in Shine	2,530	2,530		1
Fair value of NCI	1,650		1,650	2
	4,180	2,530	1,650	
Net assets of Shine at acq. date:				
Ordinary shares	3,000			3
Retained earnings	1,000			4

	(4,000)	(2,400)	(1,600)
Goodwill	180	130	50

	€000
Non-controlling interest (W2)	
Fair value at acquisition date	1,650

JOURNAL ENTRIES

	€000	€000
1. Dr. Goodwill	2,530	
Cr. Investment in Shine		2,530
Investment in Shine		
2. Dr. Goodwill	1,650	
Cr. NCI		1,650
Fair value of NCI at acquisition date		
3. Dr. Ordinary shares	3,000	
Cr. Goodwill		3,000
Ordinary shares of Shine at acquisition date		
4. Dr. Retained earnings Shine	1,000	
Cr. Goodwill		1,000
Retained earnings of Shine at acquisition date		

WORKINGS (T Account Method)

Goodwill

Debit		Credit	
Investment in Shine (Jnl. 1)	2,530	Ordinary shares (Jnl. 3)	3,000
NCI at fair value (Jnl. 2)	1,650	Retained earnings (Jnl. 4)	1,000
		Goodwill (SoFP)	180
	4,180		4,180

Non-controlling Interests

Debit		Credit	
SoFP	1,650	Goodwill (Jnl. 2)	1,650

Chapter 4

The Consolidated Statement of Financial Position: Accounting for Subsidiaries

LEARNING OBJECTIVES

After reading this chapter you should be able to:
- Understand how a wholly-owned subsidiary is accounted for in the consolidated SoFP;
- Understand the effect of **non-controlling interests** on the consolidated SoFP;
- Account for goodwill in the consolidated SoFP;
- Describe a method for the preparation of a consolidated SoFP;
- Demonstrate an understanding of the consolidation procedures; and
- Complete questions which support the above theory and practice.

Introduction

In order to understand consolidated financial statements, it is generally considered to be more beneficial to first study the preparation of a consolidated statement of financial position (SoFP), as the application of double entry facilitates the understanding of the processes and adjustments involved.

This chapter outlines the preparation of a **basic** consolidated statement of financial position of a parent and subsidiary. Associates, joint ventures and trade investments will be examined in **Chapters 6** and **7**.

Both a parent and its subsidiary prepare their own individual financial statements, i.e. each entity prepares a separate set of accounts reflecting the activity of that entity for a defined period (usually a year) and its SoFP at a specified date. As stated in **Chapter 1**, the requirements to prepare consolidated financial statements are specified by both international accounting standards and EU law. The directors of the parent are responsible for the preparation of these consolidated financial statements. Group companies must use uniform accounting policies for reporting like transactions and other events in similar circumstances. For example, valuation of inventories at the lower of cost and net realisable value (IAS 2 *Inventories*).[1] All group entities should prepare their own financial statements to the same reporting date. However,

---

[1] See Chapter 11, "Inventories", of *International Financial Accounting and Reporting* by Ciaran Connolly (4th Edition, Chartered Accountants Ireland, 2013) ('*Connolly*').

when the end of the reporting period of the parent is different from that of a subsidiary, the subsidiary must prepare additional financial statements as of the same date as the financial statement of the parent, unless it is impracticable to do so (IFRS 10, para B92).

Note: if it is impracticable to do so, the parent must consolidate the financial information of the subsidiary using its most recent financial statements adjusted for the effects of **significant transactions or events** that occurred between the date of the subsidiary's financial statements and the consolidated financial statements (IFRS 10, para B93).

The Cornerstone of Full Consolidation

Where a parent entity has an investment in the share capital of a subsidiary, the non-current asset section of the financial statements of the parent will include an asset termed 'Investment in S Ltd'. However, this will not give the users of those financial statements information about the assets and liabilities of that subsidiary and how they contribute to the net assets of the group as a whole. Consolidated financial statements, on the other hand, present information about a group **as if it were a single entity**. In the consolidated statement of financial position, the investment in S Ltd is replaced by its assets and liabilities. This is the cornerstone of full consolidation, and it bears repeating:

Key Note: when accounting for a subsidiary (S Ltd) in the consolidated SoFP, the investment in S Ltd is **replaced** by **all** its assets and liabilities (net assets). See **Examples 4.1** and **4.2** below.

Goodwill

IFRS 3 (para 32) states that an acquirer must recognise goodwill at the date of acquisition calculated as the excess of (a) over (b) as follows:
(a) The aggregate of:
    (i)   the consideration transferred measured at fair value;
    (ii) the amount of any non-controlling interest in the acquiree;
    (iii) in a business combination achieved in stages, the acquisition-date fair value of the acquirer's previously held equity interest in the acquiree. (*Note: this element does not feature in many questions.*)
(b) The fair value of the net assets of the acquiree.

Note: the calculation of goodwill throughout this textbook follows this format.

As explained in **Chapter 3**, in consolidated financial statements, goodwill can be derived from two sources:

1. **Goodwill attributable to the parent**

   This arises where the cost of the investment in a subsidiary (recorded at fair value) exceeds the group's share of the fair value of the net assets (as represented by share capital and reserves) of the subsidiary. If the reverse applies, there is a gain from a bargain purchase.

2. **Goodwill attributable to the non-controlling interests**

   This arises when the fair value of the non-controlling interests at acquisition date exceeds the non-controlling interests' share of the fair value of the net assets of the subsidiary at acquisition date.

Accounting Treatment: SoFP

(a) Goodwill is recorded as an intangible non-current asset in the consolidated SoFP and only written down when its value becomes impaired.[2] Any impairment is accounted for as follows:

   Dr. Retained earnings (Parent)
   Dr. Non-controlling interests
   Cr. Goodwill

   With the total impairment apportioned according to the ownership interests (group structure) in the subsidiary.

(b) A gain from a bargain purchase (which is recognised through profit or loss immediately) is credited to the retained earnings of the parent.

This chapter again shows you how to calculate goodwill attributable to the parent, goodwill attributable to the non-controlling interests and a gain from a bargain purchase as well as how to account for these items in both the consolidated workings and the consolidated statement of financial position.

Calculation of Goodwill

The goodwill account comprises the following:

1. The debit entries are:
   (a) the cost of the investment in the subsidiary;
   (b) the non-controlling interest at acquisition date. **This figure is either the fair value of the non-controlling interest or their share of the fair value of the net assets of the subsidiary according to the terms of the question**.

2. The credit entry comprises the total of the net assets of the subsidiary at acquisition date (measured at fair value) as represented by share capital and reserves.

   There will also be a credit entry for any impairment of goodwill.

---

[2] See **Connolly**, Chapter 10, "Impairment".

Key Note: this, pro forma, is a blueprint for **every** calculation of goodwill or gain from a bargain purchase in a subsidiary throughout this text.

PRO FORMA: GOODWILL ACCOUNT

Pro Forma: Goodwill

Debit		Credit	
Investment in S	X	Share capital S (a)	X
NCI (c)	X	Reserves S (b)	X
		Impairment of goodwill (d)	X

(a) 100% of the share capital of S Ltd at the date of acquisition.
(b) 100% of each reserve of S Ltd at the date of acquisition.
(c) This figure is either the fair value of the non-controlling interest or their share of the fair value of the net assets of the subsidiary at acquisition date.
(d) This entry is necessary only when goodwill becomes impaired

Note: S Ltd may have a number of different reserves at acquisition date, e.g. share premium, revaluation reserve, retained earnings, etc.

Columnar Presentation

	€000	€000
Investment in S Ltd		X
Non-controlling interests		X
		X
S Ltd net assets at acquisition date		
Ordinary shares	X	
Reserves	X	X
Goodwill		X

Introducing Full Consolidation, including Goodwill

Preparing a Consolidated SoFP – The T Account Method

Using the T account method, the following steps are common to every consolidated SoFP preparation:
1. Calculate the group structure, which is always based on the number of shares acquired.
2. Open a T account for each heading in the statements of financial position of P Ltd and S Ltd and enter the balances.
3. Open a goodwill account. An account for non-controlling interests (NCI) will also be used in cases where the parent has not acquired a 100% interest in the subsidiary.

4. Prepare the journal entries.
5. Close all T accounts and extract the consolidated SoFP.

Authors' Note: each consolidated SoFP example and question will be followed by a solution using both the T accounts method and also the 'columnar' method, which is also frequently employed. It must be stressed that all methods should produce an **identical** consolidated SoFP.

The following example incorporates full consolidation, which involves replacing the investment in S Ltd by all of its assets and liabilities in the consolidated SoFP and calculating and treating goodwill.

EXAMPLE 4.1: CONSOLIDATING A WHOLLY-OWNED SUBSIDIARY

P Ltd and S Ltd
STATEMENTS OF FINANCIAL POSITION
as at 30 June 2013

	P Ltd €000	S Ltd €000
Assets		
Non-current assets:		
Property, plant and equipment	2,800	1,900
Investment in S Ltd	1,300	–
Current assets	850	460
Total assets	**4,950**	**2,360**
Equity and liabilities		
Equity		
Ordinary share capital (€1)	1,000	400
Retained earnings	2,600	1,200
Total equity	3,600	1,600
Non-current liabilities	900	500
Current liabilities	450	260
Total equity and liabilities	**4,950**	**2,360**

Note: P Ltd acquired 400,000 ordinary shares in S Ltd on 1 January 2012 when the retained earnings of S Ltd were €800,000.

SOLUTION GUIDELINES

1. The key date for the calculation of goodwill is the date of acquisition, i.e. 1 January 2012.
2. Share capital plus reserves of a company are represented by net assets – the terms are interchangeable.

3. Only the post-acquisition profits of S Ltd are consolidated with the profits of P Ltd. The group's share of pre-acquisition profits of S Ltd are capitalised or frozen at the date of acquisition.
4. Group structure:
   Group $\frac{400,000}{400,000} = 100\%$
5. All assets and liabilities of S Ltd are consolidated.

Solution

WORKINGS (Columnar Method)

(W1) Goodwill	€000	€000
Cost of investment in S		1,300
Non-controlling interests		nil
		1,300
Net assets of S Ltd at acquisition date:		
Ordinary shares	400	
Retained earnings	800	1,200
Goodwill		100

JOURNAL ENTRIES (common to both methods)

		€000	€000
1.	Dr. Goodwill	1,300	
	Cr. Investment in S		1,300
	Cost of investment in S		
2.	Dr. Ordinary shares	400	
	Cr. Goodwill		400
	Share capital of S Ltd at acquisition date		
3.	Dr. Retained earnings S	800	
	Cr. Goodwill		800
	Pre-acquisition retained earnings of S		
4.	Dr Retained earnings S	400	
	Cr. Retained earnings P		400
	Group's share of post-acquisition retained earnings of S = 100% × (1,200 – 800)		

WORKINGS (T Account Method)

Property, Plant and Equipment

Debit		Credit	
P	2,800		
S	1,900	SoFP	4,700
	4,700		4,700

Investment in S

Debit		Credit	
P	1,300	Goodwill (Jnl. 1)	1,300

Current Assets

Debit		Credit	
P	850		
S	460	SoFP	1,310
	1,310		1,310

Ordinary Shares

Debit		Credit	
Goodwill (Jnl. 2)	400	P	1,000
SoFP	1,000	S	400
	1,400		1,400

Retained Earnings P

Debit		Credit	
		P at reporting date	2,600
SoFP	3,000	Share of S post-acq. (Jnl. 4)	400
	3,000		3,000

Note: The closing balance on the retained earnings of the parent represents the consolidated retained earnings and will do so throughout the remainder of this text.

Retained Earnings S

Debit		Credit	
Goodwill (Jnl. 3)	800		
Retained earnings P (Jnl. 4)	400	S at reporting date	1,200
	1,200		1,200

Note: the consolidated retained earnings, i.e. €3,000 can be defined as the retained earnings of P Ltd at the reporting date **plus** the group's share of the **post-acquisition** retained earnings of S Ltd.

P Ltd   2,600
S Ltd 100% (1,200 – 800)   400
                                               3,000

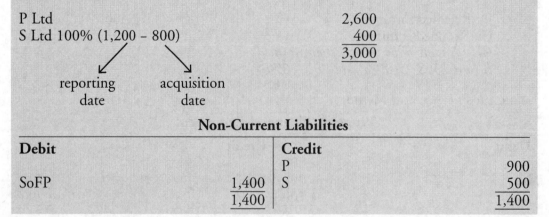

reporting   acquisition
  date   date

Non-Current Liabilities

Debit		Credit	
		P	900
SoFP	1,400	S	500
	1,400		1,400

Current Liabilities

Debit		Credit	
		P	450
SoFP	710	S	260
	710		710

Goodwill

Debit		Credit	
Investment in S Ltd (Jnl. 1)	1,300	Ordinary shares S Ltd (Jnl. 2)	400
NCI	Nil	Retained earnings S Ltd (Jnl. 3)	800
		SoFP – goodwill	100
	1,300		1,300

WORKINGS (Columnar Method)

	P Ltd €000	S Ltd €000	Adjustment €000		Consol. SoFP €000
Property, Plant & Equipment	2,800	1,900	0		4,700
Investment in S Ltd (W1)	1,300	0	(1,300)	(Jnl. 1)	0
Goodwill (W1)	0	0	100		100
Current assets	850	460	0		1,310
	4,950	2,360	(1,200)		6,110
Ordinary shares	1,000	400	(400)	(Jnl. 2)	1,000
Retained earnings (W2)	2,600	1,200	(800)	(Jnl. 3)	3,000
Non-current liabilities	900	500	0		1,400
Current liabilities	450	260	0		710
	4,950	2,360	(1,200)		6,110

(W2) Retained earnings

P Ltd at reporting date		2,600
S Ltd at reporting date	1,200	
At acquisition date	(800)	
Post-acquisition × 100%	400	400
		3,000

CONSOLIDATED STATEMENT OF FINANCIAL POSITION
as at 30 June 2013

Assets	€000
Non-current assets	
Property, plant and equipment	4,700
Goodwill	100
Current assets	1,310
Total assets	**6,110**

Equity and liabilities
Equity

Ordinary share capital	1,000
Retained earnings	3,000
Total equity	4,000
Non-current liabilities	1,400
Current liabilities	710
Total equity and liabilities	**6,110**

Introducing Non-controlling Interests

Where a parent does not acquire 100% of the equity shares of a subsidiary, **non-controlling interests (NCI)** arise. These are the balance of the shares in the subsidiary owned by shareholders outside the parent.

Definition of Non-controlling Interests

'Non-controlling interests' is "equity in a subsidiary not attributable, directly or indirectly, to a parent" (IFRS 10 *Consolidated Financial Statements*, Appendix A).

Accounting for Non-controlling Interests

The consolidated SoFP should show separately the total non-controlling interests at the reporting date which comprises:
(a) the value at the date of acquisition;
  plus
(b) their share of the post-acquisition reserves of the subsidiary.

Note: there will be a deduction for their share of goodwill impairment when relevant.

This amount should be presented within 'equity', separately from the parent shareholders' equity, in the statement of financial position as follows:

PRO FORMA: CONSOLIDATED SoFP (EXTRACT) INCLUDING
NON-CONTROLLING INTERESTS

CONSOLIDATED STATEMENT OF FINANCIAL POSITION
as at 31 May 2013

	31 May 2013 €	31 May 2012 €
Equity		
Share capital	X	X
Share premium	X	X
Retained earnings	X	X
Total shareholders' equity	X	X
Non-controlling interests (NCI)	X	X
Total equity	X	X

The non-controlling interest is calculated using a T account as follows:

PRO FORMA: NON-CONTROLLING INTEREST ACCOUNT

Non-controlling Interests			
Debit		**Credit**	
Impairment of goodwill (Note 3)	X	Goodwill (Note 1)	X
SoFP	X	Reserves S (Note 2)	X

Note 1: This entry is either the fair value of the non-controlling interest at acquisition date or their share of the fair value of the net assets of the subsidiary at acquisition date, according to the terms of the question.
Note 2: This entry is the NCI share of the post-acquisition reserves of the subsidiary.
Note 3: This entry occurs only when there is impairment of goodwill, part of which is attributable to the NCI.

COLUMNAR PRESENTATION

	€000
Measurement at acquisition date	X
Share of subsidiary's post-acquisition reserves	X
Share of goodwill impairment (if applicable)	(X)
	X

Remember: A subsidiary may have only one reserve, i.e. retained earnings or it could have others also such as share premium, revaluation reserve, general reserve, etc.

The treatment of non-controlling interests (NCI) is outlined in **Examples 4.2** and **4.3**, which also involve full consolidation and goodwill.

EXAMPLE 4.2: CONSOLIDATING A SUBSIDIARY WITH NON-CONTROLLING INTERESTS
Preparation of a Consolidated SoFP
where Pompey Ltd owns less than 100% of the voting shares of Saints Ltd

STATEMENTS OF FINANCIAL POSITION as at 30 June 2013	Pompey Ltd €000	Saints Ltd €000
Assets		
Non-current assets		
Property, plant and equipment	8,500	4,300
Investment in S Ltd	2,450	–
Current assets	2,700	1,400
Total assets	**13,650**	**5,700**

Equity and liabilities
Equity

Ordinary share capital (€1)	5,000	2,000
Retained earnings	4,950	1,900
Total equity	9,950	3,900
Non-current liabilities	1,800	700
Current liabilities	1,900	1,100
Total equity and liabilities	**13,650**	**5,700**

Pompey Ltd acquired 1,500,000 shares in Saints Ltd on 1 November 2011 when the retained earnings of S Ltd were €1,200,000.

Pompey Ltd elects to measure non-controlling interests at their proportionate interest in the net assets of Saints Ltd at the date of acquisition.

Solution

Group Structure

Group   1,500,000/2,000,000   =   75%
Non-controlling Interest (NCI)   =   25%

Note: the group structure is always based on the number of shares acquired.

Solution Guidelines

1. Although the group owns only 75% of Saints Ltd in this case, **all** the assets and liabilities of Saints Ltd are still consolidated with those of Pompey Ltd.
2. Non-controlling interests are credited with:
   (a) their share of the fair value of the net assets of the subsidiary at acquisition date;
   plus
   (b) their share of the post-acquisition retained earnings of the subsidiary.

3. In the consolidated SoFP, the non-controlling interest figure is shown under equity but *after* the shareholder's equity. Non-controlling interest is not a liability of a group because it does not constitute a liability under IAS 37 *Provisions, Contingent Liabilities and Contingent Assets,* as there is not a present obligation arising from past events, the settlement of which would result in an outflow of economic benefits.[3]

---

[3] See **Connolly**, Chapter 14, "Provisions, Contingent Liabilities and Contingent Assets".

	€000	€000
(W1) Goodwill		
Cost of investment in Saints	2,450 (Jnl.1)	
Non-controlling interests 25% X (2,000 + 1,200)	800 (Jnl. 2)	3,250
Net assets of Saints at acquisition date:		
Ordinary shares	2,000	
Retained earnings	1,200	3,200
Goodwill		50

JOURNAL ENTRIES (common to both methods)

	€000	€000
1. Dr. Goodwill	2,450	
Cr. Investment in Saints		2,450
Cost of investment in Saints		
2. Dr. Goodwill	800	
Cr. NCI		800
NCI share of net assets of Saints at acquisition date		
3. Dr. Ordinary shares	2,000	
Cr. Goodwill		2,000
Ordinary shares of Saints		
4. Dr. Retained earnings Saints	1,200	
Cr. Goodwill		1,200
Pre-acquisition retained earnings of Saints		
5. Dr. Retained earnings Saints	700	
Cr. Retained earnings Pompey (75%)		525
Cr. NCI (25%)		175

Apportionment of post-acquisition retained earnings of Saints
$$(1,900 - 1,200)$$

Reporting date   Acquisition date

WORKINGS (T Account Method)

Property, Plant and Equipment

Debit		Credit	
P	8,500		
S	4,300	SoFP	12,800
	12,800		12,800

Investment in S Ltd

Debit		Credit	
P	2,450	Goodwill (Jnl. 1)	2,450

Current Assets

Debit		Credit	
P	2,700		
S	1,400	SoFP	4,100
	4,100		4,100

Ordinary Shares

Debit		Credit	
Goodwill (Jnl. 3)	2,000	P	5,000
SoFP	5,000	S	2,000
	7,000		7,000

Note: The ordinary share capital of the group is Pompey Ltd's share capital.

Retained Earnings P

Debit		Credit	
		P at reporting date	4,950
SoFP	5,475	Share of S post-acq. (Jnl. 5)	525
	5,475		5,475

Retained Earnings S

Debit		Credit	
Goodwill (Jnl. 4)	1,200		
P – share of post-acq. (Jnl. 5)	525	S	1,900
NCI (Jnl. 5) – share of post-acq.	175		
	1,900		1,900

Non-Current Liabilities

Debit		Credit	
		P	1,800
SoFP	2,500	S	700
	2,500		2,500

Current Liabilities

Debit		Credit	
		P	1,900
SoFP	3,000	S	1,100
	3,000		3,000

Goodwill

Debit		Credit	
		Ordinary shares S (Jnl. 3)	2,000
Investment in S (Jnl. 1)	2,450	Retained earnings S (Jnl. 4)	1,200
NCI (Jnl. 2)	800	SoFP: Goodwill	50
	3,250		3,250

Non-controlling Interests

Debit		Credit	
		Goodwill (Jnl. 2)	800
SoFP	975	Share of S post-acq. (Jnl. 5)	175
	975		975

WORKINGS (Columnar Method)

	Pompey €000	Saints €000	Adjustment €000	Consol. SoFP €000
Property, plant and equipment	8,500	4,300	0	12,800
Investment in S Ltd (W1)	2,450	0	(2,450) (Jnl. 1)	0
Goodwill (W1)	0	0	50	50
Current assets	2,700	1,400	0	4,100
	13,650	5,700	(2,400)	16,950
Ordinary share capital	5,000	2,000	(2,000) (Jnl. 3)	5,000
Retained earnings (W2)	4,950	1,900	(1,375)	5,475
Non-controlling interests (W3)	0	0	975	975
Non-current liabilities	1,800	700	0	2,500
Current liabilities	1,900	1,100	0	3,000
	13,650	5,700	(2,400)	16,950

(W2) Retained earnings	€000	€000
Pompey at reporting date		4,950
Saints at reporting date	1,900	
at acquisition date	(1,200)	
post-acquisition	700	
Group's share: 75%		525
		5,475

(W3) Non-controlling interests
Share of Saint's net assets at acquisition date:

Ordinary shares	500	(W1)
Retained earnings	300	(W1)
Share of Saint's post-acquisition earnings	175	Jnl. 5
	975	

Pompey Limited
CONSOLIDATED STATEMENT OF FINANCIAL POSITION
as at 30 June 2013

Assets	€000
Non-current assets	
Property, plant and equipment	12,800
Goodwill	50
Current assets	4,100
Total assets	**16,950**
Equity and liabilities	
Equity	
Ordinary share capital	5,000
Retained earnings	5,475
Total shareholders' equity	10,475
Non-controlling interests	975
Total equity	11,450
Non-current liabilities	2,500
Current liabilities	3,000
Total equity and liabilities	**16,950**

EXAMPLE 4.3: PREPARATION OF A CONSOLIDATED SoFP WHERE THERE IS GOODWILL
ATTRIBUTABLE TO THE NON-CONTROLLING INTERESTS

STATEMENTS OF FINANCIAL POSITION
as at 31 May 2013

	Jack Ltd	Jill Ltd
	€000	€000
Sundry net assets	11,250	5,800
Investment in Jill Ltd	4,000	–
	15,250	5,800

Ordinary shares	7,500	3,000
Retained earnings	7,750	2,800
	15,250	5,800

Jack Ltd acquired 90% of the ordinary shares of Jill Ltd on 1 January 2012 when the retained earnings of Jill Ltd were €1,300,000. At the date of acquisition, the fair value of the non-controlling interests was €450,000.

(W1) Goodwill

		€000	€000	€000	Jnl.
		Total	Jack	NCI	
Cost of investment in Jill		4,000	4,000		1
Non-controlling interests		450		450	2
		4,450	4,000	450	
Net assets of Jill at acquisition date					
Ordinary shares	3,000				3
Retained earnings (Jnl. 4)	1,300	4,300	3,870	430	
Goodwill		150	130	20	

JOURNAL ENTRIES (common to both methods)

		€000	€000
1.	Dr. Goodwill	4,000	
	Cr. Investment in Jill		4,000
	Investment in subsidiary		
2.	Dr. Goodwill	450	
	Cr. NCI		450
	Fair value of NCI at acquisition date		
3.	Dr. Ordinary shares	3,000	
	Cr. Goodwill		3,000
	Ordinary shares Jill at acquisition date		
4.	Dr. Retained earnings Jill	1,300	
	Cr. Goodwill		1,300
	Retained earnings Jill at acquisition date		
5.	Dr. Retained earnings Jill	1,500	
	Cr. Retained earnings Jack (90%)		1,350
	Cr. NCI (10%)		150
	Post-acquisition retained earnings of Jill		
	(2,800–1,300)		

WORKINGS (T Account Method)

Sundry Net Assets

Debit		Credit	
Jack	11,250		
Jill	5,800	SoFP	17,050
	17,050		17,050

Investment in Jill

Debit		Credit	
Jack	4,000	Goodwill (Jnl. 1)	4,000

Ordinary Shares

Debit		Credit	
Goodwill (Jnl. 3)	3,000	Jack	7,500
SoFP	7,500	Jill	3,000
	10,500		10,500

Retained Earnings Jack

Debit		Credit	
		Jack at reporting date	7,750
SoFP	9,100	Share of Jill post-acq. (Jnl. 5)	1,350
	9,100		9,100

Retained Earnings Jill

Debit		Credit	
Goodwill (Jnl. 4)	1,300	Jill at reporting date	2,800
Retained earnings Jack (Jnl. 5)	1,350		
NCI (Jnl. 5)	150		
	2,800		2,800

Goodwill

Debit		Credit	
Investment in Jill (Jnl. 1)	4,000	Ord. shares Jill (Jnl. 3)	3,000
NCI (Jnl. 2)	450	Pre-acq. ret. earnings (Jnl. 4)	1,300
		Goodwill: SoFP	150
	4,450		4,450

Non-controlling Interests

Debit		Credit	
		Goodwill (Jnl. 2)	450
SoFP	600	Retained earnings Jill (Jnl. 5)	150
	600		600

WORKINGS (Columnar Method)

	Jack	Jill	Adjustments	Consol. SoFP	
	€000	€000	€000	€000	Jnl.
Sundry net assets	11,250	5,800		17,050	
Investment in Jill (W1)	4,000		(4,000)		1
Goodwill (W1)			150	150	
	15,250	5,800	(3,850)	17,200	
Ordinary shares	7,500	3,000	(3,000)	7,500	3
Retained earnings (W2)	7,750	2,800	(1,450)	9,100	
Non-controlling interests (W3)			600	600	
	15,250	5,800	(3,850)	17,200	

(W2) Retained earnings

	€000	€000
Jack at reporting date		7,750
Jill at reporting date	2,800	
at acquisition date	(1,300)	
Post-acquisition	1,500	
Group's share (90%)		1,350
SoFP		9,100

(W3) Non-controlling interest

Fair value at date of acquisition	450	2
Share of post-acquisition retained earnings of Jill	150	5
	600	

Jack Limited
CONSOLIDATED STATEMENT OF FINANCIAL POSITION
as at 31 May 2013

	€000
Goodwill	150
Sundry net assets	17,050
	17,200
Ordinary share capital	7,500
Retained earnings	9,100
	16,600
Non-controlling interests	600
	17,200

EXAMPLE 4.4: CALCULATION AND TREATMENT OF A GAIN ON A BARGAIN PURCHASE

STATEMENTS OF FINANCIAL POSITION OF PORTAL LTD AND SASH LTD
as at 31 August 2013

	Portal Ltd €000	Sash Ltd. €000
Investment in Sash	8,600	–
Sundry net assets	18,750	9,700
	27,350	9,700
Ordinary share capital	15,000	5,000
Retained earnings	12,350	4,700
	27,350	9,700

Note 1: Portal Ltd. acquired 90% of the ordinary shares of Sash Ltd on 31 August 2013.
Note 2: Non-controlling interests at acquisition date is valued at their share of the net assets of Sash Ltd.

Requirement Prepare the consolidated statement of financial position of Portal Ltd. as at 31 August 2013.

Solution

(W1) Gain from a bargain purchase	€000	€000	Jnl.
Investment in Sash		8,600	1
NCI at acquisition date 10% (5,000 + 4,700)		970	2
		9,570	
Net assets of Sash Ltd. at acquisition date:			
Ordinary shares	5,000		3
Retained earnings	4,700	9,700	4
Gain from a bargain purchase		130	

JOURNAL ENTRIES (common to both methods)

1. Dr. Goodwill   8,600
    Cr. Investment in Sash   8,600
    Investment in Sash

2. Dr. Goodwill   970
    Cr. NCI   970
    Value of NCI at acquisition date

3. Dr. Ordinary shares   5,000
    Cr. Goodwill   5,000
    Ordinary shares Sash at acquisition date

4. Dr. Retained earnings   4,700
    Cr. Goodwill   4,700
    Retained earnings Sash at acquisition date

5. Dr. Goodwill   130
    Cr. Retained earnings Portal   130
    Immediate recognition of gain on bargain purchase

WORKINGS (T Account Method)

Investment in S

Debit		Credit	
P	8,600	Goodwill (Jnl. 1)	8,600

Sundry Net Assets

Debit		Credit	
P	18,750		
S	9,700	SoFP	28,450
	28,450		28,450

Ordinary Shares

Debit		Credit	
Goodwill (Jnl. 3)	5,000	P	15,000
SoFP	15,000	S	5,000
	20,000		20,000

Retained Earnings Portal

Debit		Credit	
		P at reporting date	12,350
		Goodwill–gain on	
SoFP	12,480	bargain purchase	130
	12,480		12,480

Retained Earnings Sash

Debit		Credit	
Goodwill (Jnl. 2)	4,700	S at reporting date	4,700

Non-controlling Interests

Debit		Credit	
SoFP	970	Goodwill (Jnl. 2)	970

Goodwill

Debit		Credit	
Investment in S (Jnl. 1)	8,600	Ordinary shares S (Jnl. 3)	5,000
NCI (Jnl. 2)	970	Retained earnings S (Jnl. 4)	4,700
Retained earnings P (gain from a bargain purchase)	130		
	9,700		9,700

Note: in this example the date of acquisition and the reporting date are the same. As a consequence there are no post-acquisition profits in Sash, and therefore Portal and NCI cannot be credited with their shares.

WORKINGS (Columnar Method)

	Portal	Sash	Adjustments		Consol. SoFP
	€000	€000	€000		€000
Investment in Sash	8,600	-	(8,600)	Jnl. 1	
Sundry net assets	18,750	9,700			28,450
Total assets	**27,350**	**9,700**	**(8,600)**		**28,450**
Ordinary shares	15,000	5,000	(5,000)	Jnl. 3	15,000
Retained earnings (*W2*)	12,350	4,700	(4,570)		12,480
NCI (*W3*)			970		970
Total equity and liabilities	**27,350**	**9,700**	**(8,600)**		**28, 450**

(W2) Retained earnings	€000	€000
Portal at reporting date		12,350
Gain on bargain purchase (Jnl. 5)		130
Sash at reporting date	4,700	
Sash at acquisition date	(4,700)	
Post-acquisition	Nil	
Group's share (90%)		Nil
SoFP		12,480

(W3) Non-controlling interests	
Value at acquisition date (Jnl. 2)	970

Portal Limited
CONSOLIDATED STATEMENT OF FINANCIAL POSITION
as at 31 August 2013

	€000
Sundry net assets	28,450
	28,450
Ordinary share capital	15,000
Retained earnings	12,480
	27,480
Non-controlling interests	970
	28,450

IFRS 5 *Discontinued Operations*

When a subsidiary is acquired with the intention of resale, it gets special treatment in the **consolidated SoFP**. The subsidiary is consolidated in the normal way in the workings. However, in the consolidated SoFP its total assets and liabilities are shown separately as follows:

Assets held for sale	€000
Liabilities held for sale	€000

And in the SPLOCI – P/L

Profit/loss on discontinued operation	€000

See below **Appendix 1**, Question D.

SUMMARY

1. All the assets and liabilities of a subsidiary are consolidated with those of the parent. This applies whether the parent acquires 100%, 90%, 70%, etc., of the voting shares of a subsidiary.
2. **Goodwill** (in the absence of a business combination achieved in stages) is calculated as **A − B**.

   Where **A** is the aggregate of:
   - (i) the cost of the investment in the subsidiary (at fair value); and
   - (ii) the amount of any non-controlling interest at the date of acquisition;

   and **B** is the net assets of the subsidiary (at fair value) at the date of acquisition.

   Accounting treatment: goodwill should be treated as an intangible asset in the consolidated SoFP and only written down if its value becomes impaired. A **gain from a bargain purchase** arises where **B** above exceeds **A**.

   Accounting treatment: the gain should be credited to the retained earnings of the acquirer in the consolidated SoFP.
3. When a parent acquires less than 100% of the voting shares of a subsidiary, the balance of the shares are owned by the **non-controlling interests (NCI)**.
4. The consolidated SoFP should disclose under equity the non-controlling interests calculated as follows:

	€000
Share of **net assets** of S at date of acquisition (at fair value)	
or **fair value** of interest at date of acquisition	X
Any impairment of goodwill	(X)
Share of post-acquisition retained reserves of S	X
	X

5. Consolidated retained earnings can be defined as the retained earnings of the parent at the reporting date plus the group's share of the **post-acquisition** retained earnings of the subsidiary at the same date.

Conclusion

You should now be in a position to prepare a consolidated SoFP involving calculating non-controlling interests and goodwill, and present the SoFP in a form suitable for publication in accordance with IAS 1 *Presentation of Financial Statements.*[4]

QUESTIONS

Question 4.1

Explain the difference between goodwill and a gain on a bargain purchase.

Solution

Goodwill arises where the sum of:
1. the cost of the investment in a subsidiary; and
2. the amount of any non-controlling interest at the date of acquisition exceeds the net assets of the subsidiary at the date of acquisition.

A gain on a bargain purchase arises when the net assets of the subsidiary at the date of acquisition exceeds the sum of:
1. the cost of the investment in a subsidiary; and
2. the amount of any non-controlling interest at the date of acquisition.

Note: both the cost of the investment in the subsidiary and the net assets of the subsidiary at acquisition date are recorded at fair value.

Question 4.2

What are the components of the following figures in the consolidated statement of financial position?
(a) retained earnings
(b) non-controlling interests.

Solution

(a) Consolidated retained earnings comprise the retained earnings of the parent at the **reporting date** plus the group's share of the post-acquisition retained earnings of the subsidiary to that date.
(b) NCI comprises

	€000
Share of **net assets** of S at date of acquisition (at fair value) **or fair value** of interest at date of acquisition	X
Any impairment of goodwill	(X)
Share of post-acquisition retained reserves of S	X
	X

---

[4] See also **Connolly**, Chapter 2 "Presentation of Financial Statements".

Question 4.3

The following are the summarised statements of financial position of Red Ltd and Blue Ltd at 30 June 2013:

	Red Ltd €000	Blue Ltd €000
Sundry net assets	8,400	5,700
Investment in Blue Ltd	3,680	–
	12,080	5,700
Ordinary share capital	5,000	3,000
Retained earnings	7,080	2,700
	12,080	5,700

Red Ltd acquired 2,400,000 ordinary shares in Blue Ltd on 1 December 2011 when the retained earnings of Blue Ltd were €1,500,000. Red Ltd elects to measure non-controlling interests at their proportionate interest in the net assets of Blue Ltd at the date of acquisition.

Requirement Calculate the following, which would appear in the consolidated statement of financial position of the Red Ltd group as at 30 June 2013:
(a) Goodwill
(b) Retained earnings
(c) Non-controlling interests.

Solution to Question 4.3

	€000	€000
(W1) Goodwill		
Investment in Blue		3,680
NCI 20% × (3,000 + 1,500)		900
		4,580
Net assets of Blue at acquisition date		
Ordinary share capital	3,000	
Retained earnings	1,500	4,500
Goodwill		80
(W2) Retained earnings		
Retained earnings Red at reporting date		7,080
Share of post-acquisition retained earnings of Blue		
80% × (2,700–1,500)		960
		8,040
(W3) Non-controlling interests		
Share of net assets of Blue at acquisition date *(W1)*		900
Share of post-acquisition retained earnings Blue		
20% × 1,200 *(W2)*		240
		1,140

Goodwill

Debit		Credit	
		Ordinary shares Blue	3,000
Investment in Blue Ltd	3,680	Retained earnings Blue (pre-acq).	1,500
NCI	900	Goodwill	80
	4,580		4,580

Retained Earnings Red

Debit		Credit	
		Red at reporting date	7,080
SoFP	8,040	Share of Blue post-acq.[1]	960
	8,040		8,040

[1]See W2.

Retained Earnings Blue

Debit		Credit	
Goodwill	1,500	Blue at reporting date	2,700
Retained earnings Red	960		
NCI[2]	240		
	2,700		2,700

[2] NCI share of Blue post-acq. 20% (2,700 – 1,500)

Non-controlling Interests

Debit		Credit	
		Goodwill (W1)	900
SoFP	1,140	Post-acq. retained earnings Blue	240
	1,140		1,140

Note: the following questions, **Questions 4.4** and **4.5**, are longer, review-type questions, which underpin the content of **Chapter 4** and involve dealing with more than one reserve in the SoFP of the subsidiary. Each solution contains:
1. Journal entries.
2. The T account method workings.
3. The columnar method workings.
4. The consolidated SoFP.

Question 4.4

The following are the statements of financial position of Black Ltd and White Ltd as at 31 July 2013:

	Black Ltd €000	White Ltd €000
Assets		
Non-current assets		
Property, plant and equipment	7,600	3,040
Investment in White Ltd	1,280	
Current assets	2,280	920
Total assets	**11,160**	**3,960**
Equity and liabilities		
Equity		
Ordinary share capital	4,000	1,000
Share premium	1,000	200
Retained earnings	3,620	1,630
Total equity	8,620	2,830
Non-current liabilities	1,300	500
Current liabilities	1,240	630
Total equity and liabilities	**11,160**	**3,960**

Black Ltd acquired 600,000 ordinary shares in White Ltd on 1 November 2011 when White Ltd had the following reserves:

	€000
Share premium	200
Retained earnings	800

Black Ltd elects to measure non-controlling interests at their proportionate interest in the net assets of White Ltd at the date of acquisition.

Requirement Prepare the consolidated statement of financial position of the Black Ltd group as at 31 July 2013.

Solution to Question 4.4

Group structure:

Group	600,000/1,000,000	= 60%
Non-controlling Interest (NCI)		= 40%

[AU: Edit OK?]

WORKINGS (Columnar Method)
(W1) Goodwill

	€000	€000	Jnl.
Investment in White		1,280	1
NCI 40% × (1,000 + 200 + 800)		800	2
		2,080	

Net assets of White at acquisition date:

Ordinary share capital	1,000		
Share premium	200		
Retained earnings	800	2,000	3 and 4
Goodwill		80	

JOURNAL ENTRIES (common to both methods)

	€000	€000

1. Dr. Goodwill   1,280
    Cr. Investment in White   1,280
    Investment in subsidiary

2. Dr. Goodwill   800
    Cr. NCI   800
    NCI share of net assets of White at acquisition date

3. Dr. Ordinary shares   1,000
    Cr. Goodwill   1,000
    Share capital of White at acquisition date

4. Dr. Share premium   200
    Dr. Retained earnings White   800
    Cr. Goodwill   1,000
    Reserves of White at acquisition date

5. Dr. Retained earnings White   830
    Cr. Retained earnings Black (60%)   498
    Cr. Non-controlling interest (40%)   332
    Post-acquisition retained earnings of White
    (1,630 – 800)

WORKINGS (T Account Method)

Property, Plant and Equipment

Debit		Credit	
Black	7,600		
White	3,040	SoFP	10,640
	10,640		10,640

Investment in White Ltd

Debit		Credit	
Black	1,280	Goodwill (Jnl. 1)	1,280

Current Assets

Debit		Credit	
Black	2,280		
White	920	SoFP	3,200
	3,200		3,200

Ordinary Shares

Debit		Credit	
Goodwill (Jnl. 3)	1,000		
		Black	4,000
SoFP	4,000	White	1,000
	5,000		5,000

Share Premium

Debit		Credit	
Goodwill (Jnl. 4)	200	Black	1,000
SoFP	1,000	White	200
	1,200		1,200

Retained Earnings Black

Debit		Credit	
		Black at reporting date	3,620
SoFP	4,118	Share of White post-acq. (Jnl. 5)	498
	4,118		4,118

Retained Earnings White

Debit		Credit	
Goodwill (Jnl. 4)	800	White at reporting date	1,630
Retained earnings Black (Jnl. 5)	498		
NCI (Jnl. 5)	332		
	1,630		1,630

Non-current Liabilities

Debit		Credit	
		Black	1,300
SoFP	1,800	White	500
	1,800		1,800

Current Liabilities

Debit		Credit	
		Black	1,240
SoFP	1,870	White	630
	1,870		1,870

Goodwill

Debit		Credit	
Investment in White (Jnl. 1)	1,280	Ord. shares (Jnl. 3)	1,000
NCI (Jnl. 2)	800	Share premium (Jnl. 4)	200
		Retained earnings (Jnl. 4)	800
		Goodwill SoFP	80
	2,080		2,080

Non-controlling Interests

Debit		Credit	
		Goodwill (Jnl. 2)	800
SoFP	1,132	Post-acq. ret. earnings White (Jnl. 5)	332
	1,132		1,132

WORKINGS (Columnar Method)

	Black	White	Adjustment		Consol. SoFP
	€000	€000	€000		€000
Property, plant and equipment	7,600	3,040	0		10,640
Investment in White *(W1)*	1,280	0	(1,280)	(Jnl. 1)	0
Goodwill *(W1)*	0	0	80		80
Current assets	2,280	920	0		3,200
Total Assets	**11,160**	**3,960**	**(1,200)**		**13,920**
Ordinary shares	4,000	1,000	(1,000)	(Jnl. 3)	4,000
Share premium *(W2)*	1,000	200	(200)	(Jnl. 4)	1,000
Retained earnings *(W3)*	3,620	1,630	(1,132)		4,118
Non-controlling interests *(W4)*	0	0	1,132		1,132
Non-current liabilities	1,300	500	0		1,800
Current liabilities	1,240	630	0		1,870
Total equity and liabilities	**11,160**	**3,960**	**(1,200)**		**13,920**

(W2) Share premium	€000	€000	Jnl.
Black Ltd at reporting date		1,000	
White Ltd at reporting date	200		
at acquisition date	(200)		4
Post-acquisition		0	
Consolidated SoFP		1,000	

(W3) Retained earnings

	€000
Black Ltd at reporting date	3,620

White Ltd: At reporting date	1,630	
At acquisition date	(800)	4
Post-acquisition	830	
Group share: 60%		498
SoFP		4,118

(W4) Non-controlling interests

Share of net assets at acquisition date:

Ordinary shares	1,000	
Share premium	200	
Retained earnings	800	
	2,000	
NCI share (40%)	800	2
Share of post-acq. retained earnings White (40% × 830)	332	5
	1,132	

Black Ltd
CONSOLIDATED STATEMENT OF FINANCIAL POSITION
as at 31 July 2013

Assets	**€000**
Non-current assets	
Property, plant and equipment	10,640
Goodwill	80
Current Assets	3,200
Total assets	**13,920**
Equity and liabilities	
Equity	
Ordinary share capital	4,000
Share premium	1,000
Retained earnings	4,118
Total shareholders' equity	9,118
Non-controlling interests	1,132
Total equity	10,250
Non-current liabilities	1,800
Current liabilities	1,870
Total equity and liabilities	**13,920**

Question 4.5

Planet Plc acquired 80,000 of the ordinary shares in Sun Ltd at a cost of €160,000 on 1 May 2012. The following are the statements of financial position as at 30 April 2013:

	Planet Plc €000	Sun Ltd €000
Assets		
Non-current Assets		
Property, plant and equipment	218	140
Investment in Sun Ltd	160	–
	378	140
Current Assets		
Inventories	111	65
Trade receivables	30	15
Cash	19	2
	160	82
Total assets	**538**	**222**
Equity and liabilities		
Equity		
Ordinary shares (€1)	300	100
Share premium	20	10
General reserve	68	15
Retained earnings	50	35
Total equity	438	160
Current liabilities		
Trade payables	50	32
Taxation	50	30
	100	62
Total equity and liabilities	**538**	**222**

The following additional information is available:

At 1 May 2012 the balances on the reserves of Sun Ltd were as follows:

	€000
Share premium	10
General reserve	10
Retained earnings	30

The fair value of the non-controlling interests amounted to €42,000 at 1 May 2012.

Requirement Prepare a consolidated statement of financial position of Planet Plc and its subsidiary Sun Ltd as at 30 April 2013.

Solution to Question 4.5

Group structure:

Group	80,000/100,000	= 80%
Non-controlling interest (NCI)		= 20%

WORKINGS (Columnar Method)

(W1) Goodwill	Total €000	Planet €000	NCI €000	Jnl.
Investment in Sun	160	160		1
Fair value of NCI	42		42	2
	202	160	42	
Net assets of Sun at acquisition date:				
Ordinary shares	100			3
Share premium	10			4
General reserve	10			4
Retained earnings	30			4
	150	120	30	
Goodwill	52	40	12	

JOURNAL ENTRIES (common to both methods)

	€000	€000
1. Dr. Goodwill	160	
Cr. Investment in Sun		160
Investment in Sun		
2. Dr. Goodwill	42	
Cr. NCI		42
Fair value of NCI at acquisition date		
3. Dr. Ordinary shares	100	
Cr. Goodwill		100
Share capital of Sun at acquisition date		
4. Dr. Share premium	10	
Dr. General reserve	10	
Dr. Retained earnings	30	
Cr. Goodwill		50
Reserves of Sun at acquisition date		
5. Dr. General reserve	1	
Cr. NCI		1
Post-acquisition general reserve of Sun		
NCI share 20% × (15 – 10)		
6. Dr. Retained earnings Sun	5	
Cr. Retained earnings Planet (80%)		4
Cr. NCI (20%)		1
Post-acquisition retained earnings of Sun		
(35 – 30)		

WORKINGS (T Account Method)

Property, Plant and Equipment

Debit		Credit	
Planet	218		
Sun	140	SoFP	358
	358		358

Investment in Sun Ltd

Debit		Credit	
Planet	160	Goodwill (Jnl. 1)	160

Inventories

Debit		Credit	
Planet	111		
Sun	65	SoFP	176
	176		176

Trade Receivables

Debit		Credit	
Planet	30		
Sun	15	SoFP	45
	45		45

Cash

Debit		Credit	
Planet	19		
Sun	2	SoFP	21
	21		21

Ordinary Shares

Debit		Credit	
Goodwill (Jnl. 3)	100	Planet	300
SoFP	300	Sun	100
	400		400

Share Premium

Debit		Credit	
Goodwill (Jnl. 4)	10	Planet	20
SoFP	20	Sun	10
	30		30

General Reserve

Debit		Credit	
Goodwill (Jnl. 4)	10	Planet at reporting date	68
Jnl. 5 (NCI)	1	Sun at reporting date	15
SoFP	72		
	83		83

Retained Earnings Planet

Debit		Credit	
SoFP	54	Planet at reporting date	50
		Post-acq. ret. earnings. Sun (Jnl. 6)	4
	54		54

Retained Earnings Sun

Debit		Credit	
Goodwill (Jnl. 4)	30	Sun at reporting date	35
Ret. earnings Planet (Jnl. 6)	4		
NCI (Jnl. 6)	1		
	35		35

Trade Payables

Debit		Credit	
		Planet	50
SoFP	82	Sun	32
	82		82

Taxation

Debit		Credit	
		Planet	50
SoFP	80	Sun	30
	80		80

Goodwill

Debit		Credit	
Investment in Sun Ltd (Jnl. 1)	160	Ordinary shares (Jnl. 3)	100
NCI (Jnl. 2)	42	Share premium (Jnl. 4)	10
		General reserve (Jnl. 4)	10
		Retained earnings (Jnl. 4)	30
		SoFP – Goodwill	52
	202		202

Non-controlling Interest (NCI)

Debit		Credit	
SoFP	44	Goodwill (Jnl. 2)	42
		General reserve Sun (Jnl. 5)	1
		Retained earnings Sun (Jnl. 6)	1
	44		44

WORKINGS (Columnar Method)

	Planet Plc. €000	Sun Ltd €000	Adjustment €000		Consol. SoFP €000
Property, plant and equipment	218	140	0		358
Goodwill (*W1*)	0	0	52		52
Investment in Sun Ltd (*W1*)	160	0	(160)	(Jnl. 1)	0
Inventories	111	65	0		176
Trade receivables	30	15	0		45
Cash	19	2	0		21
Total assets	**538**	**222**	**(108)**		**652**
Ordinary shares	300	100	(100)	(Jnl. 3)	300
Share premium *(W2)*	20	10	(10)	(Jnl. 4)	20
General reserve *(W3)*	68	15	(11)		72
Retained earnings *(W4)*	50	35	(31)		54
Non-controlling interests *(W5)*	0	0	44		44
Trade payables	50	32	0		82
Taxation	50	30	0		80
Total equity and liabilities	**538**	**222**	**(108)**		**652**

(W2) Share premium	€000	€000	Jnl.
Planet Ltd at reporting date		20	
Sun Ltd at reporting date	10		
at acquisition date	(10)		4
Post-acquisition	nil		
Consolidated SoFP		20	

(W3) General reserve			
Planet Ltd at reporting date		68	
Sun Ltd at reporting date	15		
at acquisition date	(10)		4
Post-acquisition	5		
Group share: 80%		4	
Consolidated SoFP		72	

(W4) Retained earnings			Jnl.
Planet Ltd at reporting date		50	
Sun Ltd at reporting date	35		
at acquisition date	(30)		4
Post-acquisition	5		
Group share: 80%		4	
Consolidated SoFP		54	

(W5) Non-controlling interests		
Fair value at acquisition date	42	2
Share of Sun post-acq. general reserve (20%)	1	5
Share of Sun post-acq. retained earnings (20%)	1	6
	44	

Planet Plc
CONSOLIDATED STATEMENT OF FINANCIAL POSITION
as at 30 April 2013

Assets	**€000**
Non-current Assets	
Property, plant and equipment	358
Goodwill	52
	410
Current Assets	
Inventories	176
Receivables	45
Cash	21
	242
Total assets	**652**
Equity and liabilities	
Equity	
Ordinary shares	300
Share premium	20
General reserve	72
Retained earnings	54
Total shareholders' equity	446
Non-controlling interest	44
Total equity	490
Current Liabilities	
Trade payables	82
Taxation	80
	162
Total equity and liabilities	**652**

Chapter 5

The Consolidated Statement
of Financial Position: Complications

LEARNING OBJECTIVES

After reading this chapter you should be able to:
- demonstrate an understanding of the various complications;
- prepare journal entries to account for each complication; and
- undertake questions on the preparation of a consolidated statement of financial position of a parent and subsidiary, which includes a combination of complications.

Introduction

Beware! At the end of **Chapter 4** you were in a position to prepare and present a basic consolidated SoFP. However, you should avoid the temptation to become complacent as in this chapter we will introduce accounting issues that will make the preparation of the consolidated SoFP more complex and intricate.

As stated, the basics of preparing a consolidated SoFP are explained in **Chapter 4**. These basics would remain the same irrespective of how many subsidiaries are acquired, i.e.:
1. Consolidate all the assets and liabilities of **each subsidiary** with those of the parent.
2. Debit goodwill with:
   (a) the cost of the investment in the subsidiary; and
   (b) either the fair value of the non-controlling interest or their share of the fair value of the net assets of the subsidiary at acquisition date.
3. Credit goodwill with 100% of the share capital of the subsidiary and each of its reserves (net assets) at the **date of acquisition**, and any impairment of goodwill.
4. Credit non-controlling interests:
   (a) either the fair value of the non-controlling interest or their share of the fair value of the net assets of the subsidiary at acquisition date; and
   (b) their share of the post-acquisition reserves of the subsidiary.
5. Debit non-controlling interests with their share of any goodwill impairment.
6. Share capital and reserves are represented by net assets.

However, in the world of business, group entities trade with one another and subsidiaries pay dividends to parents. Frequently, there are amounts owing by one group entity to another at the reporting date. Such events give rise to a set of adjustments which will be termed 'complications'. **Every examination question on consolidated financial statements contains a combination of complications so their understanding is essential.**

The key factor in considering these complications is that consolidated financial statements present information about a group **as if it were a single entity** (see **Chapter 1**). Therefore, for example, if the parent (P Ltd) owes the subsidiary (S Ltd) €20,000 at the period end for goods purchased, it is correct for P Ltd to show this amount as a payable and for S Ltd to include a corresponding amount as a receivable in their **individual** financial statements. However, there is a problem in preparing a set of consolidated financial statements in this case. Under full consolidation, the net assets of S Ltd would be combined with those of P Ltd. **If this were done without adjustment, both the assets and liabilities of the group would be overstated.** In the consolidated workings, therefore, the receivables of S Ltd need to be reduced by €20,000, as do the payables of P Ltd.

	€000	€000
Dr. Trade payables	20	
Cr. Trade receivables		20
Cancel intragroup balance		

> **Key Note:** having now pointed to the fact that complications do arise, the term '**full consolidation**' is defined throughout the remainder of this text as: combining the assets and liabilities of P Ltd and S Ltd **after adjustment for the effects of any complications**.

The Complications

A number of adjustments or 'complications' frequently arise when individual group member SoFPs are consolidated to create the consolidated statement of financial position (CSoFP). The main complications can be characterised as follows:
1. Unrealised inventory profit.
2. Unrealised profit on sale of tangible non-current assets.
3. Revaluation of a subsidiary's net assets at acquisition date.
4. Proposed preference dividends by a subsidiary.
5. Proposed ordinary dividends.
6. Intragroup balances.
7. Impairment of goodwill.
8. Preference shares in issue by a subsidiary.

> **Key Note:** before dealing with the accounting treatment for each of the complications, it is important to understand that any adjustment that affects the post-acquisition retained earnings of the subsidiary will also affect the calculation of non-controlling interests (NCI). As stated in **Chapter 4**, *non-controlling interests* at the reporting date comprises their share of the net assets of the subsidiary at acquisition date or

the fair value of their interest plus their share of the post-acquisition retained earnings of the subsidiary. Post-acquisition retained earnings of the subsidiary are defined throughout the remainder of this text as the earnings after adjusting for the complications.

Complication 1 – Unrealised Inventory Profits

IAS 2 *Inventories* states that inventories should be measured at the lower of cost and net realisable value. When one group entity sells goods to another at a profit and some/all of those goods are in the inventory of the buying entity (at cost to them) at the reporting date, an element of unrealised profit is included in the closing inventory of the **group**.

EXAMPLE 5.1: TREATMENT OF UNREALISED INVENTORY PROFIT

P Ltd owns 80% of the share capital of S Ltd. P Ltd buys goods for €100 and sells them to S Ltd for €150. At the reporting date, S Ltd still has these goods in inventory. In the **individual** SoFP of S Ltd, these goods are valued at cost of €150 in accordance with IAS 2 and this is correct. Now consider the consolidated SoFP. If the inventory of S Ltd were consolidated (without adjustment) with the inventory of P Ltd, the result would be that the group bought these goods for €100 and valued its inventory at €150 which contravenes IAS 2. There is unrealised profit from a group perspective of €50.

ACCOUNTING TREATMENT

Eliminate all the unrealised profit   €   €

Dr. Retained earnings (selling company P Ltd)	50	
Cr. Inventory		50
Unrealised profit on inventory		

However, if S Ltd was the selling company and the unrealised profit arose in the inventory of P Ltd, then the adjustment would affect the non-controlling interests because S Ltd's post-acquisition retained earnings are now reduced by €50 (see also below, **Questions 5.6** and **5.7**).

Complication 2 – Unrealised Profit on Sale of Tangible Non-current Assets

This complication arises when one group company sells a non-current asset to another at a profit, and the asset is in the statement of financial position of the buying company at the period end. When looking at the group as a single entity, both the profits (from the sale of the asset) and non-current assets are overstated. IAS 16 *Property, Plant and Equipment* states that an asset should be carried at:

1. **Cost**, less accumulated depreciation and impairment; **OR**
2. **Revaluation,** being its fair value at the date of revaluation less subsequent depreciation and impairment.[1]

EXAMPLE 5.2: TREATMENT OF UNREALISED PROFIT ON SALE
OF NON-CURRENT ASSETS

P Ltd bought an item of property, plant and equipment (PPE) on 1 August 2010 at a cost of €300,000 and is depreciating it at 10% straight line. On 1 August 2012 P Ltd sold the asset to S Ltd for €280,000 who is currently depreciating it over the remaining years. A consolidated SoFP is prepared as at 31 July 2013.

1 August 2012

Carrying value of asset (€300,000 – two years' depreciation)	€240,000
Sale proceeds	€280,000
Profit on disposal	€40,000

If the consolidated SoFP as at 31 July 2013 was prepared without adjustment both the profits and the property, plant and equipment (PPE) figures would be overstated by €40,000.

ACCOUNTING TREATMENT

Eliminate unrealised profit in the selling company's accounts:

Dr.	Retained earnings (P Ltd)	€40,000	
Cr.	PPE		€40,000

This transaction is further complicated by the fact that the asset in question is subject to depreciation. At present, **the depreciation is overstated from a group perspective** calculated as follows:

Year ended 31 July 2013:

Depreciation per S Ltd financial statements (€280,000 ÷ 8)	=	€35,000
Depreciation if asset not sold at a profit (€300,000 @ 10%)	=	€30,000
Over-provision		€5,000

Write back the over-provision of depreciation in the buying company

Dr.	PPE	€5,000	
Cr.	Retained Earnings (S Ltd)		€5,000

Remember: The depreciation adjustment changes the retained earnings of S Ltd; therefore, the calculation of non-controlling interests must take this into account. (See also below, **Question 5.7.**)

---

[1] See also **Connolly**, Chapter 6, "Property, Plant and Equipment".

Complication 3 – Revaluation of a Subsidiary's Net Assets at Acquisition Date

When a parent (P Ltd) acquires a subsidiary (S Ltd), the purchase consideration is based on the **fair value** of the subsidiary's net assets acquired and not the carrying values, which are frequently significantly different, particularly in the case of tangible assets such as property.

Fair value is defined as the price that would be received to sell an asset or paid to transfer a liability in an orderly transaction between market participants at the measurement date (IFRS 13).

IFRS 3 requires that all the assets and liabilities of a subsidiary (S Ltd) be revalued (with some exceptions) for consolidation purposes to **fair value** at the date of acquisition. However, there is no obligation on S Ltd to reflect the revaluation in its own financial statements. If S Ltd has recorded the revaluation in its own financial statements, no adjustment is necessary. If not, adjustments are necessary in the consolidation workings. Any change in value is a pre-acquisition adjustment and will impact on **the calculation of goodwill**.

If any of the revalued assets are subject to depreciation, another entry must be made to account for the cumulative additional depreciation on the revaluation surplus. The practical implications of Complication 3 are all illustrated in **Example 5.3**.

EXAMPLE 5.3: REVALUATION OF NET ASSETS OF SUBSIDIARY

The following is the summarised statement of financial position of a subsidiary (S Ltd) on 1 June 2011:

	€000
Property, plant and equipment	4,400
Current assets	1,300
Total assets	**5,700**
Ordinary share capital	2,000
Retained earnings	1,800
Non-current liabilities	1,000
Current liabilities	900
Total equity and liabilities	**5,700**

P Ltd acquired 60% of the ordinary shares of S Ltd on the 1 June 2011. At the date of acquisition the fair value of the property, plant and equipment (PPE) exceeded the carrying value by €300,000 while those assets had an average remaining useful life of five years. S Ltd did not record the revaluation.

In the consolidated workings as at 31 May 2013 (the reporting date) the following adjustments would be necessary:

ACCOUNTING TREATMENT

		€000	€000
1.	**Account for surplus**		
	Dr. PPE	300	
	Cr. Goodwill		300
	Revaluation surplus		
2.	**Account for cumulative additional depreciation**		
	Dr. Retained earnings (S Ltd)	120	
	Cr. Accumulated depreciation – PPE		120
	With the cumulative additional depreciation, i.e. €300,000 × 2/5		

Remember: there is an effect on non-controlling interests because the post-acquisition retained earnings of S Ltd are reduced.
(See also below, **Question 5.7.**)

Complication 4 – Proposed Preference Dividends by a Subsidiary

Complication 4(a) This arises where a subsidiary (S Ltd) has proposed a preference dividend at the reporting date **and the parent (P Ltd) has taken credit for its share**.

If a subsidiary proposes a dividend, part of which is payable to P Ltd, the **intragroup figure must be eliminated** in the consolidated workings, otherwise both the assets and liabilities of the group would be overstated. The remainder of the dividend is payable to non-controlling interests which is a liability of the group and is shown under current liabilities in the consolidated SoFP.

EXAMPLE 5.4: TREATMENT OF PROPOSED PREFERENCE DIVIDENDS
BY A SUBSIDIARY

P Ltd owns 80% of the preference shares of S Ltd.

Extract from statements of financial position as at 31 August 2013:

	P Ltd	S Ltd
	€	€
Assets		
Dividends receivable	40,000	
Liabilities		
Proposed dividends		50,000

The proposed dividend €50,000 is payable as follows:
€40,000 to P Ltd
€10,000 to NCI

ACCOUNTING TREATMENT

Cancel the intragroup dividend   €   €

    Dr. Proposed dividends   40,000
    Cr. Dividends receivable   40,000
    With intragroup dividend

Dividends Receivable

Debit		Credit	
P	40,000	Journal (proposed dividends)	40,000

Proposed Dividends

Debit		Credit	
Journal (dividends receivable)	40,000	S	50,000
SoFP (NCI)	10,000		
	50,000		50,000

Note: the proposed dividends due of €10,000 are disclosed under current liabilities as due to non-controlling interests.

Complication 4(b) Where S Ltd has proposed a preference dividend **and P Ltd has not taken credit** for its share.

EXAMPLE 5.5: TREATMENT OF PROPOSED PREFERENCE DIVIDENDS INCLUDED IN A SUBSIDIARY ONLY

P Ltd owns 80% of the preference shares of S Ltd.

EXTRACT: STATEMENTS OF FINANCIAL POSITION
at 30 August 2013

	P Ltd	S Ltd
Proposed dividend		€50,000

The proposed dividend is again payable as follows:
€40,000 to P Ltd – this is intragroup.
€10,000 to NCI – this is a group liability.

ACCOUNTING TREATMENT

In this instance the intragroup dividend cannot as yet be cancelled because P Ltd has not taken credit for its share, therefore:

	€	€
1. Bring in dividend receivable into P's accounts		
Dr. Dividends receivable	40,000	
Cr. Retained earnings (P Ltd)		40,000
And then		
2. Cancel the intragroup dividend		
Dr. Proposed dividends	40,000	
Cr. Dividends receivable		40,000

Dividends Receivable – P Ltd

Debit		Credit	
Journal 1 (ret. earnings P Ltd)	40,000	Journal 2 (proposed dividends)	40,000

Proposed Dividends – S Ltd

Debit		Credit	
Journal 2 (divs. receivable P Ltd)	40,000	S	50,000
SoFP – NCI	10,000		
	50,000		50,000

Note: disclose €10,000 under current liabilities as due to non-controlling interests.

Complication 5 – Proposed Ordinary Dividends

Under IAS 10 *Events after the Reporting Period*, proposed ordinary dividends at the reporting date do not normally constitute a liability as there is **no obligation** to transfer economic benefits until the dividend is formally approved by the shareholders at the annual general meeting. However, some exam questions contain ordinary dividends proposed by S Ltd, which **are approved** before the year end and accounted for. If this is the case, the treatment in the consolidated workings would be the same as in the case of the preference dividends as per Complication 4 above, i.e.:

(a) where S Ltd has proposed an ordinary dividend and P Ltd **has** taken credit for its share;

or

(b) where S Ltd has proposed an ordinary dividend and P Ltd **has not** taken credit for its share.

Note: any dividends in the SoFP of the parent do not give rise to adjustments. They are liabilities of the group, and are shown in the consolidated SoFP as current liabilities, assuming they have been approved.

Complication 6 – Intragroup Balances

When looking at a group as a **single entity**, it follows that all intragroup balances should be eliminated, otherwise both the assets and liabilities of a group would be overstated.

EXAMPLE 5.6: TREATMENT OF INTRAGROUP BALANCES

In their respective statements of financial position as at 30 June 2013, P Ltd shows an amount of €50,000 owing to S Ltd while S Ltd has a corresponding receivable due from P Ltd.

ACCOUNTING TREATMENT

Cancel intragroup balances

	€000	€000
Dr. Trade payables	50	
Cr. Trade receivables		50

Sometimes group companies operate through current accounts. If this were the case, the adjustment would be:

Dr. Current a/c with S Ltd	50	
Cr. Current a/c with P Ltd		50

Intragroup balances can only be eliminated if they are **in agreement**. The balances could differ for two reasons:
1. Cash in transit.
2. Goods in transit.

When accounting for items in transit between a parent and a subsidiary, the adjustments are made in the financial statements of the **parent**.

EXAMPLE 5.7: ADJUSTMENTS FOR ITEMS IN TRANSIT

At 31 August 2013 the SoFP of P Ltd showed the following receivable:
  Current account with S Ltd: €100,000.

On the same date P Ltd was included as a payable in the SoFP of S Ltd:
  Current account with P Ltd: €60,000.

During late August, the following occurred:
(a) P Ltd sent goods to S Ltd at invoice value €30,000 at a mark-up of 25%. S Ltd did not receive the goods until 6 September 2013.
(b) S Ltd sent a cheque for €10,000 to P Ltd on 31 August 2013, which P Ltd did not receive until 3 September 2013.

Solution

JOURNAL 1 *Account for the cash in transit*   €   €

    Dr. Cash   10,000
    Cr. Current a/c with S Ltd   10,000

JOURNAL 2 *Account for the goods in transit*

    Dr. Inventory (cost price)   24,000
    Dr. Retained Earnings (P Ltd) (profit)   6,000
    Cr. Current a/c with S Ltd (total)   30,000

The current account balances are now in agreement.

JOURNAL 3 *Eliminate the intragroup balances*

    Dr. Current a/c with P Ltd   60,000
    Cr. Current a/c with S Ltd   60,000

IN T ACCOUNT FORMAT

Current Account with S Ltd

Debit		Credit	
P	100,000	Journal 1 Cash in transit	10,000
		Journal 2 Goods in transit	30,000
		Journal 3 Intra-group	60,000
	100,000		100,000

Current Account with P Ltd

Debit		Credit	
Journal 3 Intragroup	60,000	S	60,000

Complication 7 – Impairment of Goodwill

IAS 36 *Impairment of Assets* states that assets should be carried at no more than their recoverable amount. IAS 36 defines an 'impairment loss' as "the amount by which the carrying amount of an asset or a cash generating unit exceeds its recoverable amount". An asset is carried at more than its recoverable amount if its carrying value exceeds the amount to be recovered through use or sale of the asset. In simple terms, impairment occurs when the value of an asset is reduced by an amount that is greater than the normal reduction through depreciation or amortisation. If this is the case, the asset is impaired and the entity must recognise the impairment loss. Under IAS 36, goodwill acquired in a business combination must be tested for impairment **annually**.

EXAMPLE 5.8: TREATMENT OF IMPAIRMENT OF GOODWILL

On 1 May 2011, P Ltd acquired 90% of the ordinary shares of S Ltd at a cost of €1,680,000. On that date the issued share capital of S Ltd was €1,000,000 and its retained earnings €800,000. At 1 May 2011, the fair value of the non-controlling interests was €190,000

The goodwill was impaired as follows:
Year ended 30 April 2012   €20,000
Year ended 30 April 2013   €10,000

	€	€
Dr. Retained earnings (P Ltd)	30,000	
Cr. Goodwill		27,000
Cr. NCI		3,000

Note: the cumulative impairment is written off in the ratio of the group structure, i.e. 90:10, because NCI have been credited with attributable goodwill.

WORKINGS (T Account Method)

Goodwill

Debit		Credit	
Investment in S	1,680	Ord. shares S	1,000
Non-controlling interests	190	Pre-acq. retained earnings S	800
		Journal – goodwill impairment	30
		SoFP – goodwill	40
	1,870		1,870

WORKINGS (Columnar Method)

Goodwill (W1)	Total	P Ltd.	NCI
	€000	€000	€000
Investment in S Ltd.	1,680	1,680	
NCI at fair value	190		190
	1,870	1,680	190
Net assets of S Ltd. at acquisition date:			
Ordinary shares	1,000		
Retained earnings	800		
	1,800	1,620	180
Goodwill at acquisition	70	60	10
Impairment	(30)	(27)	(3)
Consolidated SoFP	40	33	7

Complication 8 – Preference Shares in Issue by a Subsidiary

Sometimes a parent acquires preference shares of a subsidiary along with the acquisition of ordinary shares. Preference shares usually carry a fixed rate of dividend which is expressed as a percentage of the nominal value. The holders of preference shares are paid before distributions are made to the ordinary shareholders and there is also preference to a distribution of assets in a winding up.

EXAMPLE 5.9: TREATMENT OF PREFERENCE SHARES IN A SUBSIDIARY

S Ltd
SUMMARISED STATEMENT OF FINANCIAL POSITION
as at 30 June 2013

	€000
Sundry net assets	4,630
Ordinary shares (€1)	1,000
10% cumulative preference shares (€1)	1,000
Retained earnings	2,630
	4,630

P Ltd acquired 80% of the ordinary shares of S Ltd on 1 July 2012 when the retained earnings of S Ltd were €2 million. The cost of the investment was €2.5 million. On the same date, it purchased 30% of the preference shares of S Ltd at a cost of €320,000. P Ltd elects to measure non-controlling interests at their proportionate interest in the net assets of S Ltd at the date of acquisition.

WORKINGS (T Account Method)

Preference Shares

Debit		Credit	
Goodwill	1,000	S	1,000

Goodwill

Debit		Credit	
Investment in S Ltd (ord. shares)	2,500	Ordinary shares	1,000
Investment in S Ltd (pref. shares)	320	Preference shares	1,000
NCI (W1)	1,300	Retained earnings	2,000
		Goodwill	120
	4,120		4,120

Non-controlling Interests

Debit		Credit	
		Goodwill	1,300
		Share of S post-acquisition	
		Retained Earnings (Note 1)	126
SoFP	1,426		
	1,426		1,426

Note 1: 20% × (2,630 − 2,000)

WORKINGS (Columnar Method)

		€000	€000
(W1) Goodwill			
Cost of investment in S Ltd – Ordinary shares		2,500	
Preference shares		320	2,820
Non-controlling interests Ordinary shares	1,000		
Retained earnings	2,000		
	3,000		
NCI share 20%			600
Preference shares (€1,000 × 70%)			700
			4,120
Net assets of S Ltd. at acquisition date			
Ordinary shares		1,000	
Preference shares		1,000	
Retained earnings		2,000	4,000
Goodwill at acquisition date			120
(W2) Non-controlling interests			
At acquisition date (see *W1*)			
Ordinary shares and retained earnings			600
Preference shares			700
Share of S Ltd post-acquisition retained earnings			
20% × (2,630 − 2,000)			126
SoFP			1,426

Conclusion

It must be emphasised that when the above complications are individually considered the adjustments are easily understood. In examination questions, however, combinations of these complications and how they affect consolidation are invariably tested. It is highly advisable that you are completely familiar with the existence and treatment of each and all of these complications. **Questions 5.6** and **5.7** below have been devised to this end and you would be wise to attempt them and study their solutions.

SUMMARY

1. Consolidated financial statements are prepared as if the group were a single entity.
2. Complications arise in the preparation of consolidated financial statements when group entities trade with each other, subsidiaries pay dividends to parents or there are amounts owing from one group entity to another at a reporting date.
3. Intragroup balances and dividends must be eliminated in full.
4. Profits and losses resulting from transactions between group entities that are recognised in assets such as inventory and property, plant and equipment must be eliminated.
5. Goodwill that arises on the acquisition of a subsidiary must be tested for impairment annually and written down to its recoverable amount if impairment occurs.
6. The assets and liabilities of a subsidiary must be revalued to fair value for consolidation purposes on acquisition by a parent. A depreciation adjustment will also be necessary if a depreciable asset is increased or decreased in value.

QUESTIONS

Question 5.1

(a) What is meant by unrealised profit on inventory?
(b) During August 2013, S Ltd sold goods to P Ltd at invoice value €250,000 on which S Ltd earned a mark-up of 25%. At the reporting date, 31 August 2013, P Ltd had one half of these goods in inventory. Show the necessary journal entry in the consolidated workings for the year ended 31 August 2013.

Solution

(a) Unrealised inventory profit arises when one group entity sells goods to another at a profit and some or all of those goods are in the inventory of the buyer at the reporting date. If the unrealised profit were not accounted for, both the profits and inventories of the group would be overstated.
(b) Calculation of unrealised profit:

	€	€
€250,000 × 1/5 × ½ = €25,000		
Dr. Retained earnings S Ltd	25,000	
Cr. Inventory		25,000

The NCI share of the profit for the year must take into account their share of the unrealised profit.

Question 5.2

(a) On 1 July 2011 P Ltd sold an item of plant to S Ltd for €280,000. P Ltd purchased the asset for €400,000 on 1 July 2008 and is depreciating it at 12.5% straight line. Record the journal entries to deal with this transaction in the consolidated workings as at 30 June 2013.

(b) Explain the accounting treatment.

Solution

(a)

	€
Cost of asset 1 July 2008	400,000
Depreciation 30 June 2009	(50,000)
30 June 2010	(50,000)
30 June 2011	(50,000)
Carrying value 30 June 2011	250,000
Sale proceeds	280,000
Profit on sale	30,000

ACCOUNTING ENTRY

Eliminate the profit

	€	€
Dr. Retained earnings P Ltd	30,000	
Cr. Property, plant and equipment		30,000

The buying entity S Ltd now depreciates the asset on cost €280,000 over the remaining useful life of five years, i.e. €56,000 per annum.

			€
Depreciation per S Ltd 30 June 2012 and 2013:			
€280,000 @ 20% (1/5) × 2 years	2 × €56,000	=	112,000
Depreciation if asset were not sold:			
€400,000 @ 12.5% × 2 years	2 × €50,000	=	100,000
Overcharge (group)			12,000

Accounting entry

	€	€
Dr. Property, plant and equipment	12,000	
Cr. Retained earnings S Ltd		12,000

(b) The sale of an asset at a profit by one group entity to another gives rise to unrealised profit which, if not eliminated on consolidation, would give rise to an overstatement of both group assets and profits. Furthermore, if the asset in question is subject to depreciation, an adjustment is necessary which will correct both the carrying value of the asset and the group profit in the consolidated financial statements.

Question 5.3

(a) P Ltd acquired 70% of the ordinary shares of S Ltd on 1 August 2011. At that date the fair values of the net assets of S Ltd were the same as their carrying values with the exception of property, plant and equipment which showed a surplus of €400,000. At the date of acquisition the average remaining useful lives of the property, plant and equipment was five years. Show the journal entries to reflect the revaluation in the consolidated workings as at 31 July 2013.

(b) Explain any assumptions you made.

Solution to Question 5.3

		€	€
(a) (i) Dr. Property, plant and equipment		400,000	
Cr. Goodwill			400,000
Increase in value of PPE at acquisition			
(ii) Dr. Retained earnings S Ltd		160,000	
Cr. Property, plant and equipment			160,000
Additional depreciation on revalued PPE (€400,000 × 2/5)			

(b) The solution assumes that the subsidiary had not recorded the revaluation surplus in its own financial statements.

Question 5.4

What is the accounting treatment for inter-company balances at a group reporting date and why is such treatment necessary?

Solution

All inter-company balances at a reporting date should be eliminated in the preparation of a consolidated statement of financial position. The aim of a consolidated statement of financial position is to show the financial position of a group as if it were a single entity. Failure to eliminate inter-company balances would result in an overstatement of both the assets and liabilities of a group.

Question 5.5

Explain the implication of impairment of goodwill on the consolidated statement of financial position.

Solution

Goodwill becomes impaired when its recoverable amount is less than the carrying amount. Impairment has the following implications for the consolidated SoFP:

1. the carrying amount of goodwill is reduced to its recoverable amount; and
2. the consolidated retained earnings are reduced by the amount of the impairment if the goodwill is attributable to the parent only. If the goodwill is attributable to both the parent and the non-controlling interests the total impairment is debited to:
   (a) the retained earnings of the parent; and
   (b) the non-controlling interests in proportion to their respective holdings in the subsidiary.

Note: the following questions, **Questions 5.6** and **5.7**, are longer, review-type questions. The solutions to both questions require many journal entries to account for the complications.

Each solution contains:
1. the journal entries;
2. the T account method workings;
3. the columnar method workings; and
4. the consolidated SoFP.

Question 5.6

Pit Plc acquired 80% of the ordinary share capital of Stop Ltd for €150,000 and 50% of the issued 10% cumulative preference shares for €10,000, both purchases being effected on 1 May 2012. There have been no changes in the issued share capital of Stop Ltd since that date. The following balances are taken from the books of the two companies at 30 April 2013:

	Pit Plc €000	Stop Ltd €000
Assets		
Non-current assets		
Property, plant and equipment	218	160
Investment in Stop	160	–
	378	160
Current assets		
Inventories	111	65
Trade receivables	30	15
Cash	19	2
	160	82
Total assets	**538**	**242**
Equity and liabilities		
Equity		
Ordinary shares (€1)	300	100
10% cumulative pref. shares (€1)	–	20

Share premium	20	10
General reserve	68	15
Retained earnings	50	44
Total equity	438	189
Current Liabilities		
Trade payables	50	30
Taxation	50	21
Proposed dividends		2
	100	53
Total equity and liabilities	**538**	**242**

The following additional information is available:
1. Inventories of Pit Plc include goods purchased from Stop Ltd for €20,000. Stop Ltd charged out these goods at cost plus 25%.
2. Proposed dividend of Stop Ltd represents a full year's preference dividend. No interim dividends were paid during the year by either company.
3. Payables of Pit Plc include €6,000 payable to Stop Ltd in respect of goods purchased. Receivables of Stop Ltd include €10,000 due from Pit Plc. The parent company sent a cheque for €4,000 to its subsidiary on 29 April 2013 which was not received by Stop Ltd until May 2013.
4. At 1 May 2012 the balances on the reserves of Stop Ltd were as follows:

	€000
Share premium	10
General reserve	10
Retained earnings	30

5. Goodwill is impaired during the year ended 30 April 2013 in the amount of €2,000.
6. Pit Plc elects to measure non-controlling interests at their proportionate interest in the net assets of Stop Ltd at the date of acquisition.

Requirement Prepare a consolidated statement of financial position for Pit Plc and its subsidiary Stop Ltd at 30 April 2013.

Solution to Question 5.6

(W1) *Goodwill*

	€000		€000	€000
Investment in Stop Ltd				160
Non-controlling interests at acquisition date:				
Ordinary shares	100			
Share premium	10			
General reserve	10			
Retained earnings	30	150 × 20%	30	
Preference shares		20 × 50%	10	40
				200

Stop Ltd net assets at acquisition date:

Ordinary shares	100	
Preference shares	20	
Share premium	10	
General reserve	10	
Retained earnings	30	170
Goodwill at acquisition date		30
Impairment		2
SoFP		28

JOURNAL ENTRIES

	€000	€000
1. Dr. Goodwill	160	
Cr. Investment in Stop		160
Investment in Stop		
2. Dr. Goodwill	40	
Cr. NCI		40
Non-controlling interests at acquisition date (W1)		
3. Dr. Ordinary shares	100	
Dr. Preference shares	20	
Cr. Goodwill		120
Share capital of Stop at acquisition date		
4. Dr. Share premium	10	
Dr. General reserve	10	
Dr. Retained earnings	30	
Cr. Goodwill		50
Reserves of Stop at acquisition date		
5. Dr General reserve	1	
Cr. NCI (20%)		1
NCI share of post-acquisition general reserve – Stop 20% × (15 – 10)		
6. Dr. Retained earnings Stop	10	
Cr. Retained earnings Pit (80%)		8
Cr. NCI (20%)		2
Post-acquisition retained earnings Stop		

Retained earnings at reporting date	44	
Retained earnings at acquisition date	30	
	14	
Journal 7 Unrealised profit	4	
Post-acquisition	10	

7. Dr. Retained earnings (Stop)   4
    Cr. Inventory   4
    Being unrealised profit €20,000 × 1/5 – the margin
        must be applied – not the mark-up

8. Dr. Dividends receivable   1
    Cr. Retained earnings (Pit)   1
    Being share of preference dividend receivable from Stop

9. Dr. Proposed dividends   1
    Cr. Dividends receivable   1
    Cancellation of inter-company dividend

10. Dr. Cash (P Ltd)   4
    Cr. Trade payables   4
    Being cash in transit brought back into Pit's accounts

11. Dr. Trade payables   10
    Cr. Trade receivables   10
    Cancellation of intragroup debt

12. Dr. Retained earnings (Pit)   2
    Cr. Goodwill   2
    *Cumulative impairment of goodwill to reporting dat*e

WORKINGS (T Account Method)

Property, Plant and Equipment

Debit		Credit	
P	218		
S	160	SoFP	378
	378		378

Investment in S

Debit		Credit	
P	160	Goodwill (Jnl. 1)	160

Inventories

Debit		Credit	
P	111	Unrealised profit (Jnl. 7)	4
S	65	SoFP	172
	176		176

Trade Receivables

Debit		Credit	
P	30	Intragroup (Jnl. 11)	10
S	15	SoFP	35
	45		45

Cash

Debit		Credit	
P	19		
S	2		
Cash in transit (Jnl. 10)	4	SoFP	25
	25		25

Ordinary Shares

Debit		Credit	
Goodwill (Jnl. 3)	100	P	300
SoFP	300	S	100
	400		400

Preference Shares

Debit		Credit	
Goodwill (Jnl. 3)	20	S	20

Share Premium

Debit		Credit	
Goodwill (Jnl. 4)	10	P	20
		S	10
SoFP	20		
	30		30

General Reserve

Debit		Credit	
Goodwill (Jnl. 4)	10	P	68
Post-acq. NCI (Jnl. 5)	1	S	15
SoFP	72		
	83		83

Retained Earnings P

Debit		Credit	
Goodwill impaired (Jnl. 12)	2	P at reporting date	50
SoFP	57	Post-acq. of S (Jnl. 6)	8
		Divs. receivable (Jnl. 8)	1
	59		59

Retained Earnings S

Debit		Credit	
Goodwill (Jnl. 4)	30	At reporting date	44
Share of post-acq. (group) (Jnl. 6)	8		
Share of post-acq. NCI (Jnl. 6)	2		
Unrealised profit (Jnl. 7)	4		
	44		44

Trade Payables

Debit		Credit	
Intragroup (Jnl. 11)	10	P	50
SoFP	74	S	30
		Cash in transit (Jnl. 10)	4
	84		84

Taxation

Debit		Credit	
SoFP	71	P	50
		S	21
	71		71

Dividends Proposed

Debit		Credit	
Intragroup (Jnl. 9)	1	S	2
SoFP	1		
	2		2

Dividends Receivable

Debit		Credit	
Retained earnings P (Jnl. 8)	1	Intragroup (Jnl. 9)	1

Goodwill

Debit		Credit	
Investment in S (Jnl. 1)	160	Goodwill impaired (Jnl. 12)	2
NCI (Jnl. 2)	40	Ordinary shares (Jnl. 3)	100
		Pref. shares (Jnl. 3)	20
		Share prem. (Jnl. 4)	10
		Gen. reserve (Jnl. 4)	10
		Ret. earnings (Jnl. 4)	30
		SoFP: Goodwill	28
	200		200

Non-controlling Interests

Debit		Credit	
SoFP	43	Goodwill (Jnl. 2)	40
		Post-acq. gen reserve (Jnl. 5)	1
		Post-acq. ret. earnings (Jnl. 6)	2
	43		43

WORKINGS (Columnar Method)

	Pit	Stop	Adjustments	Consol. SoFP
	€000	€000	€000	€000
Property, plant and equipment	218	160	0	378
Goodwill (*W1*)	0	0	28	28
Investment in Stop	160	0	(160) (Jnl. 1)	0
Inventories	111	65	(4) (Jnl. 7)	172
Trade receivables	30	15	(10) (Jnl. 11)	35
Dividends receivable			1(1) (Jnl. 8/9)	0
Cash	19	2	4 (Jnl. 10)	25
Total assets	**538**	**242**	**(142)**	**638**
Ordinary shares	300	100	(100) (Jnl. 3)	300
Preference shares	0	20	(20) (Jnl. 3)	0
Share premium (*W2*)	20	10	(10) (Jnl. 4)	20
General reserve (*W3*)	68	15	(11)	72
Retained earnings (*W4*)	50	44	(37)	57
Non-controlling interests (*W5*)	0	0	43	43
Trade payables	50	30	4 (10) (Jnl. 10/11)	74
Taxation	50	21		71
Proposed dividend	0	2	(1) (Jnl. 9)	1
Total equity and liabilities	**538**	**242**	**(142)**	**638**

(*W2*) *Share premium:*	€000		€000
Pit at reporting date			20
Stop at reporting date	10		
at acquisition date	(10)		
Post-acquisition	nil		-
Consolidated SoFP			20

(*W3*) *General reserve*			
Pit at reporting date			68
Stop at reporting date	15		
at acquisition date	(10)		
Post-acquisition	5 × 80%		4
Consolidated SoFP			72

(W4) Retained earnings	€000	€000
Pit at reporting date		50
Journal 8 – dividend receivable		1
Journal 12 – goodwill impairment		(2)
Stop at reporting date	44	
Journal 7 – unrealised inventory profit	(4)	
Adjusted	40	
At acquisition date	(30)	
Post -acquisition	10	
Group's share 80%		8
Consolidated SoFP		57

(W5) Non-controlling interests		
Value at acquisition date (W1)		
Ordinary shares	100	
Share premium	10	
General reserve	10	
Retained earnings	30	
	150 × 20%	30
Preference shares	20 × 50%	10
		40
Share of post-acquisition general reserve (Jnl. 5)		1
20% × (15 – 10)		
Share of post-acquisition retained earnings (Jnl. 6)		2
		43

Pit Plc
CONSOLIDATED STATEMENT OF FINANCIAL POSITION
as at 30 April 2013

Assets	€000
Non-current assets	
Property, plant and equipment	378
Goodwill	28
	406
Current assets	
Inventory	172
Trade receivables	35
Cash	25
	232
Total assets	**638**

Equity and liabilities
Equity

Ordinary shares	300
Share premium	20
General reserve	72
Retained earnings	57
Total shareholders' equity	449
Non-controlling interests	43
Total equity	492

Current liabilities

Trade payables	74
Taxation	71
Proposed preference dividend	1
	146
Total equity and liabilities	**638**

Question 5.7

STATEMENT OF FINANCIAL POSITION
as at 31 August 2013

	Push Ltd €000	Shove Ltd €000
Assets		
Non-current assets		
Property, plant and equipment	110	350
Loans	180	–
Investments in Shove	295	
	585	350
Current assets		
Inventory	300	190
Trade receivables	270	90
Cash	160	50
	730	330
Total assets	**1,315**	**680**
Equity and liabilities		
Equity		
Ordinary shares (€1)	840	200
Retained earnings	265	140
Total equity	1,105	340
Non-current liabilities		
Long-term loans	–	170

Current liabilities		
Trade payables	210	170
Total equity and liabilities	**1,315**	**680**

Additional information:
1. Push Ltd acquired 150,000 shares in Shove Ltd for €295,000 on 1 September 2011, at which date Shove Ltd had a balance on retained earnings of €60,000.
2. At the date of acquisition the property, plant and equipment of Shove Ltd had a fair value which exceeded the carrying value by €100,000. At that date the remaining useful life of the property, plant and equipment was five years.
3. Included in Push Ltd's loans is one of €130,000 to Shove Ltd.
4. Push Ltd supplied goods to the value of €125,000 for which it has not yet been paid. These goods cost Push Ltd €100,000 and Shove Ltd still had 4/5ths of them in inventory at 31 August 2013.
5. On 1 September 2012, Push Ltd supplied machinery to Shove Ltd at a price of €198,000. The machine had cost €180,000 one year earlier. It is group policy to depreciate machinery over 10 years.
6. The fair value of the non-controlling interests at 1 September 2011 was €95,000.

Requirement Prepare the consolidated statement of financial position of the Push Ltd group as at 31 August 2013.

Solution to Question 5.7

Group Structure
Group 75%: 150,000/200,000
NCI: 25%

WORKINGS (Columnar Method)

(W1) *Goodwill*

	Total €000	Push €000	NCI €000	Jnl.
Investment in Shove	295	295		1
Fair value of NCI at acquisition date	95		95	2
	390	295	95	
Net assets of Shove at acquisition date:				
Ordinary shares	200			3
Revaluation surplus	100			6
Retained earnings	60	360	270	90	4
SoFP		30	25	5

JOURNAL ENTRIES	€000	€000

1. Dr. Goodwill   295
   Cr. Investment in Shove   295
   Transfer of investment.

2. Dr. Goodwill   95
   Cr. NCI   95
   Fair value of NCI at acquisition date

3. Dr. Ordinary shares   200
   Cr. Goodwill   200
   Ordinary shares of Shove at acquisition date

4. Dr. Retained earnings Shove   60
   Cr. Goodwill   60
   Retained earnings Shove at acquisition date

5. Dr. Retained earnings Shove   44
   Cr. Retained earnings Push   33
   Cr. NCI   11
   Apportionment of Shove **post-acquisition**
   retained earnings 75:25

Shove retained earnings per question	140
Pre-acquisition	(60)
Journal 7 – additional depreciation	(40)
Journal 12 – depreciation write back	4
	44

6. Dr. Property, Plant and Equipment   100
   Cr. Goodwill   100
   With revaluation surplus

7. Dr. Retained earnings Shove   40
   Cr. PPE   40
   With additional depreciation – 100,000 × 2/5

8. Dr. Long-term loans   130
   Cr. Loans   130
   With cancellation of inter-company loans

9. Dr. Trade payable   125
   Cr. Trade receivables   125
   With cancellation of inter-company debt

10. Dr. Retained earnings Push   20
    Cr. Inventory   20
    With unrealised inventory profit 4/5 × 25,000

11. Dr. Retained earnings Push   36
    Cr. Property, plant and equipment   36
    With unrealised profit € 198,000 – (€ 180,000 × 90%)

12. Dr. Property, plant and equipment   4
    Cr. Retained earnings Shove   4
    With write back of over-depreciation

Depreciation per Shove $\dfrac{198,000}{9 \text{ years}}$ = 22,000

Depreciation on historic cost $\dfrac{180,000}{10}$ = 18,000

WORKINGS (T Account Method)

Property, Plant and Equipment

Debit		Credit	
P	110	Extra depreciation (Jnl. 7)	40
S	350	Unrealised profit (Jnl. 11)	36
Revaluation surplus (Jnl. 6)	100		
Depreciation write back (Jnl. 12)	4	SoFP	488
	564		564

Loans

Debit		Credit	
P	180	Intragroup (Jnl. 8)	130
		SoFP	50
	180		180

Investment in S

Debit		Credit	
P	295	Goodwill (Jnl. 1)	295

Inventory

Debit		Credit	
P	300	Unrealised profit (Jnl. 10)	20
S	190	SoFP	470
	490		490

Trade Receivables

Debit		Credit	
P	270	Intragroup (Jnl. 9)	125
S	90	SoFP	235
	360		360

Cash

Debit		Credit	
P	160		
S	50	SoFP	210
	210		210

Trade Payables

Debit		Credit	
Intragroup (Jnl. 9)	125	P	210
SoFP	255	S	170
	380		380

Long-term Loans

Debit		Credit	
Intragroup (Jnl. 8)	130	P	–
SoFP	40	S	170
	170		170

Ordinary Shares

Debit		Credit	
Goodwill (Jnl. 3)	200	P	840
SoFP	840	S	200
	1,040		1,040

Retained Earnings Push

Debit		Credit	
Unrealised inventory profit (Jnl. 10)	20	P	265
Unrealised PPE profit (Jnl. 11)	36	Share of Shove post-acq.	
SoFP	242	retained earnings (Jnl. 5)	33
	298		298

Retained Earnings Shove

Debit		Credit	
Pre-acquisition (Jnl. 4)	60		
Extra depr. (Jnl. 7)	40	S	140
Post-acq. earnings (Jnl. 5)	44	Depr. write back (Jnl. 12)	4
	144		144

Goodwill

Debit		Credit	
Investment in S Ltd (Jnl. 1)	295	Revaluation (Jnl. 6)	100
NCI (Jnl. 2)	95	Ordinary shares (Jnl. 3)	200
		Ret. earnings (Jnl. 4)	60
		SoFP Goodwill (*W1*)	30
	390		390

Non-controlling Interests

Debit		Credit	
		Fair value at acq. date (Jnl. 2)	95
SoFP	106	Share of S post-acq. (Jnl. 5)	11
	106		106

WORKINGS (Columnar Method)

	Push €000	Shove €000	Adjustments €000	Consol. SoFP €000
Property, plant and equipment (*W2*)	110	350	100 (40) (36) 4	488
Loans	180		(130)(Jnl. 8)	50
Goodwill (*W1*)			30	30
Investment in Shove (*W1*)	295		(295)(Jnl. 1)	
Inventory	300	190	(20)(Jnl. 10)	470
Trade receivables	270	90	(125)(Jnl. 9)	235
Cash	160	50		210
Total assets	**1,315**	**680**	**(512)**	**1,483**
Ordinary shares	840	200	(200)(Jnl. 3)	840
Retained earnings (*W3*)	265	140	(163)	242
Non-controlling interests (*W4*)			106	106
Long-term loans		170	(130)(Jnl. 8)	40
Trade payables	210	170	(125)(Jnl. 9)	255
Total equity and liabilities	**1,315**	**680**	**(512)**	**1,483**

(W2) Property, plant and equipment

	€000
Push	110
Shove	350
Revaluation surplus (Jnl. 6)	100
Depreciation on revaluation surplus (Jnl. 7)	(40)
Unrealised profit on sale of machinery (Jnl. 11)	(36)
Depreciation write back on unrealised profit (Jnl. 12)	4
SoFP	488

(W3) Retained earnings

	€000	€000	Jnl.
Push at reporting date		265	
Unreahsed inventory profit		(20)	10
Unrealised profit on sale of PPE		(36)	11
Adjusted		209	
Shove at reporting date	140		
Additional depreciation on revalued asset	(40)		7
Depreciadon write back	4		12
Revised	104		
At acquisition date	(60)		
Post-acquisition	44		
Group's share 75%		33	5
Consolidated SoFP		242	

(W4) Non-controlling interests

	€000	€000	Jnl.
Fair value at acquisition date (*W1*)		95	2
Share of post-acquisition retained earnings of Shove		11	5
		106	

Push Ltd
CONSOLIDATED STATEMENT OF FINANCIAL POSITION
as at 31 August 2013

Assets	€000
Non-current assets	
Property, plant and equipment	488
Goodwill	30
Loans	50
	568

Current assets

Inventory	470
Trade receivables	235
Cash	210
	915
Total assets	**1,483**

Equity and liabilities

Ordinary share capital	840
Retained earnings	242
Total shareholders' equity	1,082
Non-controlling interest	106
Total equity	1,188

Non-current liabilities

Long term loans	40

Current liabilities

Trade payables	255
Total equity and liabilities	**1,483**

Chapter 6

The Statement of Financial Position: Accounting for Associates

LEARNING OBJECTIVES

After reading this chapter you should be able to:
- define an associate;
- explain the concept of significant influence;
- explain the meaning of the equity method of accounting and its application; and
- illustrate the equity method through completion of relevant questions.

Introduction

IAS 28 *Investments in Associates and Joint Ventures* prescribes the same method of accounting in the financial statements of the investor for:

      (a) investments in associates, and

      (b) investments in joint ventures

but, because of the different nature between the two entities, **Chapter 6** deals with 'Accounting for Associates' while 'Accounting for Joint Ventures' will be the subject of **Chapter 7**.

An associate is defined in IAS 28 (para 3) as an entity over which the investor has **significant influence**, which is the power to participate in the financial and operating policy decisions of the investee but is not control or joint control of those policies.

Accounting for an investment in an associate using the equity method, as explained below, is the same whether the investor is an individual entity or a member of a group.

Your focus must now change from consolidating **all** the assets and liabilities of a subsidiary (**full consolidation**) to consolidating **none** of the assets and liabilities of an associate (**equity accounting**). As detailed in **Chapter 2**, an investor can only exercise significant influence over the financial and operating policies of an associate as it owns only between 20% and 50% of its voting shares whereas if can exercise control over a subsidiary. It is logical, therefore, that a different accounting treatment be given to an investment in an associate (A Ltd).

When consolidating a subsidiary (S Ltd) the investment in S Ltd is replaced in the consolidated SoFP by its net assets. In the case of an associate, the investment in A Ltd is carried to the consolidated SoFP (albeit at a valuation – see below) since the net assets of A Ltd are *not* consolidated. Thus, the treatments for subsidiaries and associates are effectively opposite in nature. (See also **Questions 6.6** and **6.7**.)

Prior to the introduction of accounting standards, a long-term investment in another entity was treated either as a trade investment or an investment in a subsidiary. A trade investment was accounted for as a non-current asset and the investing company took credit in profit or loss for dividends received/receivable. However, it was considered that the interests of the shareholders of the investing company were not served by merely accounting for dividends received/receivable from an entity in which it had a significant holding, as this would not measure accurately either the associate's performance or the share of the profit of the associate in which the investing company had a significant investment. The **equity method** was devised to give such information and to reflect it in the financial statements of the investor.

Why Would an Investor Acquire an Interest in an Associate?

Many entities acquire interests in associates for such reasons as:
(a) attempting to ensure the supply of a vital raw material;
(b) securing a return on investment by way of a stream of dividends;
(c) gaining management expertise.

How Significant Influence is 'Evidenced'

Take an example of a shareholder in an associate company speaking to a director of its investor:

> "Can you tell me why your company is in a position to exercise significant influence over the affairs of my company?"

IAS 28 at paragraph 6 details the ways in which significant influence by an investor is evidenced, meaning that it can be shown that it exists as follows:
"(a) representation on the board of directors or equivalent governing body of the investee;
(b) participation in policy-making processes, including participation in decisions about dividends or other distributions;
(c) material transactions between the investor and the investee;
(d) interchange of managerial personnel; or
(e) provision of essential technical information."

While any one of the above would be evidence of significant influence, representation on the board of directors of the investee is the strongest evidence. The investing company should be influential in the direction taken by the associate through participation in policy decisions such as strategy, dividends, capital expenditure, etc.

Accounting for Associates

The **equity method** is a method of accounting whereby the investment is initially recognised at cost and adjusted thereafter for the post-acquisition change in the investor's share of the investee's net assets. The investor's profit or loss includes its share of the investee's profit or loss, and the investor's other comprehensive income includes its share of the investee's other comprehensive income. In more simple terms, in the statement of financial position of the investor, the investment in an associate is topped up each year by the investor's share of the post-acquisition retained earnings (and any other reserves) of the associate and reduced by any impairment loss to the carrying amount of the investment.

Application of Equity Accounting

> ***Key Note:*** **none** of the individual assets and liabilities of an associate are consolidated. HOWEVER, the investment in an associate is carried to the consolidated SoFP at a valuation.

The carrying amount of an investment in a consolidated statement of financial position is demonstrated in **Example 6.1** below:

EXAMPLE 6.1: VALUATION OF CARRYING AMOUNT OF INVESTMENT IN AN ASSOCIATE

P Ltd purchased 40% of the ordinary shares of A Ltd on 1 August 2011 when A Ltd's issued ordinary share capital was €300,000 and its retained earnings €500,000. The cost of the investment was €340,000.

A Ltd
DRAFT STATEMENT OF FINANCIAL POSITION
as at 31 July 2013

	€
Sundry net assets	1,100,000
Ordinary share capital	300,000
Retained earnings	800,000
	1,100,000

The carrying value of the investment in A Ltd was impaired during the year ended 31 July 2013 by €5,000.

Requirement Show the value of the investment in A Ltd in the consolidated statement of financial position of the P Ltd group as at 31 July 2013.

Solution

	€	€
Cost of investment		340,000
Plus		
Share of post-acquisition retained profits and reserves of A Ltd (to end of reporting period):		
Retained earnings at end of reporting period	800,000	
Less Retained earnings at acquisition date	(500,000)	
Post-acquisition retained earnings	300,000	
Investor's share: 40%		120,000
Less		
Impairment to carrying value of investment		(5,000)
Carrying amount of investment		455,000

Accounting for an associate can be achieved by means of **two journal entries** in the financial statements of the investor, thus:

	€	€
1. Dr. Investment in A Ltd	120,000	
Cr. Retained earnings P Ltd		120,000
With the investor's share of the post-acquisition earnings and any other reserves of A Ltd to reporting date		
2. Dr. Retained earnings P Ltd	5,000	
Cr. Investment in A Ltd		5,000
With the cumulative impairment to the reporting date		

(**Note:** goodwill that forms part of the carrying amount of an investment in an associate is not separately recognised and therefore is not tested for impairment separately under IAS 36 *Impairment of Assets*. Instead, the entire carrying amount of the investment is tested for impairment as a single asset by comparing its recoverable amount with its carrying amount.)

Complications (when Accounting for an Associate)

Complication 1 – Unrealised Inventory Profit

Unrealised inventory profit can arise from transactions between a investor and an associate. An associate is *not* a group company but the **investors' share** of unrealised profit between P Ltd and A Ltd must be eliminated in the consolidated workings (see **Example 6.2**).

EXAMPLE 6.2: TREATMENT OF UNREALISED INVENTORY PROFIT

P Ltd has a 40%-owned associate (A Ltd), both of which have a reporting date of 31 August 2013.

P Ltd sells goods at a profit to A Ltd

During August 2013, P Ltd sold goods to A Ltd at invoice value €60,000 on which P Ltd made a gross profit of 20%. All of the goods were in the inventory of A Ltd at the reporting date.

ACCOUNTING TREATMENT

Eliminate Group Share of Unrealised Profit

	€	€
Dr. Retained earnings P Ltd	4,800	
Cr. Investment in A Ltd.		4,800

(being unrealised profit €60,000 × 1/5 × 100% × 40%)

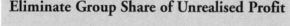

Selling Price	Margin	In Inventory	Group Share

A Ltd sells goods at a profit to P Ltd

During August 2013, A Ltd sells goods to P Ltd at invoice value €120,000 on which A Ltd made a markup of 50%. One half of the goods were in the inventory of P Ltd at the reporting date.

	€	€
Dr. Retained earnings P Ltd — SOFP – Investment	8,000	
Cr. Inventory — SOFP		8,000

(being unrealised profit €120,000 $\times \dfrac{1}{3} \times \dfrac{1}{2} \times$ 40%)

Complication 2 – Dividends

If an associate (A Ltd) has proposed a dividend before the period end, a portion of that dividend is naturally payable to the investor:

(a) if P Ltd has taken credit for its share of the dividend in its SPLOCI – P/L, **this figure should not be included in the consolidated SPLOCI;**

(b) the parent does, however, take credit in the consolidated SPLOCI – P/L for its share of the profits of A Ltd, **which includes its share of A Ltd's dividend**. The dividend is credited to the investment account instead when the equity financial statements are prepared.

Complication 3 – Inter-company Balances

Inter-company balances between a parent (P Ltd) and an associate (A Ltd) at the reporting date **should not be eliminated. Any amounts in P Ltd's SoFP owing to/from A Ltd should be carried to the consolidated SoFP. A Ltd is not a group company**.

Share of Loss of Associate

If an investor's share of losses of an associate equals or exceeds its interest in the associate, the investor must discontinue recognising its share of further losses.

Conclusion

Beware! As **none** of the assets and liabilities of an associate (A Ltd) are consolidated, when preparing consolidated workings, do *not* include any balances from A Ltd.

SUMMARY

1. IAS 28 defines an associate as "an entity, over which the investor has **significant influence**."
2. Significant influence normally arises when the investing entity or group acquires between 20% and 50% of the voting power of the investee. Conversely, if the investor holds less than 20% of the voting power of the investee, it is presumed that the investor does not have significant influence, unless such influence can be demonstrated.
3. The **equity method** is used for the treatment of an associate in the financial statements of the investor.
4. None of the assets and liabilities of an associate are consolidated with those of a parent and subsidiary.
5. The investment in an associate is included in the consolidated statement of financial position at a valuation calculated as follows:

	€
Cost of investment	X
Plus	
Group's share of the post-acquisition retained profits and any other reserves of A Ltd	X
Less	
Cumulative impairment of carrying value of investment	(X)
	X

6. The valuation would be the same in the financial statements of an investor (without a subsidiary) who does not prepare consolidated financial statements.

QUESTIONS

Question 6.1

What percentage of the voting rights of an investee must an investing entity or group purchase in order to acquire an associate?

Solution

If an investor holds between 20% and 50% of the voting power of an investee, it is presumed that the investor has significant influence over the investee and therefore an associate is acquired, unless this assumption can be rebutted.

Question 6.2

Explain the term 'significant influence' in the context of an investment in an associate.

Solution

Significant influence is the power to participate in the financial and operating policy decisions of the investee but not to control or jointly control them.

Question 6.3

What method is used to account for an associate in the financial statements of the investor?

Solution

An investment in an associate is accounted for using the equity method.

Question 6.4

How is an investment in an associate accounted for in a consolidated statement of financial position?

Solution

An investment in an associate is carried to the consolidated statement of financial position at a valuation, calculated as follows:

	€
Cost of investment	X
Group's share of post-acquisition retained profits and reserves of A Ltd	
and reserves of A Ltd	X
Less impairment of investment	(X)
	X

Question 6.5

Explain the treatment of assets and liabilities of an associate in the consolidated statement of financial position.

Solution

None of the assets and liabilities of an associate are consolidated with those of a parent and subsidiary.

Note: **Questions 6.6** and **6.7** are longer, review-type questions. They include an associate and also provide an opportunity to revise the principles of full consolidation of a subsidiary. Each of their solutions contains:
1. the journal entries;
2. the T account method workings;
3. the columnar method workings; and
4. the consolidated SoFP.

Question 6.6

The following are the summarised statements of financial position of Pearl Ltd, Sapphire Ltd and Amethyst Ltd as at 31 July 2013:

	Pearl Ltd €000	Sapphire Ltd €000	Amethyst Ltd €000
Assets			
Non-current assets			
Property, plant and equipment	12,830	7,690	5,130
Investment in Sapphire Ltd	5,040	–	–
Investment in Amethyst Ltd	1,390	–	–
Current assets	4,490	2,680	1,770
Total assets	**23,750**	**10,370**	**6,900**
Equity and liabilities			
Equity			
Ordinary share capital (€1)	10,000	5,000	4,000
Retained earnings	7,930	3,210	1,250
Non-current liabilities	2,000	1,200	900
Current liabilities	3,820	960	750
Total equity and liabilities	**23,750**	**10,370**	**6,900**

The following additional information is available:
1. Pearl Ltd acquired three million of the ordinary shares of Sapphire Ltd on 1 October 2011 when the retained earnings of Sapphire Ltd were €1,800,000.

2. Pearl Ltd acquired 30% of the ordinary shares of Amethyst Ltd on 1 March 2012 when the retained earnings of Amethyst Ltd were €500,000.
3. During July 2013 Amethyst Ltd sold goods to Pearl Ltd at invoice value €60,000 on which Amethyst Ltd earned a mark-up of 20%. Pearl Ltd had 60% of these goods in inventory at the reporting date and the invoice was not settled until 30 August 2013.
4. The investment in Amethyst Ltd was impaired by €10,000 during the year ended 31 July 2013.
5. Non-controlling interests at 1 October 2011 was measured at their share of the net assets of Sapphire Ltd.

Requirement Prepare the consolidated statement of financial position of the Pearl Ltd group as at 31 July 2013.

Solution to Question 6.6

Group Structure

	Sapphire	Amethyst
Group	60%	30%
Non-group interests	40%	

WORKINGS (Columnar Method)

	€000	€000	Jnl.
(W1) Goodwill			
Investment in Sapphire	5,040		1
Non-controlling interests 40% (5,000 +1,800)	2,720	7,760	2
Net assets of Sapphire at acquisition date			
Ordinary shares	5,000		3
Retained earnings	1,800	6,800	4
SoFP		960	

JOURNAL ENTRIES

	€000	€000
1. Dr. Goodwill	5,040	
Cr. Investment in Sapphire		5,040
Investment in Sapphire		
2. Dr. Goodwill	2,720	
Cr. NCI		2,720
Value of NCI at acquisition date		

3. Dr. Ordinary shares   5,000
   Cr. Goodwill   5,000
   Ordinary shares of Sapphire at acquisition date
4. Dr. Retained earnings Sapphire   1,800
   Cr. Goodwill   1,800
   Retained earnings of Sapphire at acquisition date
5. Dr. Retained earnings Sapphire   1,410
   Cr. Retained earnings Pearl (60%)   846
   Cr. NCI (40%)   564
   Post-acquisition retained earnings Sapphire (3,210 – 1800)
6. Dr. Retained earnings (Pearl)   1.8
   Cr. Inventories   1.8
   Unrealised profit €60,000 × 1/6 × 60% × 30%
7. Dr. Retained earnings (Pearl)   10
   Cr. Investment in Amethyst   10
   Impairment of investment
8. Dr. Investment in Amethyst   225
   Cr. Retained earnings (Pearl)   225
   Group's share of post-acquisition earnings of Amethyst
   30% × (1,250 – 500)

WORKINGS (T Account Method)

Note: none of the assets and liabilities of Amethyst Ltd are consolidated.

Property, Plant and Equipment

Debit		Credit	
P	12,830		
S	7,690	SoFP	20,520
	20,520		20,520

Investment in Sapphire

Debit		Credit	
P	5,040	Goodwill (Jnl. 1)	5,040

Investment in Amethyst

Debit		Credit	
P	1,390	Impairment (Jnl. 7)	10
Post-acq. profits (Jnl. 8)	225	SoFP	1,605
	1,615		1,615

Current Assets

Debit		Credit	
P	4,490	Unrealised profit (Jnl. 6)	1.8
S	2,680	SoFP	7,168.2
	7,170		7,170

Ordinary Shares

Debit		Credit	
Goodwill (Jnl. 3)	5,000	P	10,000
SoFP	10,000	S	5,000
	15,000		15,000

Retained Earnings Pearl

Debit		Credit	
Unrealised profit (Jnl. 6)	1.8	Pearl at reporting date	7,930
Investment impairment (Jnl. 7)	10	Share of S post-acq. (Jnl. 5)	846
SoFP	8,989.2	Share of A post-acq. (Jnl. 8)	225
	9,001		9,001

Retained Earnings Sapphire

Debit		Credit	
Pre-acquisition (Jnl. 4)	1800	Sapphire at reporting date	3,210
Post-acquisition – P (Jnl. 5)	846		
NCI (Jnl. 5)	564		
	3,210		3,210

Non-current Liabilities

Debit		Credit	
		P	2,000
SoFP	3,200	S	1,200
	3,200		3,200

Current Liabilities

Debit		Credit	
		P	3,820
SoFP	4,780	S	960
	4,780		4,780

Goodwill

Debit		Credit	
Investment in S Ltd (Jnl. 1)	5,040	Ordinary shares (Jnl. 3)	5,000
NCI (Jnl. 2)	2,720	Retained earnings (Jnl. 4)	1,800
		SoFP: Goodwill	960
	7,760		7,760

Non-controlling Interests

Debit		Credit	
		Goodwill (acq. date) (Jnl. 2)	2,720
SoFP	3,284	Share of S post-acq. (Jnl. 5)	564
	3,284		3,284

WORKINGS (Columnar Method)

	Pearl €000	Sapphire €000	Adjustments €000	Consol. SoFP €000
Property, plant and equipment	12,830	7,690		20,520
Investment in Sapphire (*W1*)	5,040		(5,040) (Jnl. 1)	—
Investment in Amethyst (*W2*)	1,390		225 (10)	1,605
Goodwill (W1)			960	960
Current assets	4,490	2,680	(1.8) (Jnl. 6)	7,168.2
Total assets	**23,750**	**10,370**	**(3,866.8)**	**30,253.2**
Ordinary share capital	10,000	5,000	(5,000) (Jnl. 3)	10,000
Retained earnings (*W3*)	7,930	3,210	(2,150.8)	8,989.2
Non-controlling interests (*W4*)			3,284	3,284
Non-current liabilities	2,000	1,200		3,200
Current liabilities	3,820	960		4,780
Total equity and liabilities	**23,750**	**10,370**	**(3,866.8)**	**30,253.2**

	€000
(W2) Investment in Amethyst	
Cost	1,390
Share of Amethyst post-acquisition profit (Jnl. 8)	225
Impairment of investment (Jnl. 7)	(10)
SoFP	1,605
(W3) Retained earnings	
Pearl at reporting date	7,930
Journal 6 (unrealised profit)	(1.8)
Journal 7 (investment impaired)	(10)
Journal 8 (share of post-acq. of A Ltd)	225

Sapphire: at reporting date	3,210	
at acquisition date	(1,800)	
post-acquisition	1,410	
Group's share: 60%		846
Consolidated SoFP		8,989.2

(W4) Non-controlling interests

Value at acquisition date (W1) and (Jnl. 2)	2,720
Share of Sapphire post-acquisition profit (Jnl. 5)	564
	3,284

Pearl Ltd
STATEMENT OF FINANCIAL POSITION
as at 31 July 2013

	€000
Assets	
Non-current assets	
Property, plant and equipment	20,520
Goodwill	960
Investment in associate	1,605
Current assets	7,168.2
Total assets	**30,253.2**
Equity and liabilities	
Equity	
Ordinary share capital	10,000
Retained earnings	8,989.2
Total shareholders' equity	18,989.2
Non-controlling interests	3,284
Total equity	22,273.2
Non-current liabilities	3,200
Current liabilities	4,780
Total equity and liabilities	**30,253.2**

Question 6.7

The following are the Statements of Financial Position of Purple Plc, Silver Ltd and Amber Ltd as at 30 June 2013:

	Purple Plc €000	Silver Ltd €000	Amber Ltd €000
Assets			
Non-current assets			
Property plant and equipment	10,350	9,520	16,200
Investment in Silver Ltd	5,450	–	–
Investment in Amber Ltd	4,950	–	–
	20,750	9,520	16,200
Current Assets			
Inventories	1,600	1,020	780
Trade receivables	970	600	490
Cash	150	50	20
	2,720	1,670	1,290
Total assets	**23,470**	**11,190**	**17,490**
Equity and liabilities			
Equity			
Ordinary €1 shares	12,500	4,000	8,700
Share premium	1,000	800	1,500
Retained earnings	8,680	5,260	6,440
Total equity	22,180	10,060	16,640
Current liabilities			
Trade payables	1,290	1,130	850
Total equity and liabilities	**23,470**	**11,190**	**17,490**

The following additional information is available:
1. Purple Plc acquired 70% of the ordinary shares of Silver Ltd on 1 July 2010 when its reserves were:

	€000
Share premium account	800
Retained earnings	2,500

2. At 1 July 2010 the fair value of the property, plant and equipment of Silver Ltd. exceeded the book value by €100,000. This surplus has not been reflected in the financial statements of Silver Ltd. At that date the average remaining useful life of the assets was five years.
3. Purple Plc acquired 30% of the ordinary shares of Amber Ltd on 1 September 2010 when the reserves of Amber Ltd were:

	€000
Share premium	1,500
Retained earnings	2,600

4. During March 2013 Silver Ltd sold goods to Purple Plc at invoice value €200,000 on which Silver Ltd made a gross profit of 20%. One half of these goods remained in the inventories of Purple Plc at 30 June 2013.

5. Impairment has occurred as follows during the year under review:
   (a) on goodwill on acquisition of Silver Ltd   €50,000
   (b) on carrying value of investment in Amber Ltd   €100,000
6. At 1 July 2010 the fair value of the non-controlling interests was €2,290,000.

Requirement Prepare the consolidated statement of financial position of the Purple Plc group as at 30 June 2013.

Solution to Question 6.7

WORKINGS (Columnar Method)

		Total €000	Purple €000	NCI €000	Jnl.
(W1) Goodwill					
Investment in Silver		5,450	5,450		1
Fair value of NCI at acquisition date		2,290		2,290	2
		7,740	5,450	2,290	
Net assets of Silver at acquisition date:					
Ordinary shares	4,000				3
Share premium	800				4
Revaluation surplus	100				6
Retained earnings	2,500	7,400	5,180	2,220	4
Goodwill at acquisition date		340	270	70	
Impairment		(50)	(35)	(15)	
SoFP		290	235	55	

JOURNAL ENTRIES		€000	€000
1. Dr. Goodwill		5,450	
Cr. Investment in Silver			5,450
Investment in Silver			
2. Dr. Goodwill		2,290	
Cr. NCI			2,290
Fair value at acquisition date			
3. Dr. Ordinary shares		4,000	
Cr. Goodwill			4,000
Ordinary shares Silver at acquisition date			
4. Dr. Share premium		800	
Dr. Retained earnings		2,500	
Cr. Goodwill			3,300
Reserves of Silver at acquisition date			
5. Dr. Retained earnings Silver		2,680	
Cr. Retained earnings Purple (70%)			1,876
Cr. NCI (30%)			804
Post-acquisition retained earnings Silver			

	€000
Retained earnings Silver at reporting date	5,260
Retained earnings Silver at acquisition date	(2,500)
	2,760
Depreciation on revaluation (Jnl. 7)	(60)
Unrealised inventory profit (Jnl. 8)	(20)
Adjusted post-acquisition	2,680

6. Dr. PPE   100
    Cr. Goodwill   100
    Being increase in PPE at acquisition date from book value to fair value
7. Dr. Retained earnings (Silver)   60
    Cr. PPE   60
    Being cumulative depreciation on revaluation surplus 100,000 × 3/5
8. Dr. Retained earnings (Silver)   20
    Cr. Inventory   20
    With unrealised profit on inventory: (€200,000 × 1/5 × 50%)
9. Dr. Retained earnings Purple Ltd   35
    Dr. NCI   15
    Cr. Goodwill   50
    Impairment of goodwill on acquisition of Silver 70%:30%

Accounting for the Associate

10. Dr. Investment in Amber Ltd   1,152
    Cr. Share premium Purple Ltd (a)   nil
    Cr. Retained earnings Purple Ltd (b)   1,152
    (a) 30% × (1,500 – 1,500)
    (b) 30% × (6,440 – 2,600)
    With 30% of the post-acquisition reserves of Amber Ltd
11. Dr. Retained Earnings Purple Ltd   100
    Cr. Investment in Amber Ltd   100
    With cumulative impairment of investment in Amber Ltd

WORKINGS (T Account Method)

Property, Plant and Equipment

Debit		Credit	
P	10,350	Additional depreciation (Jnl. 7)	60
S	9,520		
Revaluation (Jnl. 6)	100	SoFP	19,910
	19,970		19,970

Investment in Silver Ltd

Debit		Credit	
P	5,450	Goodwill (Jnl. 1)	5,450

Investment in Amber Ltd

P	4,950	Impairment (Jnl. 11)	100
Share of a post-acq. profits (Jnl. 10)	1,152	SoFP	6,002
	6,102		6,102

Inventories

Debit		Credit	
P	1,600	Unrealised profit (Jnl. 8)	20
S	1,020	SoFP	2,600
	2,620		2,620

Trade Receivables

Debit		Credit	
P	970		
S	600	SoFP	1,570
	1,570		1,570

Trade Payables

Debit		Credit	
SoFP	2,420	P	1,290
		S	1,130
	2,420		2,420

Cash

Debit		Credit	
P	150	SoFP	200
S	50		
	200		200

Ordinary Shares

Debit		Credit	
Goodwill (Jnl. 3)	4,000	P	12,500
SoFP	12,500	S	4,000
	16,500		16,500

Share Premium

Debit		Credit	
Goodwill (Jnl. 4)	800	P	1,000
SoFP	1,000	S	800
	1,800		1,800

Retained Earnings Purple

Debit		Credit	
Goodwill impairment (Jnl. 9)	35	Purple at reporting date	8,680
Impairment of invest. in A (Jnl. 11)	100	Share of S post-acq. (Jnl. 5)	1,876
SoFP	11,573	Share of A post-acq. (Jnl. 10)	1,152
	11,708		11,708

Retained Earnings Silver

Debit		Credit	
Pre-acquisition (Jnl. 4)	2,500	Silver at reporting date	5,260
Post-acq. Purple (Jnl. 5)	1,876		
Post-acq. NCI (Jnl. 5)	804		
Additional depr. (Jnl. 7)	60		
Unrealised profit (Jnl. 8)	20		
	5,260		5,260

Goodwill

Debit		Credit	
Investment in Silver (Jnl. 1)	5,450	Ordinary shares (Jnl. 3)	4,000
NCI (Jnl. 2)	2,290	Share premium (Jnl. 4)	800
		Retained earnings (Jnl. 4)	2,500
		Revaluation (Jnl. 6)	100
		Impairment (Jn1. 9)	50
		SoFP – Goodwill	290
	7,740		7,740

Non-controlling Interests

Debit		Credit	
Goodwill impaired (Jnl. 9)	15	Fair value at acq. date (Jnl. 2)	2,290
SoFP	3,079	Share of S post-acq. (Jnl. 5)	804
	3,094		3,094

WORKINGS (Columnar Method)

	Purple	Silver	Adjustments	Consol. SoFP
	€000	€000	€000	€000
Property, plant and equipment (*W2*)	10,350	9,520	100 (60)	19,910
Investment in Silver	5,450		(5,450) (Jnl. 1)	0
Investment in Amber (*W3*)	4,950		1,152 (100)	6,002
Goodwill (*W1*)			290	290

Inventories	1,600	1,020	(20) (Jnl. 8)	2,600
Trade receivables	970	600		1,570
Cash	150	50		200
Total Assets	**23,470**	**11,190**	**(4,088)**	**30,572**
Ordinary shares	12,500	4,000	(4,000)(Jnl. 3)	12,500
Share premium (*W4*)	1,000	800	(800)(Jnl. 4)	1,000
Retained earnings (*W5*)	8,680	5,260	(2,367)	11,573
Non-controlling interests (*W6*)			3,079	3,079
Trade payables	1,290	1,130		2,420
Total Equity and Liabilities	**23,470**	**11,190**	**(4,088)**	**30,572**

(W2) Property, plant and equipment	**€000**	**€000**
Purple		10,350
Silver		9,520
Revaluation surplus (Jnl. 6)		100
Additional depreciation (Jnl. 7)		(60)
		19,910

(W3) Investment in Amber		
Cost of investment		4,950
Share of Amber post-acquisition profits (Jnl. 10)		1,152
Impairment of carrying value of investment (Jnl. 11)		(100)
		6,002

(W4) Share premium		
Purple at reporting date		1,000
Silver at reporting date	800	
at acquisition date	(800)	
post-acquisition	nil	
Group's share – 70%		nil
SoFP		1,000

(W5) Retained earnings	**€000**	**€000**
Purple at reporting date		8,680
Journal 9: Goodwill impairment		(35)
Journal 10: Share of Amber post-acq.		1,152
Journal 11: Impairment of investment		(100)
		9,697
Silver at reporting date	5,260	

Journal 7: Additional depreciation	(60)	
Journal 8: Unrealised profit	(20)	
Adjusted	5,180	
Silver at acquisition date	(2,500)	
Post-acquisition	2,680	
Group's share – 70%		1,876
		11,573

(W6) Non-controlling interests

Fair value at acquisition date (Jnl. 2)	2,290
Share of post-acq. earnings of Silver (Jnl. 5)	804
Share of goodwill impairment (Jnl. 9)	(15)
	3,079

Purple Plc
CONSOLIDATED STATEMENT OF FINANCIAL POSITION
as at 30 June 2013

Assets	€000
Non-current assets	
Property, plant and equipment	19,910
Goodwill	290
Investment in associate	6,002
	26,202
Non-current assets	
Inventory	2,600
Trade receivables	1,570
Cash	200
	4,370
Total assets	**30,572**
Equity and liabilities	
Equity	
Ordinary share capital	12,500
Share premium account	1,000
Retained earnings	11,573
Total shareholders' equity	25,073
Non-controlling interests	3,079
Total equity	28,152
Current liabilities	
Trade payables	2,420
Total equity and liabilities	**30,572**

Chapter 7

The Statement of Financial Position: Accounting for Joint Ventures

LEARNING OBJECTIVES

After reading this chapter you should be able to:
- Define a joint arrangement, a joint operation and a joint venture;
- Explain the concept of joint control;
- Describe the accounting treatment for a joint venture; and
- Account for a joint venture in a consolidated SoFP or the SoFP of the investor.

Stop! Before we start in to this chapter, it is important now to recall:
1. how to treat a subsidiary in the consolidated SoFP: all its assets and liabilities are consolidated with those of the parent, whether or not there are non-controlling interests;
2. how to treat an associate in the consolidated SoFP: none of its assets and liabilities are consolidated with those of the parent and the subsidiary.

Introduction

With regard to IFRS 11 *Joint Arrangements,* important terms and their definitions are as follows[1]:

Joint Arrangement An arrangement of which two or more parties have **joint control.** A joint arrangement is either a **joint operation** or a **joint venture.**

Joint Control The contractually agreed sharing of control of an arrangement which exists only when decisions about the relevant activities require the **unanimous consent** of the parties sharing control.

Joint operation A **joint arrangement** whereby the parties that have **joint control** of the arrangement have rights to the assets and obligation for the liabilities relating to the arrangement.

Joint venture A joint arrangement whereby the parties that have joint control of the arrangement have rights to the **net assets of the arrangement.**

---

[1] See also *Connolly*, Chapter 30, "Joint Arrangements".

As explained, a joint arrangement is either a joint operation or a joint venture. This can be illustrated as follows:

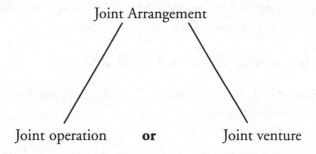

Joint Arrangement

Joint operation **or** Joint venture

> **Note:**
> * joint operations are accounted for in accordance with IFRS 11 and are not the subject of this text; whereas
> * joint ventures are accounted for in accordance with IAS 28.

As joint operations and joint ventures are accounted for according to different reporting standards, it is important to be able to distinguish between the two. The distinction between a joint operation and a joint venture depends upon the rights and obligations of the parties to the arrangement.

Characteristics of Joint Operations

The main characteristics of joint operations can be summarised as follows:
(a) Normally, they are not structured through a separate vehicle.
(b) Joint operators share all the assets relating to the arrangement in a specified proportion.
(c) Joint operators share all the liabilities of an arrangement in a specified proportion.
(d) The arrangement establishes the allocation of revenue and expenses on the basis of the relative performance of each party.

Characteristics of Joint Ventures

(a) Joint ventures *are* structured through a separate vehicle.
(b) The contractual agreement endows the parties to the arrangement with rights to the **net assets** of the arrangement. It is the vehicle that endows the rights and obligations. Without the vehicle the parties to the arrangement would have no rights or obligations to the arrangement. The assets of the arrangement are the arrangement's assets. The parties themselves have no interests in the assets. The arrangement (not the parties to it) is liable for the debts and obligations. The parties are only liable to the extent of their investment and the agreement establishes each party's share of profits or losses.

Accounting for Joint Operations (IFRS 11)

Each joint operator recognises its assets, liabilities, expenses and revenue or its share of those items in their own individual financial statements.

Accounting for Joint Ventures (IAS 28)

As explained in **Chapter 6**, IAS 28 prescribes an **identical accounting treatment** for:
(a) investments in associates; and
(b) investments in joint ventures.

The accounting treatment is known as the **equity method**. You should be aware that prior to the issue of the revised IAS 28, investments in joint ventures were accounted for under IAS 31 using proportionate consolidation. The equity method is explained comprehensively in **Chapter 6** and therefore will only be outlined at this point.

Valuation of Investment in Joint Venture in SoFP of the Venturer

As in the case of an associate, an investment in a joint venture is measured as follows:

Pro-forma Measurement

	€000
Cost of investment	X
Share of JV's post-acquisition retained profits and other reserves	X
Any impairment of investment	(X)
	X

SoFP Accounting Entries for the Equity Method in the Case of a Joint Venture

The following entries are made in the consolidated workings:

	€000	€000
1. Dr. Investment in JV	X	
Cr. Reserves		X

Investor's (venturer) share of post-acquisition retained profits and other reserves of JV

	€000	€000
2. Dr. Retained earnings investor	X	
Cr. Investment in JV		X

Impairment of investment in JV

See **Example 7.2** below.

EXAMPLE 7.1: CONSOLIDATING A PARENT, A SUBSIDIARY AND JOINT VENTURE

The following summarised statements of financial position have been prepared as at 31 August 2013:

	P Ltd €000	S Ltd €000	JV Ltd €000
Assets			
Non-current assets			
Property, plant and equipment	9,810	5,880	3,920
Investment in S Ltd	3,890		
Investment in JV Ltd	1,260		
Current assets	2,450	1,470	980
Total Assets	**17,410**	**7,350**	**4,900**
Equity and Liabilities			
Equity			
Ordinary share capital (€1)	10,000	3,000	1,000
Retained earnings	3,450	2,430	2,710
Total equity	13,450	5,430	3,710
Non-current liabilities	2,000	800	500
Current liabilities	1,960	1,120	690
Total Equity and Liabilities	**17,410**	**7,350**	**4,900**

The following additional information is available:
1. P Ltd acquired 2.7 million ordinary shares in S Ltd on 1 September 2011 when the retained earnings of S Ltd were €1,300,000.
2. P Ltd acquired 50% of JV Ltd on 1 March 2012 when the retained earnings of JV Ltd were €1,500,000.
3. Non-controlling interests are measured at acquisition date at their share of the net assets of S Ltd.

WORKINGS (Columnar Method)

	€000	€000	Jnl.
(W1) Goodwill			
Investment in S Ltd		3,890	1
NCI at acquisition date		430	2
10% × (3,000 + 1,300)			
		4,320	
Net assets of S Ltd. at acquisition date:			
Ordinary shares	3,000		3
Retained earnings	1,300	4,300	4
SoFP		20	

JOURNAL ENTRIES

		€000	€000
1.	Dr. Goodwill	3,890	
	Cr. Investment in S Ltd		3,890
	Investment in S Ltd		
2.	Dr. Goodwill	430	
	Cr. NCI		430
	NCI at acquisition date		
3.	Dr. Ordinary shares	3,000	
	Cr. Goodwill		3,000
	Ordinary shares S Ltd. at acquisition date		
4.	Dr. Retained earnings	1,300	
	Cr. Goodwill		1,300
	Retained earnings of S Ltd at acquisition date		
5.	Dr. Retained earnings S Ltd	1,130	
	Cr. Retained earnings P Ltd (90%)		1,017
	Cr. NCI (10%)		113

Retained earnings S: at reporting date   2,430
at acquisition date   (1,300)
Post-acquisition   1,130

6.	Dr. Investment in JV	605	
	Cr. Retained earnings		605
	Investor's share (50%) of post-acquisition		
	retained earnings of JV.		

Retained earnings JV: at reporting date   2,710
at acquisition date   (1,500)
Post-acquisition   1,210

WORKINGS (T Account Method)

Property, Plant and Equipment

Debit		Credit	
P	9,810		
S	5,880	SoFP	15,690
	15,690		15,690

Investment in S Ltd

Debit		Credit	
P	3,890	Goodwill (Jnl. 1)	3,890

Investment in JV Ltd

Debit		Credit	
P	1,260		
Share of post-acq. (Jnl. 6)	605	SoFP	1,865
	1,865		1,865

Current Assets

Debit		Credit	
P	2,450		
S	1,470	SoFP	3,920
	3,920		3,920

Ordinary Shares

Debit		Credit	
Goodwill (Jnl. 3)	3,000	P	10,000
SoFP	10,000	S	3,000
	10,000		13,000

Retained Earnings P

Debit		Credit	
		P at reporting date	3,450
		Share of S post-acq. (Jnl. 5)	1,017
SoFP	5,072	Share of JV post-acq. (Jnl. 6)	605
	5,072		5,072

Retained Earnings S

Debit		Credit	
Pre acquisition (Jnl. 4)	1,300	S at reporting date	2,430
Post-acquisition P (Jnl. 5)	1,017		
Post-acquisition NCI (Jnl. 5)	113		
	2,430		2,430

Non-current Liabilities

Debit		Credit	
		P	2,000
SoFP	2,800	S	800
	2,800		2,800

Current Liabilities

Debit		Credit	
SoFP	3,080	P	1,960
		S	1,120
	3,080		3,080

Goodwill

Debit		Credit	
Investment in S Ltd (Jnl. 1)	3,890	Ordinary shares (Jnl. 3)	3,000
NCI (Jnl. 2)	430	Retained earnings (Jnl. 4)	1,300
		SoFP: Goodwill	20
	4,320		4,320

Non-controlling Interests

Debit		Credit	
SoFP	543	Acquisition date (Jnl. 2)	430
		Share of S post-acq. (Jnl. 5)	113
	543		543

WORKINGS (Columnar Method)

	P	S	Adjustments		Consol. SoFP
	€000	€000	€000		€000
Property, plant and equipment	9,810	5,880			15,690
Investment in S (*W1*)	3,890		(3,890)	(Jnl. l)	–
Investment in JV	1,260		605	(Jnl. 6)	1,865
Goodwill (*W1*)			20		20
Current assets	2,450	1,470			3,920
Total assets	**17,410**	**7,350**	**(3,265)**		**21,495**
Ordinary shares	10,000	3,000	(3,000)	(Jnl. 3)	10,000
Retained earnings (*W2*)	3,450	2,430	(808)		5,072
Non-controlling interests (*W3*)			543		543
Non-current liabilities	2,000	800			2,800
Current liabilities	1,960	1,120			3,080
Total equity and liabilities	**17,410**	**7,350**	**(3,265)**		**21,495**

		€000	€000
(W2) Retained earnings			
P Ltd at reporting date:			3,450
Journal 6 share of JV Ltd post-acquisition earnings			605
S Ltd at reporting date		2,430	

	€000	€000	Jnl.
S Ltd at acquisition date		(1,300)	
Post-acquisition		1,130	
Group's share: 90%			1,017
SoFP			5,072

(W3) Non-controlling interest	€000	€000	Jnl.
At date of acquisition		430	2
Share of S Ltd post-acquisition retained earnings		113	5
SoFP		543	

P Limited
CONSOLIDATED STATEMENT OF FINANCIAL POSITION
as at 31 August 2013

Assets	€000
Non-current assets	
Property, plant and equipment	15,690
Investment in JV	1,865
Goodwill	20
Current assets	3,920
Total assets	**21,495**
Equity and liabilities	
Equity	
Ordinary share capital	10,000
Retained earnings	5,072
Total shareholders' equity	15,072
Non-controlling interests	543
Total equity	15,615
Non-current liabilities	2,800
Current liabilities	3,080
Total equity and liabilities	**21,495**

Conclusion

Thus far, you have studied the consolidation procedures for a subsidiary, an associate and a joint venture. A unique opportunity to revise all of these at the same time is presented in **Question 7.5**. Do not let this opportunity pass!

SUMMARY

1. There are two types of joint arrangements specified in IFRS 11:
   (a) joint operations; and
   (b) joint ventures.
2. A joint venture is a joint arrangement whereby the parties that have joint control of the arrangement have rights to the net assets of the arrangement.
3. The equity method is the accounting treatment for an interest in a joint venture in the financial statements of the investor.
4. Under the equity method, none of a joint venture's assets or liabilities are consolidated with those of a parent and subsidiary (as in the case of an associate).

The same applies in the case of an investor in a joint venture or associate who does not prepare consolidated financial statements.

QUESTIONS

Question 7.1

What is meant by a joint venture in accordance with IAS 28 *Investments in Associates and Joint Ventures*?

Solution

A joint venture is a joint arrangement whereby the parties that have joint control of the arrangement have rights to the **net assets** of the arrangement.

Question 7.2

How many categories of joint arrangements are contained in IFRS 11?

Solution

IFRS 11 recognises two categories of joint arrangement:
(a) joint operations
(b) joint ventures.

Question 7.3

What are the defining characteristics of a joint venture?

Solution

The defining characteristics are:
(a) It is normally structured through a separate vehicle.
(b) The contractual agreement gives the parties rights to the net assets of the arrangement.

Question 7.4

Describe the method of accounting for a joint venture in the financial statements of the investor.

Solution

The equity method is used to account for a joint venture in the financial statements of the investor.

> *Note:* **Question 7.5** is a long review question which involves accounting for a parent, a subsidiary, an associate, a joint venture and a trade investment. The solution contains:
> - the journal entries;
> - the T account method workings;
> - the columnar method workings; and
> - the consolidated SoFP.

Question 7.5

The following are the statements of financial position of Peach Plc, Silver Ltd, Amber Ltd and Green Ltd as at 30 June 2013:

	Peach Plc €000	Silver Ltd €000	Amber Ltd €000	Green Ltd €000
Assets				
Non-current assets				
Property, plant and equipment	10,350	9,520	16,200	6,400
Investment in Silver Ltd	5,450	–	–	–
Investment in Amber Ltd	4,950	–	–	–
Investment in Green Ltd	3,200	–	–	–
Investment in Blue Ltd	100	–	–	–
	24,050	9,520	16,200	6,400
Current assets	2,720	1,670	1,290	660
Total assets	**26,770**	**11,190**	**17,490**	**7,060**
Equity and liabilities				
Equity				
Ordinary €1 shares	14,500	4,000	8,700	5,000
Share premium	2,200	800	1,500	–
Retained earnings	8,680	5,260	6,440	1,630

Total equity	25,380	10.060	16,640	6,630
Current liabilities	1,390	1,130	850	430
Total equity and liabilities	**26,770**	**11,190**	**17,490**	**7,060**

The following additional information is available:
1. Peach Plc acquired 70% of the ordinary shares of Silver Ltd on 1 July 2010 when Silver's reserves were:

	€000
Share premium account	800
Retained earnings	2,500

2. Peach Plc acquired 30% of the ordinary shares of Amber Ltd on 1 July 2011 when the reserves of Amber Ltd were:

	€000
Share Premium	1,500
Retained earnings	2,600

3. Peach Plc acquired 50% of the ordinary shares of Green Ltd on 1 July 2012. Red Ltd and Peach Ltd jointly own and jointly control the relevant activities of Green Ltd. Retained earnings of Green Ltd at 1 July 2012 were €970,000.
4. During the year ended 30 June 2013 impairment occurred as follows:
   (a) goodwill on acquisition of Silver   €50,000
   (b) carrying value of investment in Amber   €100,000
5. At 1 July 2010 the fair value of the non-controlling interests in Silver was €2,250,000.
6. The investment in Blue Ltd. was designated on acquisition as 'not held for trading'. The fair value at 30 June 2013 was €120,000.

Requirement Prepare the consolidated statement of financial position as at 30 June 2013.

Solution to Question 7.5

SOLUTION GUIDELINES

- All of Silver's assets and liabilities are consolidated – *full consolidation.*
- None of Amber's assets and liabilities are consolidated – *the equity method.*
- None of Green's assets and liabilities are consolidated – *the equity method.*
- The investment in Blue Ltd is a trade investment and is carried to the consolidated SoFP at fair value at the reporting date.

(W1) Goodwill

	Total	Peach	NCI	
	€000	**€000**	**€000**	**Jnl.**
Investment in Silver	5,450	5,450		1
Fair value of NCI at acq. date	2,250		2,250	2
	7,700	5,450	2,250	
Net assets of Silver at acq. date:				

Net assets of Silver at acq. date:					
Ordinary shares	4,000				3
Share premium	800				4
Retained earnings	2,500				4
	7,300	(7,300)	(5,110)	(2,190)	
Goodwill at acquisition date		400	340	60	
Impairment (70% : 30%)		(50)	(35)	(15)	9
SoFP		350	305	45	

JOURNAL ENTRIES

	€000	€000
1. Dr. Goodwill	5,450	
Cr. Investment in Silver		5,450
Transfer of investment in Silver		
2. Dr. Goodwill	2,250	
Cr. NCI		2,250
Fair value of NCI at acquisition date		
3. Dr. Ordinary shares	4,000	
Cr. Goodwill		4,000
Ordinary shares of Silver at acquisition date		
4. Dr. Share premium	800	
Dr. Retained earnings	2,500	
Cr. Goodwill		3,300
Reserves of Silver at acquisition date		
5. Dr. Retained earnings Silver	2,760	
Cr. Retained earnings Peach (70% × 2,760)		1,932
Cr. NCI (30% × 2,760)		828

Post-acquisition profits of Silver

Silver: retained earnings at reporting date	5,260
retained earnings at acquisition date	2,500
Post-acquisition	2,760

6. Dr. Investment in Amber Ltd   1,152
    Cr. Share premium Peach 30% (1,500 – 1,500)   0
    Cr. Retained earnings Peach 30% (6,440 – 2,600)   1,152
    Share of post-acquisition reserves of Amber Ltd

7. Dr. Retained earnings (Peach Ltd)   100
    Cr. Investment in Amber Ltd   100
    Impairment of investment

8. Dr. Investment in Green Ltd   330
    Cr. Retained earnings (Peach Ltd)   330
    Share of Green's post-acquisition profits 50% × (1,630 – 970)

9. Dr. Retained earnings Peach   35
    Dr. NCI   15
    Cr. Goodwill   50
    Impairment of goodwill (70:30) in Silver

10. Dr. Investment in Blue   20
    Cr. Revaluation reserve   20
    Increase in fair value of investment (120 – 100)

WORKINGS (T Account Method)

Property, Plant and Equipment

Debit		Credit	
P	10,350		
S	9,520		
		SoFP	19,870
	19,870		19,870

Investment in Silver Ltd

Debit		Credit	
P	5,450	Goodwill (Jnl. 1)	5,450

Investment in Amber Ltd

Debit		Credit	
P	4,950	Impairment (Jnl. 7)	100
Share of post-acq. (Jnl. 6)	1,152	SoFP	6,002
	6,102		6,102

Investment in Green Ltd

Debit		Credit	
P	3,200		
Share of post-acq. (Jnl. 8)	330	SoFP	3,530
	3,530		3,530

Investment in Blue

Debit		Credit	
P	100		
Revaluation reserve (Jnl. 10)	20	SoFP	120
	120		120

Current Assets

Debit		Credit	
P	2,720		
S	1,670	SoFP	4,390
	4,390		4,390

Ordinary Shares

Debit		Credit	
Goodwill (Jnl. 3)	4,000	P	14,500
SoFP	14,500	S	4,000
	18,500		18,500

Share Premium

Debit		Credit	
Goodwill (Jnl. 4)	800	P	2,200
SoFP	2,200	S	800
	3,000		3,000

Revaluation Reserve

Debit		Credit	
SoFP	20	Investment in Blue (Jnl. 10)	20

Retained Earnings P

Debit		Credit	
Impairment of invest. in A (Jnl. 7)	100	P at reporting date	8,680
Goodwill impairment (Jnl. 9)	35	Share of S post-acq (Jnl. 5)	1,932
SoFP	11,959	Share of G post-acq. (Jnl. 8)	330
		Share of A post-acq. (Jnl. 6)	1,152
	12,094		12,094

Retained Earnings Silver

Debit		Credit	
Pre-acquisition (Jnl. 4)	2,500	S at reporting date	5,260
Post-acq. P (Jnl. 5)	1,932		
Post-acq. NCI (Jnl. 5)	828		
	5,260		5,260

Current Liabilities

Debit		Credit	
SoFP	2,520	P	1,390
		S	1,130
	2,520		2,520

Goodwill

Debit		Credit	
Investment in S Ltd (Jnl. 1)	5,450	Ordinary shares (Jnl. 3)	4,000
NCI (Jnl. 2)	2,250	Share premium (Jnl. 4)	800
		Retained earnings (Jnl. 4)	2,500
		Impairment (Jnl. 9)	50
		Goodwill (SoFP)	350
	7,700		7,700

Non-controlling Interests

Debit		Credit	
Goodwill impairment (Jnl. 9)	15	Fair value at acq. date (Jnl. 2)	2,250
SoFP	3,063	Share of S post-acq. (Jnl. 5)	828
	3,078		3,078

Workings (Columnar Method)

	Peach €000	Silver €000	Adjustments €000	Consol. SoFP €000
Property, plant and equipment	10,350	9,520		19,870
Investment in S (*W1*)	5,450		(5,450) (Jnl. l)	–
Investment in A (*W2*)	4,950		1,152, (100)	6,002
Investment in G	3,200		330 (Jnl. 8)	3,530
Investment in B	100		20 (Jnl. 10)	120
Goodwill (*W1*)			350	350
Current assets	2,720	1,670		4,390
Total assets	**26,770**	**11,190**	**(3,698)**	**34,262**
Ordinary shares	14,500	4,000	(4,000) (Jnl. 3)	14,500
Share premium (*W3*)	2,200	800	(800) (Jnl. 4)	2,200
Revaluation reserve			20 (Jnl. 10)	20
Retained earnings (*W4*)	8,680	5,260	(1,981)	11,959
NCI (*W5*)			3,063	3,063
Current liabilities	1,390	1,130		2,520
Total equity & liabilities	**26,770**	**11,190**	**(3,698)**	**34,262**

	€000	€000
(W2) Investment in Amber Ltd		
At cost		4,950
Share of post-acquisition profits (Jnl. 6)		1,152
Impairment of investment (Jnl. 7)		(100)
Carrying value of investment		6,002
(W3) Share premium		
Peach Ltd at reporting date		2,200
Silver Ltd at reporting date	800	
at acquisition date	(800)	
post-acquisition	nil	
Group's share (70%)		nil
SoFP		2,200
(W4) Retained earnings		
Peach at reporting date		8,680
Share of post-acq. retained earnings Amber (Jnl. 6)		1,152
Impairment of investment in Amber (Jnl. 7)		(100)
Share of post-acq. retained earnings Green (Jnl. 8)		330
Impairment of goodwill in Silver (Jnl. 9)		(35)
Silver:		
At reporting date	5,260	
At acquisition date	(2,500)	
Post-acquisition	2,760	
Group's share (70%)		1,932
SoFP		11,959
(W5) Non-controlling interests		
Fair value at acquisition date (Jnl. 2)		2,250
Share of post-acquisition earnings of Silver (Jnl. 5)		828
Impairment of goodwill on acquisition of Silver (Jnl. 9)		(15)
		3,063

Peach Plc
CONSOLIDATED STATEMENT OF FINANCIAL POSITION
as at 30 June 2013

Assets	€000
Non-current assets	
Property, plant and equipment	19,870
Investment in associate	6,002
Investment in joint venture	3,530

Investment in Blue	120
Goodwill	350
	29,872
Current assets	4,390
Total assets	**34,262**

Equity and liabilities
Equity

Ordinary shares	14,500
Share premium	2,200
Revaluation reserve	20
Retained earnings	11,959
Total shareholders' equity	28,679
Non-controlling interests	3,063
Total equity	31,742
Current liabilities	2,520
Total equity and liabilities	**34,262**

Chapter 8

The Consolidated Statement of Profit or Loss and Other Comprehensive Income and The Consolidated Statement of Changes in Equity

LEARNING OBJECTIVES

After studying this chapter you should be able to:
1. explain the application of full consolidation and the equity method in the context of the consolidated SPLOCI and the SoCIE;
2. demonstrate an understanding of the calculation of non-controlling interests in the subsidiary's profit/loss and its total comprehensive income for a reporting period; and
3. prepare and present a basic consolidated statement of profit or loss and other comprehensive income and a consolidated statement of changes in equity incorporating a parent, a subsidiary, an associate, an joint venture and a trade investment.

Introduction

By the end of the chapter, you should have a more complete picture of consolidation.

In **Chapters 3 to 7** we dealt with the preparation and presentation of consolidated statements of financial position (SoFP), including the treatment of:
- investments in subsidiaries;
- investments in associates;
- investments in joint ventures; and
- trade investments.

This chapter will illustrate the preparation and presentation of:
1. the consolidated statement of profit or loss and other comprehensive income (SPLOCI) and
2. the consolidated statement of changes in equity (SoCIE) for each type of investment.

Other Comprehensive Income

It is a fundamental principle of accounting that all gains and losses, other than those arising from transactions with owners acting in their capacity as owners, should be included in the calculation of profit or loss for a reporting period. However, company law and specific international accounting standards allow or require some gains/losses to be taken through other comprehensive income (OCI) to reserves. Any gain/loss taken to reserves is included under **other comprehensive income** in the statement of profit or loss and other comprehensive income, for example:
- changes in revaluation reserves (e.g. property revaluation);
- exchange differences on translating foreign operations;
- actuarial gains and losses (re-measurements) arising in a defined benefit pension scheme.

Definition of Other Comprehensive Income

'Other comprehensive income' "comprises items of income and expense (including reclassification adjustments) that are not recognised in profit or loss as required or permitted by other IFRSs" (IAS 1 *Presentation of Financial Statements*, para 7).

Definition of Total Comprehensive Income

'Total comprehensive income' (TCI) is the change in equity during a period resulting from transactions and other events, other than those changes resulting from transactions with owners in their capacity as owners (IAS 1, para 1).

The Consolidated Statement of Profit or Loss and Other Comprehensive Income

IAS 1 specifies the format and content of the statement of profit or loss and other comprehensive income (SPLOCI) and the statement of changes in equity (SoCIE) and requires that particular disclosures are made in these statements or in the notes to the statements.

IAS 1 also states that an entity must present all items of income and expense recognised in a period using either one of two methods:

Method 1: in a single statement of profit or loss and other comprehensive income; **or**
Method 2: in two statements:
     (a) a statement of profit or loss for the year; and
     (b) a statement of profit or loss and other comprehensive income for the year beginning with profit or loss for the year and showing components of other comprehensive income.

Key Note: this text adopts Method 1, a single consolidated statement of profit or loss and other comprehensive income in its examples, questions and solutions.

Non-controlling Interests

The **profit or loss for the reporting period** and the **total comprehensive income** for the same period must be apportioned between the shareholders of the parent and the non-controlling interests as follows:

PRO FORMA: CONSOLIDATED STATEMENT OF PROFIT OR LOSS AND OTHER COMPREHENSIVE INCOME

	€
Revenue	X
Cost of sales	(X)
Gross profit	X
Distribution costs	(X)
Administrative expenses	(X)
Finance costs	(X)
Profit before tax	X
Income tax expense	X
Profit for the year	X
Other comprehensive income:	
Gains on property revaluation	X
Total comprehensive income for the year	X
Profit for the year attributable to:	
Owners of the parent	X
Non-controlling interests	X
	X
Total comprehensive income for the year attributable to:	
Owners of the parent	X
Non-controlling interests	X
	X

The Consolidated Statement of Changes in Equity

An entity must present a statement of changes in equity (SoCIE) showing:
(a) the carrying amount for each component of equity both at the beginning and the end of each reporting period;
(b) the total comprehensive income for the period showing separately the total amounts attributable to owners of the parent and to non-controlling interests;

(c) transactions with shareholders in their capacity as owners, e.g issues of shares, distributions to owners.

PRO FORMA: CONSOLIDATED STATEMENT OF CHANGES IN EQUITY

	Share capital	Revaluation reserve	Retained earnings	Total	Non-controlling interests	Total Equity
	€	€	€	€	€	€
Balance at 1 July 2012	X	X	X	X	X	X
Issue of shares	X			X		X
Dividends			(X)	(X)		(X)
Total comprehensive income for the year		X	X	X	X	X
Balance at 30 June 2013	X	X	X	X	X	X

Note: a majority of examination questions involving the preparation of a consolidated SPLOCI will also require preparation of the consolidated SoCIE.

Accounting Treatment of a Subsidiary in the Consolidated SPLOCI

As previously stated in **Chapter 4,** subsidiaries are accounted for using full consolidation. This means that all the income and expenses of a subsidiary are consolidated with those of the parent company.

Key Note: however, a parent can only consolidate the post-acquisition income and expenses of a subsidiary, or any other acquired entity. Therefore, a vital distinction needs to made between:
• a subsidiary acquired *before* the start of a reporting year (see **Example 8.1**); and
• a subsidiary acquired during a reporting year (see **Example 8.2**).

Accounting Treatment of Non-controlling Interests

The **profit/loss** and the **total comprehensive income** of a subsidiary for a reporting period must be apportioned between the shareholders of the parent and the non-controlling interests (NCI). The following points should be noted:

1. The non-controlling interests in the profit/loss of subsidiary is based on the entity's profit/loss **after tax** (this figure may need to be adjusted for 'complications', e.g. unrealised inventory profits, etc., which will be covered in **Chapter 9**).
2. The non-controlling interests in the total comprehensive income of a subsidiary for a reporting period is calculated as follows:

	€
Interest in profit/loss of subsidiary (as in 1 above)	X
Plus/Minus: NCI share of other comprehensive gains and losses	X
NCI in total comprehensive income	X

EXAMPLE 8.1: SUBSIDIARY ACQUIRED BEFORE THE START
OF THE REPORTING PERIOD

STATEMENTS OF PROFIT OR LOSS AND OTHER COMPREHENSIVE INCOME
for the Year Ended 31 August 2013

	Pop Ltd €000	Snap Ltd €000
Revenue	4,600	1,800
Cost of sales	(3,200)	(1,300)
	1,400	500
Distribution costs	(270)	(70)
Administrative expenses	(320)	(90)
Finance costs	(60)	(30)
Profit before tax	750	310
Income tax expense	(280)	(90)
Profit for the year	470	220
Other comprehensive income		
Property revaluation surplus	100	50
Total comprehensive income for the year	570	270

Pop Ltd acquired 80% of the ordinary shares of Snap Ltd when its retained earnings were €120,000. The date of acquisition was 1 September 2010.

Retained earnings 1 September 2012

Pop Ltd   €860,000
Snap Ltd   €340,000

Requirement Prepare for the year ended 31 August 2013:
(a) the consolidated statement of profit or loss and other comprehensive income;
(b) the consolidated statement of changes in equity, insofar as the information
     permits.

Solution
JOURNAL ENTRY

	€000	€000
1. Dr. PPE (SoFP)	150	
Cr. SPLOCI – OCI		150

Property revaluation surplus

Note: Pop will be credited with €140,000 and non-controlling interests will be credited with €10,000 through total comprehensive income for the year.
       Pop: €100,000 + (80% × €50,000)
       NCI: 20% × €50,000.

WORKINGS (Columnar Method)

	Pop	Snap	Adjustments	Consol. SPLOCI
	€000	€000	€000	€000
Revenue	4,600	1,800		6,400
Cost of sales	(3,200)	(1,300)		(4,500)
Gross profit	1,400	500		1,900
Distribution costs	(270)	(70)		(340)
Administrative expenses	(320)	(90)		(410)
Finance costs	(60)	(30)		(90)
Profit before tax	750	310		1,060
Income tax expense	(280)	(90)		(370)
Profit for the year	470	220		690

(W1) Non-controlling interest in profit of Snap Ltd
Profit after tax Snap Ltd   220
NCI × 20%   44

(W2) Non-controlling interest in total comprehensive income of Snap Ltd
As per (W1) above   44
Revaluation surplus – Snap Ltd:
    €50,000 × 20%   10
                                                            54

Pop Limited
CONSOLIDATED STATEMENT OF PROFIT OR LOSS AND OTHER COMPREHENSIVE INCOME
for the Year Ended 31 August 2013

	€000
Revenue	6,400
Cost of sales	(4,500)
Gross profit	1,900
Distribution costs	(340)
Administrative expenses	(410)
Finance costs	(90)
Profit before tax	1,060
Income tax expense	(370)
Profit for the year	**690**
Other comprehensive income	
Property revaluation surplus	150
Total comprehensive income for the year	**840**

Profit attributable to:	
Owners of the parent	646
Non-controlling interest	44
	690
Total comprehensive income attributable to:	
Owners of the parent	786
Non-controlling interests	54
	840

STATEMENT OF CHANGES IN EQUITY (EXTRACT)
for the Year Ended 31 August 2013

	Ordinary Shares €000	Revaluation Reserve €000	Retained Earnings €000	NCI €000	Total €000
Balance 1 September 2012			1,036 (*W3*)		
TCI for the year		140	646	54	840
Balance 31 August 2013			1,682		

(W3) Group retained earnings 1 September 2012

The group retained earnings at the start of a reporting period can be defined as the retained earnings of the parent at that date **plus** the group's share of the post-acquisition retained earnings of the subsidiary to the same date.

		€000
Pop Ltd		860
Snap Ltd	80% (340–120)	176
		1,036

1/9/12   Acquisition date

Subsidiary Acquired during a Reporting Period

It is a basic principle of consolidated financial statements that income and expenses of a subsidiary **are only consolidated from the date of acquisition**. When a subsidiary is acquired during a reporting period, its income and expenses must be **time-apportioned** and only those income and expenses earned and incurred **after the date of acquisition** can be consolidated. *Beware:* a particular income or expense could fall into one period only.

Non-controlling Interest in a Subsidiary Acquired during a Reporting Period

The non-controlling interests in the profits of the subsidiary must also be time-apportioned.

EXAMPLE 8.2: SUBSIDIARY ACQUIRED DURING A REPORTING PERIOD

STATEMENTS OF PROFIT OR LOSS
for the Year Ended 30 September 2013

	Pit Ltd €	Stop Ltd €
Revenue	860,000	220,000
Cost of sales	520,000	130,000
Gross profit	340,000	90,000
Distribution costs	(80,000)	(10,000)
Administrative expenses	(90,000)	(30,000)
Finance costs	(30,000)	(5,000)
Profit before tax	140,000	45,000
Income tax expense	(50,000)	(18,000)
Profit for the year	90,000	27,000

Pit Ltd acquired 80% of the ordinary shares of Stop Ltd on 31 March 2013.

Retained earnings 1 October 2012
Pit Ltd   €310,000
Stop Ltd   €186,000

Requirement Prepare for the year ended 30 September 2013:
(a) The consolidated statement of profit or loss;
(b) The consolidated statement of changes in equity, insofar as the information permits.

Solution

Stop Ltd became a subsidiary of Pit Ltd on 31 March 2013 (i.e. half way through the reporting period); therefore all its income and expenses must be **time-apportioned × 6/12.**

WORKINGS (Columnar Method)

	Pit	**Stop**	**Adjustments**	**Consol. SPLOCI**
	€	€	€	€
Revenue	860,000	220,000	(110,000)	970,000
Cost of sales	(520,000)	(130,000)	65,000	(585,000)
Gross profit	340,000	90,000	(45,000)	385,000
Distribution costs	(80,000)	(10,000)	5,000	(85,000)
Administrative expenses	(90,000)	(30,000)	15,000	(105,000)
Finance costs	(30,000)	(5,000)	2,500	(32,500)
Profit before tax	140,000	45,000	(22,500)	162,500
Income tax expense	(50,000)	(18,000)	9,000	(59,000)
Profit for the year	90,000	27,000	(13,500)	103,500

Non-controlling interests
In profits of Stop Ltd
   Post-acquisition profit after tax   €27,000 × 6/12   =   €13,500
   NCI × 20%   €2,700

CONSOLIDATED STATEMENT OF PROFIT OR LOSS
for the Year Ended 30 September 2013

	€
Revenue	970,000
Cost of sales	(585,000)
Gross profit	385,000
Distribution costs	(85,000)
Administrative expenses	(105,000)
Finance costs	(32,500)
Profit before tax	162,500
Income tax expense	(59,000)
Profit for the year	103,500

Profit for the year attributable to:
Owners of the parent   100,800
Non-controlling interest   2,700
                                                                     103,500

CONSOLIDATED STATEMENT OF CHANGES IN EQUITY (EXTRACT)

	Ordinary Shares	Ret. Earnings	NCI	Total
		€	€	€
Balance at 1 October 2012		310,000 *(W1)*		
Profit for the year		100,800	2,700	103,500
Balance at 30 September 2013		410,800		

(W1) Retained Earnings
Pit Ltd   310,000

Note: Stop Ltd cannot be included in the opening retained earnings of the group as it was bought during the reporting period, i.e. there were no post-acquisition earnings at the start of the reporting period.

Introducing an Associate

Accounting Treatment

As previously explained in **Chapter 6**, the investment in an associate is accounted for using the equity method. In the consolidated statement of financial position, the investment in the associate is valued as follows:

	€
Cost of investment	X
Plus: group's share of post-acquisition retained profits and reserves	X
Less: impairment of investment	(X)
	X

In the consolidated SPLOCI **none of the individual income and expenses of an associate are consolidated**; however, the associate is dealt with through a one-line item which is added to the consolidated profit before tax figure, as follows:

	€
Share of profit of associate (profit after tax)	X

Note: the consolidated SPLOCI would also have to recognise the share of any other comprehensive income of an associate.

Example 8.3 illustrates a consolidated SPLOCI and SoCIE involving a parent, a subsidiary and an associate.

EXAMPLE 8.3: ASSOCIATE ACQUIRED BEFORE THE START OF THE REPORTING PERIOD

STATEMENTS OF PROFIT OR LOSS
for the Year Ended 31 July 2013

	Pot Ltd €000	Stove Ltd €000	Apron Ltd €000
Revenue	4,840	3,610	1,790
Cost of sales	(3,230)	(2,410)	(1,260)
Gross profit	1,610	1,200	530
Distribution costs	(380)	(295)	(110)
Administrative expenses	(350)	(185)	(130)
Finance costs	(140)	(95)	(55)
Profit before tax	740	625	235
Income tax expense	(310)	(250)	(95)
Profit for the year	430	375	140

(a) Pot Ltd acquired 80% of the ordinary shares of Stove Ltd and 40% of the ordinary shares of Apron Ltd when Stove Ltd's retained earnings were €630,000 and those of Apron Ltd were €140,000. The investments were made on 1 November 2010 and 31 August 2011.

(b) The retained earnings of the companies at 1 August 2012 were:

Pot Ltd	€2,650,000
Stove Ltd	€1,410,000
Apron Ltd	€360,000

Non-controlling interest is measured at acquisition date at their share of the net assets of Stove Ltd.

Requirement Prepare:

(a) the consolidated statement of profit or loss for the year ended 31 July 2013;

(b) the consolidated statement of changes in equity for the same period, insofar as the information permits.

Solution

JOURNAL ENTRY

	€000	€000
1. Dr. Investment in Apron (SoFP)	56	
Cr. SPLOCI – P/L		56

Share of profit of associate for reporting year
(€140,000 × 40%) (W1)

WORKINGS (Columnar Method)

	Pot	Stove	Adjustments	Consol. SPLOCI
	€000	€000	€000	€000
Revenue	4,840	3,610		8,450
Cost of sales	(3,230)	(2,410)		(5,640)
Gross profit	1,610	1,200		2,810
Distribution costs	(380)	(295)		(675)
Administrative expenses	(350)	(185)		(535)
Finance costs	(140)	(95)		(235)
Share of profit of Apron *(W1)*			56 (Jnl. 1)	56
Profit before tax	740	625	56	1,421
Income tax expense	(310)	(250)		(560)
Profit for the year	430	375	56	861

CONSOLIDATED STATEMENT OF PROFIT OR LOSS
for the year ended 31 July 2013

	€000
Revenue	8,450
Cost of sales	(5,640)
Gross profit	2,810
Distribution costs	(675)
Administrative expenses	(535)
Finance costs	(235)
Share of profit of associate *(W1)*	56
Profit before tax	1,421
Income tax expense	(560)
Profit for the year	861
Profit attributable to:	
Owners of the parent	786
Non-controlling interests *(W2)*	75
	861

(W1) Share of profit of associate

	€000
Profit after tax Apron Ltd	140
Group's share × 40%	56

(W2) Non-controlling interests

Profit after tax Stove Ltd	375
NCI × 20%	75

CONSOLIDATED STATEMENT OF CHANGES IN EQUITY (EXTRACT)

	Ordinary Shares €000	Retained Earnings €000	NCI €000	Total €000
Balance 1 August 2012		3,362 (W3)		
Profit for the year		786	75	861
Balance 31 July 2013		4,148		

(W3) Retained Earnings at 1 August 2012

Pot Ltd	2,650
Share of post-acquisition profits:	
Stove Ltd: Group's share: 80% (1,410 – 630)	624
Apron Ltd: Group's share: 40% (360 – 140)	88
	3,362

Note: both Stove Ltd and Apron Ltd are included in the opening retained earnings of the group as both entities were acquired before the reporting period.

Key Note: if an associate is acquired during a reporting period, its profit after tax must be time-apportioned and only the group's share of the post-acquisition element should be included in the consolidated SPLOCI.

Joint Ventures

As discussed in **Chapter 7** a joint venture is an entity that is subject to joint control whereby the parties to the arrangement have rights to the net assets of the arrangement. An investment in a joint venture is accounted for in the financial statements of the investor using the **equity method**. In a consolidated statement of profit or loss and other comprehensive income there are included:

    (a) the investor's share of the profit or loss for the year; and
    (b) the investor's share of any other comprehensive income.

This treatment is identical to that of an associate (see **Example 8.3** above and **8.4** below.)

EXAMPLE 8.4: JOINT VENTURE ACQUIRED BEFORE THE
START OF THE REPORTING PERIOD

The following are the statements of profit or loss of Pete Ltd, Sue Ltd and JV Ltd for the period ending 31 May 2013:

	Pete Ltd €000	Sue Ltd €000	JV Ltd €000
Revenue	12,600	8,900	4,800

Cost of sales	(8,800)	(6,670)	(3,600)
Gross profit	3,800	2,230	1,200
Distribution costs	(590)	(410)	(150)
Administrative expenses	(1,240)	(530)	(260)
Finance costs	(440)	(220)	(90)
Profit before tax	1,530	1,070	700
Income tax expense	(300)	(210)	(140)
Profit for the year	1,230	860	560

Pete Ltd acquired 90% of the ordinary shares of Sue Ltd on 1 November 2010.

Pete Ltd and Rob Ltd each acquired 50% of the ordinary shares of JV Ltd on 1 June 2011. JV Ltd is subject to joint control by its two investing companies.

Non-controlling interests are measured at acquisition date at their share of the net assets of Sue Ltd.

Requirement Prepare the consolidated statement of profit or loss for the period ended 31 May 2013.

Solution

JOURNAL ENTRY

	€000	€000
1. Dr. Investment in JV (SoFP)	280	
Cr. SPLOCI – P/L		280

Share of profit of joint venture for reporting year
(€560,000 × 50%)

WORKINGS (Columnar Method)

	Pete	Sue	Adjustment		Consol. SPLOCI
	€000	€000	€000		€000
Revenue	12,600	8,900			21,500
Cost of sales	(8,800)	(6,670)			(15,470)
Gross profit	3,800	2,230			6,030
Distribution costs	(590)	(410)			(1,000)
Administrative expenses	(1,240)	(530)			(1,770)
Finance costs	(440)	(220)			(660)
Share of profit of JV Ltd			280	(Jnl. 1)	280
Profit before tax	1,530	1,070	280		2,880
Income tax expense	(300)	(210)			(510)
Profit for the year	1,230	860	280		2,370

CONSOLIDATED STATEMENT OF PROFIT OR LOSS
for the Year Ended 31 May 2013

	€000
Revenue	21,500
Cost of sales	(15,470)
Gross profit	6,030
Distribution costs	(1,000)
Administrative expenses	(1,770)
Finance costs	(660)
Share of profit of joint venture (W1)	280
Profit before tax	2,880
Income tax expense	(510)
Profit for the year	2,370
Profit for the year attributable to:	
Owners of the parent	2,284
Non-controlling interests (*W2*)	86
	2,370

(W1) Share of profit of joint venture:
JV Ltd – profit after tax €560,000 × 50% = €280,000

(W2) Non-controlling interests
Sue Ltd – profit after tax €860,000 × 10% = €86,000

Key Note: when a joint venture is acquired during a reporting period, the group's share of its profit for the year must be time-apportioned.

Trade (or Simple) Investments

A trade investment occurs when the investor acquires less than 20% of the voting rights of the investee and there is no significant influence over its policies (see **Chapter 2**). In a consolidated statement of profit or loss and other comprehensive income, a group records as income dividends received or receivable from a trade investment. Under IFRS 9 the gain/loss on re-measuring the investment to fair value at the reporting date is taken to the SPLOCI – P/L if "held for trading" in arriving at the profit before tax or to other comprehensive income (SPLOCI – OCI) if designated "not held for trading" or measured at fair value through other comprehensive income.

Conclusion

At this stage of your progress through the text you have studied a significant proportion of the preparation of consolidated financial statements. If you have attempted all of the questions so far in the text, you should now be proficient in what many students call, simply, 'consolidation'.

SUMMARY

1. In accordance with IAS 1 the statement of profit or loss and other comprehensive income must be either:
   (i) a single statement of profit or loss and other comprehensive income; or
   (ii) a statement of profit or loss followed by a statement of other comprehensive income for the year, beginning with profit or loss for the year and showing components of other comprehensive income.
2. In the consolidated SPLOCI all the income and expenses of subsidiary are consolidated with those of the parent (but only from the date of acquisition).
3. The following must be disclosed in respect of non-controlling interests in a subsidiary:
   (a) profit for the year attributable to the NCI;
   (b) total comprehensive income for the year attributable to the NCI.
4. Non-controlling interests in a subsidiary's profit for the year are calculated on its profit after tax.
5. Under the equity method none of the individual income and expenses of an associate or a joint venture are consolidated with those of a parent and subsidiary. The share of the profit after tax of an associate or a joint venture is included as a line item in the consolidated SPLOCI – P/L as follows:

Share of profit of associate	€X
Share of profit of joint venture	€X

6. The consolidated statement of changes in equity must disclose:
   (a) the opening and closing balances for each item classed as equity;
   (b) total comprehensive income for the reporting period split between reserves, retained earnings and non-controlling interests; and
   (c) transactions with shareholders in their capacity as owners.
7. The consolidated retained earnings at the beginning of a reporting period can be defined as:
   The retained earnings of the parent at the start of the reporting date
       Plus
   The group's share of the post-acquisition retained earnings of the other entities at the same date.

   Note: a subsidiary, associate or joint venture acquired during a reporting period cannot be included in the group retained earnings at the beginning of that period.

QUESTIONS

Question 8.1

How is a subsidiary accounted for in a consolidated statement of profit or loss and other comprehensive income and how is such treatment effected?

Solution

A subsidiary is accounted for in a consolidated SPLOCI using full consolidation. This means that all the income and expenses of subsidiary earned and incurred after the date of acquisition are consolidated with those of the parent.

Question 8.2

Explain how non-controlling interests are disclosed both in the consolidated SPLOCI and SoCIE.

Solution

SPLOCI   There must be disclosed:
(a) the profit/loss of the subsidiary for the reporting period attributable to the non-controlling interests; and
(b) the total comprehensive income of the subsidiary for the period attributable to the non-controlling interests.

SoCIE   Normally, the consolidated SoCIE discloses with regard to the non-controlling interests:
(a) the opening and closing balances;
(b) their share of the total comprehensive income of the subsidiary for the year; and
(c) any dividend paid to them.

Question 8.3

Explain the effect of the equity method on the consolidated SPLOCI.

Solution

Both an associate and a joint venture are accounted for using the equity method which entails including the group's share of the profits of both as follows:

	€000
Share of profit of associate	X
Share of profit of joint venture	X

The group's share of any other comprehensive income of both an associate and a joint venture would also be included as part of Other Comprehensive Income.

Question 8.4

List the usual components of a consolidated SoCIE.

Solution

The usual components are
- the opening and closing balances for each component of equity;
- the total comprehensive income for the year; and
- transactions with shareholders in their capacity as owners.

Note: **Questions 8.5** and **8.6** are longer review-type questions. **Question 8.5** and its solution provides a comprehensive coverage of the consolidated SPLOCI and SoCIE as it incorporates a parent, a subsidiary, an associate, a joint venture and a trade investment.

Question 8.6 will test your knowledge of how to prepare a SoCIE only, while incorporating a parent, a subsidiary and an associate.

Question 8.5

STATEMENTS OF PROFIT OR LOSS AND OTHER COMPREHENSIVE INCOME
for the Year Ended 31 July 2013

	Wind Ltd €000	Rain Ltd €000	Ice Ltd €000	Hail Ltd €000
Revenue	15,850	12,680	9,510	6,340
Cost of sales	(11,880)	(9,490)	(7,130)	(4,760)
Gross profit	3,970	3,190	2,380	1,580
Dividend received	80			
Distribution costs	(320)	(250)	(190)	(120)
Administrative expenses	(510)	(400)	(290)	(180)
Finance costs	(130)	(110)	(70)	(50)
Profit before tax	3,090	2,430	1,830	1,230
Income tax expense	(620)	(480)	(350)	(240)
Profit for the year	2,470	1,950	1,480	990
Other comprehensive income:				
Property revaluation surplus	400			
Movement in fair value of financial asset through OCI		(100)		
Total comprehensive income for the year	2,870	1,850	1,480	990

1. Wind Ltd has made the following investments:
   (a) 60% of the ordinary shares of Rain Ltd on 1 April 2009 when the retained earnings of Rain Ltd were €450,000;

(b) 30% of the ordinary shares of Ice Ltd on 1 February 2013;

(c) 50% of the ordinary shares of Hail Ltd on 1 August 2012 when its retained earnings were €1,010,000. Weather Ltd acquired the other 50% on the same date. Wind Ltd and Weather Ltd exercise joint control over the policies of Hail Ltd;

(d) 10% of the ordinary shares of Storm Ltd on 1 August 2012;

(e) the dividend received by Wind Ltd was from Storm Ltd.

2. Retained earnings at 1 August 2012   **€000**

Wind Ltd	8,130
Rain Ltd	1,970
Ice Ltd	930
Hail Ltd	1,250

There was no change in the fair value of the investment in Storm Ltd during the reporting period.

Requirement Prepare for the year ended 31 July 2013:

(a) the consolidated statement of profit or loss and other comprehensive income; and

(b) the consolidated statement of changes in equity.

Solution to Question 8.5

JOURNAL ENTRIES

	€000	€000
1. Dr. Investment in Ice (SoFP)	222	
Cr. SPLOCI – P/L		222
Share of profit of associate for reporting year		
(€1,480,000 × 30% × 6/12) (W1)		
2. Dr. Investment in Hail (SoFP)	495	
Cr. SPLOCI – P/L		495
Share of profit of joint venture for reporting year		
(€990,000 × 50%) (W2)		
3. Dr. PPE (SoFP)	400	
Cr. SPLOCI – OCI		400
Property revaluation surplus		
4. Dr. SPLOCI – OCI	100	
Cr. Financial asset (SoFP)		100
Loss in fair value		

Note: Wind will be credited with €340,000 and non-controlling interests will be debited with €40,000 through total comprehensive income for the year.

Wind: €400,000 - (60% × €100,000)

NCI: 40% × (€100,000).

WORKINGS (Columnar Method)

	Wind	Rain	Adjustments		Consol. SPLOCI
	€000	€000	€000		€000
Revenue	15,850	12,680			28,530
Cost of sales	(11,880)	(9,490)			(21,370)
Gross profit	3,970	3,190			7,160
Dividend received	80				80
Distribution costs	(320)	(250)			(570)
Administrative expenses	(510)	(400)			(910)
Finance costs	(130)	(110)			(240)
Share of profit of associate *(W1)*			222	(Jnl. 1)	222
Share of profit of joint venture *(W2)*			495	(Jnl. 2)	495
Profit before tax	3,090	2,430	717		6,237
Income tax expense	(620)	(480)			(1,100)
Profit for the year	2,470	1,950	717		5,137

(W1) *Share of profit of associate:*
Profit after tax of Ice Ltd: €1,480 × 6 months × 30% = 222
(W2) *Share of profit of joint venture*
€990 × 50% = 495

Wind Ltd
CONSOLIDATED STATEMENT OF PROFIT OR LOSS AND OTHER COMPREHENSIVE INCOME
for the Year Ended 31 July 2013

	€000
Revenue	28,530
Cost of sales	(21,370)
Gross profit	7,160
Dividend received	80
Distribution costs	(570)
Administrative expenses	(910)
Finance costs	(240)
Share of profit of associate	222
Share of profit of joint venture	495
Profit before tax	6,237
Income tax expense	(1,100)
Profit for the year	5,137
Other comprehensive income:	
Property revaluation surplus	400
Loss on investments not held for trading	(100)
Total comprehensive income for the year	5,437
Profit for the year attributable to:	
Owners of the parent	4,357
Non-controlling interests *(W3)*	780
	5,137

Total comprehensive income attributable to:

	€000
Owners of the parent	4,697
Non-controlling interests *(W4)*	740
	5,437

€000

(W3) Non-controlling Interests – Profit

Profit after tax of Rain Ltd €1,950 × 40%   =   780

(W4) Non-controlling Interests – TCI

Profit after tax of Rain Ltd €1,950 × 40%   =   780

Less: Share of loss on investment measured at fair
value through OCI €100 × 40%   (40)
  740

CONSOLIDATED STATEMENT OF CHANGES IN EQUITY (EXTRACT)
for the Year Ended 31 July 2013

	Ord. Shares €000	Rev. Res. €000	Ret. Earnings €000	NCI €000	Total €000
Balance 1 August 2012			9,042 *(W4)*		
TCI for the year		340 *(W5)*	4,357	740	5,437
Balance 31 July 2013			13,399		

(W4) Retained Earnings at 1 August 2012

Wind	8,130
Rain 60% (1,970 – 450)	912
Ice (acquired during reporting year)	nil
Hail (acquired during reporting year)	nil
	9,042

	€000
(W5) Property revaluation surplus Wind	400
Decrease in fair value of financial asset (100 × 60%)	(60)
	340

Question 8.6

1. The following extracts have been taken from the consolidated statement of profit or
loss and other comprehensive income of Munster Ltd for the year ended 30 June 2013:

	€000
Profit for the year attributable to:	
Owners of the parent	3,160
Non-controlling interests	220
	3,380
Total comprehensive income for the year attributable to:	
Owners of the parent	3,430
Non-controlling interests	250
	3,680

2. Munster Ltd acquired 90% of the ordinary shares of Leinster Ltd on 1 December 2010 when the retained earnings of Leinster Ltd were €850,000.
3. Munster Ltd acquired 45% of the ordinary shares of Connaught Ltd on 1 May 2012 when the retained earnings of Connaught Ltd were €300,000.
4. Retained earnings 1 July 2012

	€000
Munster Ltd	3,154
Leinster Ltd	2,100
Connaught Ltd	700

5. The property of Leinster Ltd was revalued at the reporting date showing a surplus of €300,000.

Requirement Prepare the consolidated statement of changes in equity for the year ended 30 June 2013.

Solution

JOURNAL ENTRY

	€000	€000
1. Dr. PPE (SoFP)	300	
Cr. SPLOCI – OCI		300
Property revaluation surplus (Leinster)		

Note: Munster will be credited with €270,000 and non-controlling interests will be credited with €30,000 through total comprehensive income for the year.

Group retained earnings 1 July 2012	€000
Munster Ltd	3,154
Leinster Ltd 90% × (2,100 – 850)	1,125
Connaught Ltd 45% × (700 – 300)	180
	4,459

CONSOLIDATED STATEMENT OF CHANGES IN EQUITY (EXTRACT)
for the Year Ended 30 June 2013

	Ord. Shares €000	Reval. Reserve €000	Ret. Earnings €000	NCI €000	Total €000
Balance 1 July 2012			4,459		
TCI for the year		270(*W1*)	3,160	250	3,680
Balance 30 June 2013			7,619		

	€000
(*W1*) *Property revaluation surplus (Leinster)*	
€300,000 × 90%	270

Chapter 9

Consolidated Statement of Profit or Loss and Other Comprehensive Income and Consolidated Statement of Changes in Equity: Complications

LEARNING OBJECTIVES

After studying this chapter you should be able to:
- demonstrate an understanding of the rationale for each complication or adjustment;
- explain the accounting treatment for each complication in the preparation of the consolidated SPLOCI and SoCIE; and
- undertake a question with complications that will demonstrate a comprehensive understanding of the preparation of a consolidated SPLOCI and SoCIE.

Introduction

It is time to deal with 'complications' again. In this instance, however, we will examine how each one affects the consolidated SPLOCI and/or the consolidated SoCIE.

At end of this chapter, you should be in a position to understand, within the context of consolidated financial statements, the link between the SoFP, on one hand, and the SPLOCI and the SoCIE, on the other, as well as, in particular, the effect of complications.

As discussed in **Chapter 5**, in the world of business, group entities trade with one another and subsidiaries pay dividends to parents. As a consequence adjustments may need to be made to **consolidated** financial statements to reflect intragroup trading and other items such as intragroup dividends or amounts owing by one group entity to another at the reporting date. These adjustments are more commonly known as 'complications'.

The complications relevant to this chapter are:
1. Unrealised inventory profit
2. Unrealised profit on sale of tangible non-current assets
3. Revaluation of a subsidiary's net assets at acquisition date
4. Intragroup dividends
5. Intragroup transactions
6. Impairment of goodwill. Gain from a bargain purchase.

Statement of Changes in Equity (SoCIE)

The statement of changes in equity is the link between the statement of profit or loss and other comprehensive income and the statement of financial position, particularly in the case of retained earnings and non-controlling interests.

Key Note: the retained earnings at a reporting date per the SoCIE must equal the corresponding figure in the SoFP. Accordingly, **any complication that affects retained earnings in the consolidated SoFP workings must have the same cumulative effect on the consolidated SPLOCI and the SoCIE.**

In **Chapter 8**, we saw that the **group retained earnings brought forward** were defined as:

The retained earnings of the parent at the start of a reporting period

Plus

The **group's share** of the post-acquisition retained earnings of the subsidiary and any other entities as at that date.

Therefore, any complication that changes the opening retained earnings of the group must be accounted for accordingly:

(a) **If the adjustment affects the parent – account for all of the adjustment.**
(b) **If the adjustment affects another company – account for the group's share only.**

In dealing with each complication as listed above, we will show:

(a) the effect on the consolidated SoFP for **revision** purposes and, more importantly, to demonstrate the **link** between the SoFP and the SPLOCI/SoCIE; and
(b) the combined effect on the consolidated SPLOCI and the SoCIE.

(*Note*: the examples used in **Chapter 5** are repeated where relevant.)

Complication 1 – Unrealised Inventory Profit

This complication arises where one group entity sells goods at a profit to another group entity and some or all of those goods are in the inventory of the buying entity at the reporting date. This results in an element of unrealised profit being included in zthe closing inventory of the buying entity. This would be in contravention of IAS 2 *Inventories* if no adjustment were made in preparing the group accounts because IAS 2 states that inventories should be measured at the **lower** of cost and net realisable value.

EXAMPLE 9.1: TREATMENT OF UNREALISED INVENTORY PROFIT

A parent (P Ltd) buys goods for €100 and sells them to a subsidiary (S Ltd) for €150. At the reporting date, S Ltd still has these goods in inventory and has valued them at cost (€150) in accordance with IAS 2. However, if the inventory of S Ltd were consolidated (without adjustment) with the inventory of P Ltd the result would be that the group bought these goods for €100 and valued its inventory at €150 which contravenes IAS 2. There is unrealised profit from a group perspective of €50.

SoFP

Problem The retained earnings of P Ltd and the group inventories are overstated by €50.

ACCOUNTING ADJUSTMENT

Eliminate all the unrealised profit

		€	€
Dr.	Retained earnings (selling company P Ltd)	50	
Cr.	Inventory		50

SPLOCI and SoCIE

Problem The profits of P Ltd are overstated. The adjustment will affect the SPLOCI – P/L only.
The revenue and cost of sales are both overstated by the intragroup sales.

ACCOUNTING ADJUSTMENT

Add the unrealised profit €50 to the cost of sales of the selling company P Ltd. Reduce revenue and cost of sales by €150.

JOURNAL ENTRIES

	€	€
Dr. Group revenue (SPLOCI – P/L)	150	
Cr. Group cost of sales (SPLOCI – P/L)		150
Intragroup sales for the reporting year		
Dr. Cost of sales P (SPLOCI – P/L)	50	
Cr. Inventory (SoFP)		50
Unrealised profit		

Complication 2 – Unrealised Profit on Sale of Tangible Non-current Assets

This second complication arises where one group entity sells property, plant and equipment to another at a profit and the asset is in the SoFP of the buying entity at the reporting date.

IAS 16 *Property, Plant and Equipment* states that an asset should be carried at:
1. **Cost**, less accumulated depreciation and impairment; **or**
2. **Revaluation**, being its fair value at the date of revaluation less subsequent depreciation and impairment, provided that fair value can be measured reliably.

The inclusion of the asset at the selling price results in an overstatement of the non-current assets of the group and of the profits of the selling company (by the profit on the disposal of the asset). The depreciation charge may also be overstated by the buying company as the charge would be based on the incorrectly inflated group asset value.

EXAMPLE 9.2: UNREALISED PROFIT ON SALE OF TANGIBLE NON-CURRENT ASSETS

A parent, P Ltd, bought an item of property, plant and equipment (PPE) on 1 August 2010 at a cost of €300,000 and is depreciating it at 10% straight line. On 1 August 2012, P Ltd sold the asset to S Ltd for €280,000 who is currently depreciating it over the remaining eight years. Consolidated financial statements are prepared as at 31 July 2013.

1 August 2012

	€
Carrying value of asset (€300,000 − two years' depreciation)	240,000
Sale proceeds	280,000
Profit on disposal	40,000

SoFP

Problem The retained earnings and the property, plant and equipment (PPE) as at 31 July 2013 are overstated by the profit on disposal of €40,000.

ACCOUNTING ADJUSTMENT

Eliminate unrealised profit in the selling company's accounts.

Dr.	Retained earnings (P Ltd)	€40,000
Cr.	PPE	€40,000

SPLOCI and SoCIE

Problem The profits of P Ltd for the year ended 31 July 2013 are overstated by €40,000.

ACCOUNTING ADJUSTMENT

Deduct €40,000 in the SPLOCI – P/L from the profit of P Ltd.

JOURNAL ENTRY

	€	€
Dr. Expenses (SPLOCI – P/L) P	40,000	
Cr. PPE (SoFP)		40,000

Unrealised profit on sale of PPE

This transaction is further complicated by the fact that the asset in question is subject to depreciation. Currently, **the depreciation is overstated from a group perspective** calculated as follows:

Year Ended 31 July 2013

			€
Depreciation per S Ltd financial statements	280,000 ÷ 8	=	35,000
Depreciation if asset not sold at a profit	300,000 @ 10%	=	30,000
Over-provision			5,000

SoFP

Problem At 31 July 2013 both the carrying value of PPE and the retained earnings of S Ltd. are understated.

ACCOUNTING ADJUSTMENT

Write back the over-provision of depreciation in the buying company.

Dr.	PPE	€5,000	
Cr.	Retained Earnings (S Ltd)		€5,000

SPLOCI and SoCIE

Problem The depreciation charge for the year ended 31 July 2013 in the SPLOCI – P/L of S Ltd is overstated by €5,000.

ACCOUNTING ADJUSTMENT

Decrease the relevant expense (e.g. cost of sales) in S Ltd by €5,000, which will increase its profit.

JOURNAL ENTRY

	€	€
Dr. PPE (SoFP)	5,000	
Cr. Depreciation (SPLOCI – P/L) S		5,000

Over-depreciation of PPE for current year

Complication 3 – Revaluation of a Subsidiary's Net Assets at Acquisition Date

When a parent (P Ltd) acquires a subsidiary (S Ltd) the purchase consideration is based on the **fair value** of the subsidiary's net assets and not the carrying values, which are frequently significantly different, particularly in the case of tangible assets such as property.

IFRS 3 *Business Combinations* requires that the net assets of S Ltd must be revalued to **fair value** for consolidation purposes at the date of acquisition. Fair value is the price that would be received to sell an asset or paid to transfer a liability in an orderly transaction between market participants at the measurement date.

EXAMPLE 9.3: REVALUATION OF NET ASSETS

SUMMARISED STATEMENT OF FINANCIAL POSITION OF S LTD as at 31 May 2013

	€000
Property, plant and equipment	4,400
Current assets	1,300
Total Assets	**5,700**
Ordinary share capital	2,000
Retained earnings	1,800
Non-current liabilities	1,000
Current liabilities	900
Total Equity and Liabilities	**5,700**

P Ltd acquired 60% of the ordinary shares of S Ltd on 1 June 2011. At the date of acquisition, the fair value of the property, plant and equipment (PPE) exceeded the carrying value by €300,000, while those assets had an average remaining useful life of five years. S Ltd did not record the revaluation.

SoFP

Problem In the consolidated workings as at 31 May 2013, the PPE must be revalued to reflect the surplus as at the date of acquisition and two years' additional depreciation on the surplus must be provided.

ACCOUNTING ADJUSTMENT

(a) **Account for surplus**

		€000	€000
Dr.	PPE	300	
Cr.	Goodwill		300

(b) Account for additional depreciation

Dr. Retained earnings (S Ltd)   120
Cr. Accumulated depreciation – PPE   120

With the cumulative additional depreciation, i.e. $€300,000 \times \dfrac{2}{5}$

SPLOCI and SoCIE

Problem The depreciation charge for both 31 May 2012 and 31 May 2013 in the SPLOCI – P/L of S Ltd is understated.

ACCOUNTING ADJUSTMENT

In the consolidated SPLOCI for the year ended 31 May 2013, add €60,000 to depreciation charge. This adjustment will affect the NCI's share of profit for the year.
In the consolidated SoCIE for the year ended 31 May 2013, reduce the opening group retained earnings by 60% × €60,000 = €36,000 (this being the group's share, as explained above, and will recur in other complications). The adjustment affects the opening retained earnings of the subsidiary.

JOURNAL ENTRIES

	€000	€000
Dr. Depreciation (SPLOCI – P/L) S	60	
Cr. PPE (SoFP)		60
Additional depreciation for the reporting year		
Dr. Group retained earnings 1 June 2012 (SoCIE)	36	
Dr. NCI 1 June 2012 (SoCIE)	24	
Cr. PPE (SoFP)		60
Additional depreciation for the y/e 31 May 2012		

Complication 4 – Intragroup Dividends

When a subsidiary (S Ltd) declares a dividend, part of it is payable to its parent (P Ltd) and the remainder to non-controlling interests. The intragroup amounts must be eliminated in the consolidated workings, otherwise both the assets and liabilities of the group would be overstated.

EXAMPLE 9.4: INTRAGROUP DIVIDENDS
INCLUDED IN SUBSIDIARY AND PARENT ACCOUNTS

A parent (P Ltd) owns 80% of the preference shares of subsidiary (S Ltd) and S Ltd has proposed a preference dividend of €50,000 for year ended 31 August 2013. Both S Ltd and P Ltd have accounted for the dividends in their respective financial statements.

EXTRACT FROM STATEMENTS of FINANCIAL POSITION
as at 31 August 2013

Assets	**P Ltd**	**S Ltd**
Dividends receivable	€40,000	

Liabilities		
Proposed dividends		€50,000

EXTRACT FROM STATEMENTS OF PROFIT OR LOSS AND OTHER COMPREHENSIVE
INCOME for the Year Ended 31 August 2013

	P Ltd	**S Ltd**
Dividends receivable	€40,000	

SoFP

Problem The assets and liabilities of the group would be overstated if the intragroup dividend was not eliminated.

ADJUSTMENT

Dr.	Proposed dividends	€40,000	
Cr.	Dividends receivable		€40,000

SPLOCI and SoCIE

Problem The dividend receivable in the SPLOCI – P/L of P Ltd is an intragroup dividend and the group profits would be overstated if the intragroup dividend was not eliminated.

ADJUSTMENT

Do not include the dividend €40,000 in the consolidated SPLOCI – P/L.

JOURNAL ENTRY

	€	**€**
Dr. Dividends receivable (SPLOCI – P/L) P	40,000	
Cr. SoCIE – S		40,000
Intragroup dividend		

Complication 5 – Intragroup Transactions

It is perfectly legitimate for a group company to sell goods to another group company at a profit and for companies in a group to charge the other group companies for management charges, interest on loans, etc. When preparing consolidated financial statements, these 'internal' or 'intragroup' transactions must be eliminated from the consolidated figures to avoid any overstatement of income or expenditures.

EXAMPLE 9.5: INTRAGROUP TRANSACTIONS

During the year ended 31 July 2013, P Ltd sold goods valued at €300,000 to S Ltd while S Ltd paid a management fee of €100,000 to P Ltd. None of the goods were in S Ltd inventory at the end of the year and P Ltd accounted for the management fee received in 'Other Income'. There were no amounts outstanding between the entities at the year end.

SoFP

Problem As there are no sums outstanding at the end of the year, no problem arises.

SPLOCI and SoCIE

Problem Without adjustment, the revenue and cost of sales figures in the consolidated SPLOCI – P/L would both be overstated by €300,000 being the amount of the intragroup sales in P Ltd and the intragroup purchases in S Ltd. 'Other Income' (in P Ltd) would also be overstated by €100,000 as would the "Management Fee" in the administrative expenses (in S Ltd).

ACCOUNTING ADJUSTMENT (SPLOCI – P/L only)

Dr. Group revenue SPLOCI – P/L	€300,000	
Cr. Group cost of sales SPLOCI – P/L		€300,000
Intragroup sales for the reporting year		
Dr. Other income SPLOCI – P/L (P)	€100,000	
Cr. Administrative expenses SPLOCI – P/L (S)		€100,000
Intragroup management fee €100,000		

Complication 6 – Impairment of Goodwill and Gain from a Bargain Purchase

As explained in **Chapter 3**, goodwill arises when the fair value of the consideration given by the investor plus the value of the non-controlling interests at the acquisition date exceed the fair value of the net assets (capital and reserves) of the subsidiary at the acquisition date. Under IAS 36 *Impairment of Assets* goodwill must be tested annually for impairment. IAS 36 defines an 'impairment loss' as *the amount by which the carrying amount of an asset or a cash generating unit exceeds its recoverable amount.*[1] If impairment occurs, the reduction in the carrying value of goodwill should be written off in the consolidated SPLOCI – P/L. If any of the impairment relates to the non-controlling interests, that amount must be deducted in arriving at "profit for the year attributable to the non-controlling interests".

---

[1] Impairment losses have a much wider impact than those covered by this text. See **Connolly**, Chapter 10, 'Impairment'.

Example 9.6: Goodwill Impairment

Port Ltd acquired 75% of the ordinary shares of Storm Ltd on 1 September 2011 at a cost of €1.4 million when the ordinary share capital of Storm Ltd was €1 million and the retained earnings €600,000. The goodwill has been impaired as follows:

Year Ending 31 August 2012   €20,000
Year Ending 31 August 2013   €40,000

The fair value of the non-controlling interests at 1 September 2011 amounted to €480,000.

SoFP
Year Ended 31 August 2013

Dr. Retained earnings Port (75%)   €45,000
Dr. NCI (25%)   €15,000
Cr. Goodwill   €60,000
Cumulative impairment of goodwill to reporting date using group structure

SPLOCI and SoCIE
Year Ended 31 August 2013

(a) The total impairment for the reporting year €40,000 must be written off in the consolidated SPLOCI – P/L.
(b) The NCI share (€40,000 × 25%) must be deducted in arriving at profit for the year attributable to non-controlling interest.
(c) The impairment €20,000 relating to y/e 31 August 2012 must be included in the SoCIE for the year ended 31 August 2013 as follows:
  • reduce the opening group retained earnings by (75% × 20,000)   €15,000;
  • reduce the opening balance for the NCI by (25% × 20,000)   € 5,000.

Journal Entries

	€	€
Dr. SPLOCI – P/L P	40,000	
Cr. Goodwill (SoFP)		40,000

Goodwill impairment for the reporting year

Dr. Group retained earnings 1 September 2012 (SoCIE)	15,000	
Dr. NCI 1 September 2012 (SoCIE)	5,000	
Cr. Goodwill (SoFP)		20,000

Goodwill impairment for the y/e 31 August 2012

Gain from a Bargain Purchase

A gain from a bargain purchase arises when the fair value of the consideration given by the investor plus the value of the non-controlling interests at the acquisition date is less than the fair value of the net assets (capital and reserves) of the subsidiary at the acquisition date. IFRS 3 *Business Combinations* requires that such a gain should be taken to the consolidated SPLOCI – P/L immediately.

EXAMPLE 9.7: GAIN FROM A BARGAIN PURCHASE

Using the same information as in **Example 9.6** above, except that Port Ltd paid €1.1 million for the investment in Storm Ltd on 1 September 2011 and NCI at the date of acquisition date is valued at their share of the net assets of Storm Ltd.

	€	€
Investment in Storm		1,100,000
NCI at acquisition date:		
25% (1,000,000 + 600,000)		400,000
		1,500,000
Net assets of Storm at acquisition date:		
Ordinary shares	1,000,000	
Retained earnings	600,000	1,600,000
Gain		100,000

SoFP
Year Ended 31 August 2013

Problem At 31 August 2013, the gain of €100,000 must be dealt with.

ADJUSTMENT

Dr.	Goodwill	€100,000	
Cr.	Retained earnings (Port Ltd)		€100,000

SPLOCI and SoCIE
Year Ended 31 August 2013

ADJUSTMENT

The gain (€100,000) would have been included in profit or loss for the year ended 31 August 2012. Increase the group retained earnings in consolidated SoCIE at the start of the year by €100,000.

JOURNAL ENTRY

	€	€
Dr. Goodwill (SoFP)	100,000	
Cr. Group retained earnings 1 September 2012 (SoCIE)		100,000

Gain from a bargain purchase y/e 31 August 2012

SUMMARY

1. Any complication which causes an adjustment to retained earnings in the consolidated SoFP must cause the same total adjustment to the consolidated SPLOCI and SoCIE. An adjustment which changes the current year's profits will affect the consolidated SPLOCI only, whereas an adjustment which changes the group retained earnings at the start of the reporting period should be accounted for in the consolidated SoCIE.

2. Unrealised inventory profit during a reporting period is added to the cost of sales of the selling entity. Intragroup sales and cost of sales are cancelled.

3. Additional depreciation on a revaluation surplus on the net assets of a subsidiary at acquisition date is accounted for as follows:
   (a) any amount relating to the current year is added to the relevant expense of the subsidiary.
   (b) the group's share of any amount relating to prior years is deducted in arriving at the group retained earnings brought forward.

4. When one group entity sells an item of property, plant and equipment at a profit to another, the unrealised profit must be deducted from the seller's profits on consolidation. Any consequential over-provision of depreciation should be treated as follows:
   (a) any amount relating to the current year is deducted from the relevant expense of the buying entity;
   (b) the group's share of any amount relating to prior years is added in arriving at the group retained earnings brought forward if the subsidiary is the buyer, or all the amount relating to prior years if the parent is the buyer.

5. Any dividend received/receivable from the subsidiary in the SPLOCI – P/L of the parent must be excluded from consolidation.

6. Impairment of goodwill attributed to the parent only is treated as follows:
   (a) the current year's charge is included as a separate line item in the consolidated SPLOCI – P/L.
   (b) the amount relating to prior periods is deducted in arriving at group retained earnings brought forward in the consolidated SoCIE.
   Impairment of goodwill which is attributable to both the parent and the non-controlling interests is treated as follows:
   (a) the current year's **total** impairment is written off in the consolidated SPLOCI – P/L while the NCI portion is deducted in arriving at "profit for the year attributable to the non-controlling interests";
   (b) any impairment relating to previous years is deducted from opening group retained earnings and non-controlling interests in the consolidated SoCIE.

7. Any adjustment which affects the profit of the subsidiary must be taken into account when calculating non-controlling interests in the profits of the subsidiary for the year.

Conclusion

Chapters 5 and **9** combined will give you a comprehensive understanding of all the complications and the impact on consolidated financial statements, i.e. SoFP, SPLOCI and SoCIE, and you should now be in a position to tackle examination-style questions (see **Appendix 1**).

QUESTIONS

Explain the adjustments to the consolidated SPLOCI and/or the consolidated SoCIE for each of the following transactions relating to different groups, **each of which has a reporting date at 30 September 2013**:

Question 9.1

Blue Ltd, a subsidiary, sold goods at invoice value of €250,000 to its parent Green Ltd in July 2013. Blue Ltd made a gross profit of 20% on the sale and 40% of the goods were in the inventory of Green Ltd at the reporting date.

Solution

Problem There is unrealised profit included in the inventory of Green Ltd: 250,000 × 1/5 × 40% = €20,000. Group revenue and cost of sales are also overstated.

ADJUSTMENT
Increase cost of sales of Blue Ltd by €20,000 (note impact on the profit attributable to the NCI).
Reduce group revenue and cost of sales by €250,000.

JOURNAL ENTRIES

	€	€
1. Dr. Cost of sales: Blue (SPLOCI – P/L)	20,000	
Cr. Inventory (SoFP)		20,000
Unrealised inventory profit.		
2. Dr. Group revenue (SPLOCI – P/L)	250,000	
Cr. Group cost of sales (SPLOCI – P/L)		250,000
Intragroup sales for the reporting year		

Question 9.2

Pan Ltd acquired 70% of the ordinary shares of Slice Ltd on 1 October 2011. At that date, the fair value of the property, plant and equipment (PPE) of Slice Ltd exceeded the carrying value by €200,000 while the average remaining useful lives of the PPE was four years. The group depreciates PPE on a straight-line basis. Slice Ltd did not record the revaluation.

Solution

Problem Group depreciation is understated by €50,000 each year ended 30 September 2012 and 2013.

ADJUSTMENT

Increase expenses of Slice Ltd by €50,000 (€200,000 × ¼) for y/e 30 September 2013 in SPLOCI – P/L (note impact on the profit attributable to the NCI).
Decrease group retained profits at 1 October 2012 by (€50,000 × 70% (group's share)) in SoCIE. Decrease NCI at 1 October 2012 by €15,000 in the SoCIE.

JOURNAL ENTRIES

	€	€
1. Dr. Expenses: Slice (SPLOCI – P/L)	50,000	
Cr. PPE (SoFP)		50,000
Current year's additional depreciation on revaluation surplus		
2. Dr. Group retained earnings at 1/10/2012 (SoCIE)	35,000	
Dr. NCI at 1/10/2012 (SoCIE)	15,000	
Cr. PPE (SoFP)		50,000
Additional depreciation y/e 30 September 2012 on revaluation surplus		

Question 9.3

Purple Ltd acquired 100% of the ordinary shares of Silver Ltd on 1 December 2009. The consideration included goodwill of €150,000. The goodwill has been impaired as follows:

      y/e 30 September 2012   €25,000
      y/e 30 September 2013   €35,000

Solution

Problem Impairment of goodwill €60,000 must be written off

ADJUSTMENT

Charge €35,000 in consolidated SPLOCI – P/L for year ended 30 September 2013, as follows:

      Impairment of goodwill   €35,000

Reduce group retained profits brought forward at 1 October 2012 by €25,000 in consolidated SoCIE.

JOURNAL ENTRIES

	€	€
1. Dr. SPLOCI – P/L	35,000	
Cr. Goodwill (SoFP)		35,000
Current year's impairment of goodwill		

2. Dr. Group retained earnings at 1/10/2012 (SoCIE)   25,000
   Cr. Goodwill (SoFP)   25,000
   Impairment of goodwill y/e 30 September 2012

Question 9.4

Pop Ltd acquired 90% of the ordinary shares of Snap Ltd, at a gain from a bargain purchase of €130,000. The date of acquisition was 1 November 2011.

Solution

Problem The gain was in the consolidated SPLOCI – P/L in the year ended 30 September 2012.

ADJUSTMENT
Increase the group retained profit brought forward at 1 October 2012 by €130,000 in the consolidated SoCIE.

JOURNAL ENTRY

	€	€
1. Dr. Goodwill (SoFP)	130,000	
Cr. Group retained earnings at 1/10/2012 (SoCIE)		130,000

Gain from a bargain purchase y/e 30 September 2012

Question 9.5

Pip Ltd, a parent, sold an item of property, plant and equipment (PPE) to its 80% owned subsidiary Seed Ltd on 1 October 2011 at a profit of €55,000. The depreciation on this asset in the SPLOCI of Seed Ltd. was €12,000 per year for each of the years ended 30 September 2012 and 2013. The annual charge would have been €9,000 based on historic cost.

Solution

Problem (a) The unrealised profit of €55,000 on the sale of the PPE must be eliminated in the September 2013 consolidated financial statements.

ADJUSTMENT
Reduce the group retained profits brought forward by €55,000 in the consolidated SoCIE.

Problem (b) The depreciation is overstated from a group perspective by €3,000 for each of two years, i.e. year-ended 30 September 2012 and year-ended 30 September 2013.

ADJUSTMENT
Increase the profit of Seed Ltd by €3,000 in the consolidated SPLOCI.
Increase the group retained earnings brought forward by 80% × €3,000 (group's share) = €2,400 in the consolidated SoCIE. Increase the NCI at 1 October 2012 by €600 in the SoCIE.

JOURNAL ENTRIES

	€	€
1. Dr. Group retained earnings at 1 October 2012 (SoCIE)	55,000	
Cr. PPE (SoFP)		55,000
Unrealised profit on sale of PPE y/e 30 September 2012		
2. Dr. PPE (SoFP)	3,000	
Cr. Expenses: Seed (SPLOCI – P/L)		3,000
Write back of surplus depreciation for current year		
3. Dr. PPE (SoFP)	3,000	
Cr. Group retained earnings at 1 October 2012 (SoCIE)		2,400
Cr. NCI at 1 October 2012 (SoCIE)		600
Write back of surplus depreciation for y/e 30 September 2012		

Note: **Questions 9.6** and **9.7** are longer, review-type questions. **Question 9.6** requires the preparation of both a consolidated SPLCOI and SoCIE of a parent, subsidiary and associate, including many of the complications discussed in this chapter. **Question 9.7** will assist you to revise virtually all of the principles outlined in this chapter as it involves a parent, a subsidiary, associate, a joint venture and a trade investment with a combination of complications.

The solutions to both questions contain the columnar method workings and an explanation of how to account for each complication.

Question 9.6

The following are the statements of profit or loss and other comprehensive income of Pear Plc, Sloe Ltd and Apple Ltd for the year ended 30 June 2013:

STATEMENTS OF PROFIT OR LOSS AND OTHER COMPREHENSIVE INCOME

	Pear Plc €000	Sloe Ltd €000	Apple Ltd €000
Revenue	14,000	9,750	6,870
Cost of sales	(8,400)	(5,850)	(2,620)
Gross profit	5,600	3,900	4,250
Dividends receivable – Sloe Ltd	20		
– Red Ltd	10		
Distribution costs	(480)	(450)	(160)
Administrative expenses	(1,490)	(650)	(460)
Finance costs	(350)	(180)	(70)
Profit before tax	3,310	2,620	3,560
Income tax expense	(1,350)	(1,050)	(420)
Profit for the year	1,960	1,570	3,140
Other comprehensive income	500	nil	nil
Total comprehensive income for the year	2,460	1,570	3,140

The following additional information is available:

1. Pear Plc acquired 70% of the ordinary shares of Sloe Ltd on 1 July 2010 when its reserves were:

	€000
Share premium account	800
Retained earnings	2,500

2. At 1 July 2010, the fair value of the property, plant and equipment of Sloe Ltd exceeded the carrying value by €160,000. This surplus has not been reflected in the financial statements of Sloe Ltd. At that date the average remaining useful life of the non-current assets was four years.

3. Pear Plc acquired 30% of the ordinary shares of Apple Ltd on 1 July 2011 when the reserves of Apple Ltd were:

	€000
Share Premium	1,500
Retained earnings	2,600

4. During March 2013 Sloe Ltd sold goods to Pear Plc at invoice value €200,000 on which Sloe Ltd made a gross profit of 20%. One half of these goods remained in the inventory of Pear Plc at 30 June 2013.

5. Impairment of goodwill on acquisition of Sloe and the carrying value of the investment in Apple occurred as follows:

Year ended 30 June 2012	Sloe Ltd	€30,000
	Apple Ltd	€20,000
Year ended 30 June 2013	Sloe Ltd	€50,000
	Apple Ltd	€40,000

There was goodwill on acquisition of Sloe Ltd of €60,000 attributable to the non-controlling interests.

6. Pear Plc had 10 million ordinary shares of €1 each in issue on 1 July 2012. On the 31 March 2013, the company made a bonus issue of one for four out of share premium which stood at €4,000,000 on the 1 July 2012.

7. Pear Plc revalued its property during the reporting period under review giving rise to a revaluation surplus of €500,000.

8. Retained earnings at 1 July 2012:

	€000
Pear Plc	€6,750
Sloe Ltd	€3,690
Apple Ltd	€3,300

9. Pear Ltd owns 10% of the ordinary shares of Red Ltd. The fair value of the investment did not change during the year.

Requirement:
(a) Prepare the consolidated statement of profit or loss and other comprehensive income for the Pear Plc group for the year ended 30 June 2013.
(b) Prepare the consolidated statement of changes in equity for the year ended 30 June 2013 in so far as the information permits.

Solution to Question 9.6

ADJUSTMENTS (as required by the additional information)
2. Provide for additional depreciation of €40,000 per annum for three years.
   Charge €40,000 to current year's administrative expenses (note impact on NCI).
   Reduce opening retained earnings in SoCIE by 2 × €40,000 × 70% = €56,000.
   Reduce opening NCI in the SoCIE by 2 × €40,000 × 30% = €24,000.

3. Disclose in consolidated SPLOCI share of profit of associate Apple Ltd.
   Profit after tax: 3,140 × 30%   =   942
   Less investment impairment for 2013   (40)   902

4. Reduce group revenue and cost of sales by intragroup sales €200,000.
   Add unrealised inventory profit (€200,000 × 1/5 × ½ = €20,000) to cost of sales Sloe Ltd (note impact on NCI).

5. *Impairment of goodwill*   €
   Charge to consolidated SPLOCI – P/L current year's impairment   50,000
   Deduct in arriving at profit attributable to NCI (30% × 50,000)   15,000
   Reduce group retained earnings brought forward in consolidated
        SoCIE by share of previous year's impairment (70% × 30,000)   21,000
   Reduce opening NCI balance in consol. SoCIE by (30% × 30,000)   9,000

   Impairment of Investment
   Reduce share of Apple's profit in consolidated SPLOCI – P/L by   40,000
   In the consolidated SoCIE reduce group retained earnings
        brought forward by   20,000

6. In the SoCIE reduce share premium and increase ordinary share capital of Pear Plc by €2.5 million.
7. Include €500,000 under other comprehensive income in consolidated SPLOCI – OCI.
9. The dividend received by Pear Plc from Red Ltd must be included in the consolidated SPLOCI – P/L as it is a dividend from outside the group.

JOURNAL ENTRIES

> **Note:** only the elements of the following journal entries which affect the SPLOCI and the SoCIE are taken into account in this solution.

	€000	€000
1. Dr. Administrative expenses: Sloe (SPLOCI – P/L)	40	
Cr. PPE (SoFP)		40

Additional depreciation y/e 30 June 2013 on revaluation surplus

2. Dr. Group retained earnings at 1/7/2012 (SoCIE)   56
    Dr. NCI at 1/7/2012 (SoCIE)   24
    Cr. PPE (SoFP)   80
    Cumulative additional depreciation on revaluation surplus to 30/6/2012
3. Dr. Investment in Apple (SoFP)   942
    Cr. SPLOCI – P/L   942
    Share of profit of associate for the reporting year
    (€3,140,000 × 30%)
4. Dr. Share of profit of Apple (SPLOCI – P/L) (see Jnl. 3)   40
    Cr. Investment in Apple (SoFP)   40
    Impairment of investment in Apple arising in the reporting year
5. Dr. Group revenue (SPLOCI – P/L)   200
    Cr. Group cost of sales (SPLOCI – P/L)   200
    Intragroup sales for the reporting year
6. Dr. Cost of sales: Sloe (SPLOCI – P/L)   20
    Cr. Inventory (SoFP)   20
    Unrealised inventory profit arising in the reporting year
7. Dr. SPLOCI – P/L   50
    Cr. Goodwill (SoFP)   50
    Current year's impairment of goodwill on acquisition of Sloe
8. Dr. Group retained earnings at 1/7/2012 (SoCIE)   21
    Dr. NCI at 1/7/2012 (SoCIE)   9
    Cr. Goodwill (SoFP)   30
    Impairment of goodwill y/e 30/6/2012
9. Dr. Group retained earnings at 1/7/2012 (SoCIE)   20
    Cr. Investment in Apple (SoFP)   20
    Impairment of investment in Apple y/e 30/6/2012
10. Dr. Share premium (SoCIE)   2,500
    Cr. Share capital (SoCIE)   2,500
    Issue of bonus shares
11. Dr. PPE (SoFP)   500
    Cr. SPLOCI – OCI   500
    Property revaluation surplus Pear

Note: the entire revaluation surplus is attributable to Pear and it will be allocated this through its share of Total Comprehensive Income.

WORKINGS (Columnar Method)

	Pear €000	Sloe €000	Adjustment €000		Consol. SPLOCI €000
Revenue (*W1*)	14,000	9,750	(200)	(Jnl. 5)	23,550
Cost of sales (*W2*)	(8,400)	(5,850)	200 (20)	(Jnl. 5/6)	(14,070)
Gross profit	5,600	3,900	(20)		9,480
Dividends receivable from Red	10				10

Distribution costs	(480)	(450)			(930)
Administrative expenses	(1,490)	(650)	(40)	(Jnl. 1)	(2,180)
Finance costs	(350)	(180)			(530)
Impairment of goodwill			(50)	(Jnl. 7)	(50)
Share of profit of associate (*W3*)			902	(Jnl. 3/4)	902
Profit before tax	3,290	2,620	792		6,702
Income tax expense	(1,350)	(1,050)			(2,400)
Profit for the year	1,940	1,570	792		4,302

CONSOLIDATED STATEMENT OF PROFIT OR LOSS AND OTHER COMPREHENSIVE INCOME
for Year Ended 30 June 2013

	€000
Revenue (*W1*)	23,550
Cost of sales (*W2*)	(14,070)
Gross profit	9,480
Dividends receivable	10
Distribution costs	(930)
Administrative expenses	(2,180)
Finance costs	(530)
Impairment of goodwill	(50)
Share of profit of associate (*W3*)	902
Profit before tax	6,702
Income tax expense	(2,400)
Profit for the year	4,302

Other Comprehensive Income

Property revaluation surplus	500
Total Comprehensive Income for the year	**4,802**

Profit for year attributable to

Owners of the parent	3,864
Non-controlling interests (*W4*)	438
	4,302

Total comprehensive income for the year attributable to:

Owners of the parent	4,364
Non-controlling interests	438
	4,802

	€000
(W1) Revenue	
Pear	14,000
Sloe	9,750
Intra group (Jnl. 5)	(200)
	23,550
(W2) Cost of Sales	
Pear	8,400
Sloe	5,850
Intragroup (Jnl. 5)	(200)
Unrealised inventory profit (Jnl. 6)	20
	14,070
(W3) Share of Profit of Associate	
Profit after tax of Apple 3,140 × 30% (Jnl. 3)	942
Less current year's impairment of investment (Jnl. 4)	(40)
	902
(W4) Non-controlling interests	
Profit after tax (Sloe Ltd)	1,570
Less extra depreciation (1 year) (Jnl. 1)	(40)
Less unrealised inventory profit (Jnl. 6)	(20)
Adjusted	1,510
NCI × 30%	453
Less impairment of goodwill	(15)
	438

CONSOLIDATED STATEMENT OF CHANGES IN EQUITY
for the Year Ended 30 June 2013

	Ordinary Shares €000	Share Premium €000	Reval. Reserves €000	Retained Earnings €000	NCI €000	Total €000
At 1 July 2012	10,000	4,000	–	7,696 *(W5)*	X	X
TCI for year			500	3,864	438	4,802
Bonus issue	2,500	(2,500)				0

	€000
(W5) Retained earnings at 1 July 2012	
Pear Plc	6,750
Goodwill written off 2012 – Sloe Ltd (30 × 70%)	(21)
Impairment of investment in Apple Ltd 2012	(20)
Sloe Ltd	
(3,690 – 2,500) × 70%	833
extra depreciation – 2 years (80) × 70% (group's share)	(56)
Apple Ltd	
(3,300 – 2,600) × 30%	210
	7,696

Question 9.7

STATEMENTS OF PROFIT OR LOSS AND OTHER COMPREHENSIVE INCOME
for the Year Ended 30 September 2013

	Cork Ltd €000	Kerry Ltd €000	Louth Ltd €000	Meath Ltd €000
Revenue	15,460	12,370	7,700	6,180
Cost of sales	(10,820)	(8,680)	(5,400)	(4,320)
Gross profit	4,640	3,690	2,300	1,860
Other income	300	–	–	–
Distribution costs	(930)	(740)	(400)	(370)
Administrative expenses	(1,110)	(880)	(500)	(440)
Finance costs	(390)	(310)	(100)	(170)
Profit before tax	2,510	1,760	1,300	880
Income tax expense	(750)	(530)	(400)	(260)
Profit for the year	1,760	1,230	900	620
Other comprehensive income:				
Property revaluation surplus	1,000	800	–	500
Total comprehensive income for the year	2,760	2,030	900	1,120

The following additional information is available:

1. Cork Ltd acquired 90% of the ordinary shares of Kerry Ltd on 1 October 2010 when the retained earnings of Kerry Ltd were € 900,000, and its share capital €5 million.
2. During August 2013 Kerry Ltd sold goods to Cork Ltd at invoice value €120,000 on which Kerry Ltd made a mark-up of one-third. All the goods were in the inventory of Cork Ltd at the reporting date. Total sales from Kerry Ltd to Cork Ltd during the year amounted to €600,000.
3. Cork Ltd received a management fee of €300,000 from Kerry Ltd for the year under review.
4. Cork Ltd and Limerick Ltd jointly control Louth Ltd, each having rights to 50% of its net assets since 1 July 2013.
5. Cork Ltd acquired 25% of the voting rights of Meath Ltd on 1 October 2012.
6. Goodwill on acquisition of Kerry Ltd was impaired in the amount of €40,000 during the year ended 30 September 2012, while the carrying value of the investment in Meath Ltd was impaired by €20,000 during the year under review.
7. Retained earnings at 1 October 2012:

	€000
Cork Ltd	8,460
Kerry Ltd	3,500
Louth Ltd	1,500
Meath Ltd	1,940.

8. Non-controlling interests in Kerry Ltd was measured at their share of the net assets at acquisition date.

Requirement Prepare for the year ended 30 September 2013:
(a) the consolidated statement of profit or loss and other comprehensive income; and
(b) the consolidated statement of changes in equity.

Solution to Question 9.7

ADJUSTMENTS (as required by the additional information)
2. Unrealised inventory profit €120,000 × ¼ = €30,000
   Add €30,000 to cost of sales of Kerry Ltd (note impact on NCI)
   Intragroup sales €600,000
   Reduce revenue and cost of sales in consolidated SPLOCI – P/L by €600,000
3. Management fee
   Reduce other income Cork Ltd by €300,000
   Reduce administrative expenses Kerry Ltd by €300,000
4. Joint venture Louth Ltd acquired nine months into reporting period
   Consolidate profit after tax $900 \times \frac{3}{12} \times 50\%$ (say 113)
5. Share of profit of associate Meath Ltd
   Profit after tax   €620,000 × 25%   =   €155,000
   Impairment of investment (see 6)   €20,000   €135,000

   Share of revaluation surplus of Meath €500,000 × 25% = €125,000

6. Reduce group retained earnings at 1 October 2012 by €40,000
   Reduce share of profit of associate (see 5) by €20,000

7. Increase OCI by €1,925,000 which includes (25% × €500,000) €125,000 for share of Meath

JOURNAL ENTRIES
Note: only the elements of the following journal entries which affect the SPLOCI and the SoCIE are taken into account in this solution.

	€	€
1. Dr. Cost of sales: Kerry (SPLOCI – P/L)	30	
Cr. Inventory (SoFP)		30
Unrealised inventory profit		
2. Dr. Group revenue (SPLOCI – P/L)	600	
Cr. Group cost of sales (SPLOCI – P/L)		600
Intragroup sales for the reporting year		
3. Dr. Other income Cork (SPLOCI – P/L)	300	
Cr. Administrative expenses Kerry (SPLOCI – P/L)		300
Management fee paid by Kerry to Cork during the reporting year		
4. Dr. Investment in Meath (SoFP)	135	
Cr. SPLOCI – P/L		135
Share of Meath's profit for the reporting year minus impairment of investment		

5. Dr. Investment in Louth (SoFP)   113
   Cr. SPLOCI – P/L   113
   Share of profit of joint venture for three months
6. Dr. Group retained earnings 1/10/2012 (SoCIE)   40
   Cr. Goodwill (SoFP)   40
   Impairment of goodwill on acquisition of Kerry y/e 30/9/2012
7. Dr. PPE (SoFP)   1,800
   Dr. Investment in Meath (SoFP)   125
   Cr. SPLOCI – OCI   1,925
   Property revaluation surplus (W1)

Note: Cork will be credited with €1,845,000 and non-controlling interests will be credited with €80,000 through total comprehensive income for the year.

WORKINGS

	Cork Ltd €000	Kerry Ltd €000	Adjustments €000	Consol. SPLOCI €000
Revenue	15,460	12,370	(600) (Jnl. 2)	27,230
Cost of sales	(10,820)	(8,680)	(30) 600 (Jnl. 1/2)	(18,930)
Gross profit	4,640	3,690	(30)	8,300
Other income	300		(300) (Jnl. 3)	–
Distribution costs	(930)	(740)		(1,670)
Administrative expenses	(1,110)	(880)	300 (Jnl. 3)	(1,690)
Finance costs	(390)	(310)		(700)
Share of profit of associate			135 (Jnl. 4)	135
Share of profit of joint venture			113 (Jnl. 5)	113
Profit before tax	2,510	1,760	218	4,488
Income tax expense	(750)	(530)		(1,280)
Profit for the year	1,760	1,230	218	3,208

Cork Ltd
CONSOLIDATED STATEMENT OF PROFIT OR LOSS AND
OTHER COMPREHENSIVE INCOME
for the Year Ended 30 September 2013

	€000
Revenue	27,230
Cost of sales	(18,930)
Gross profit	8,300
Distribution costs	(1,670)
Administrative expenses	(1,690)
Finance costs	(700)
Share of profit of associate	135

Share of profit of joint venture	113
Profit before tax	4,488
Income tax expense	(1,280)
Profit for the year	3,208
Other comprehensive income	
Property revaluation surplus *(W1)*	1,925
Total comprehensive income for the year	5,133

Profit for the year attributable to:	
Owners of the parent	3,088
Non-controlling interests *(W2)*	120
	3,208
Total comprehensive income attributable to:	
Owners of the parent	4,933
Non-controlling interests *(W3)*	200
	5,133

(W1) Property Revaluation Surplus

Cork	1,000
Kerry (subsidiary)	800
Meath (associate) 500 × 25%	125
	1,925

(W2) NCI €000

Non-controlling interests in Kerry Ltd profit for the year	
Profit after tax Kerry Ltd	1,230
Less unrealised inventory profit	(30)
Adjusted	1,200
NCI × 10%	120

(W3) NCI

Non-controlling interests in Kerry Ltd total comprehensive income	
Interest in profit for the year *(W2)*	120
Share of property revaluation surplus Kerry Ltd (800 × 10%)	80
	200

CONSOLIDATED STATEMENT OF CHANGES IN EQUITY (EXTRACT)
For the Year Ended 30 September 2013.

	Ordinary Shares €000	Revaluation Reserve €000	Retained Earnings €000	NCI €000	Total €000
At 1 October 2012			10,760(W4)	850(W5)	
TCI for the year		1,845 (W6)	3,088	200(W3)	5,133

At 30 September 2013	1,845	13,848	1,050

(W4) Retained earnings 1 October 2012

Cork	8,460
Impairment of goodwill y/e 30 September 2012	(40)
Kerry 90% × (3,500–900)	2,340
	10,760

(W5) NCI at 1 October 2012

Ordinary shares	5,000
Retained earnings	3,500
	8,500
NCI share 10%	850

(W6) Revaluation Reserve

Cork	1,000
Kerry 90% × 800	720
Meath 25% × 500	125
	1,845

Note: neither Louth Ltd nor Meath Ltd are included in the consolidated retained earnings at 1 October 2012, as the investment in both entities occurred during the reporting year.

Note: in Appendix 1, Question B requires the preparation and presentation of a complete set of consolidated financial statements, i.e.:
(a) a consolidated Statement of Profit or Loss and Other Comprehensive Income;
(b) a consolidated Statement of Changes in Equity; and
(c) a consolidated Statement of Financial Position.

The question involves full consolidation and the equity method as well as many "complications" some of which affect the reporting year while others affect prior years. You are well advised to undertake this question in order to get the full picture of "consolidation".

Chapter 10

Foreign Operations

LEARNING OBJECTIVES

After reading this chapter you should be able to:
- identify the only recognised method for translating the financial statements of a foreign operation;
- demonstrate an understanding of the rules contained in IAS 21 for translating income, expenses, assets and liabilities of a foreign operation;
- account for exchange differences which arise under the presentation currency method; and
- prepare and present a complete set of consolidated financial statements which include the results and financial position of a foreign operation.

Introduction

Thus far, this text has focused on preparing consolidated financial statements where a parent has invested in entities whose financial statements are denominated in the same currency as the parent. This chapter now introduces a 'foreign operation', the accounts of which must be translated into the same currency as the parent before consolidation.

The emphasis of the chapter is on:
1. how to translate the financial statements of a foreign operation; and
2. how to calculate and treat resultant exchange differences.

Key Note: an important point to remember is that the principles and practices of 'consolidation' do not change just because there is a foreign operation. These principles remain the same and what you have learned thus far is totally relevant to this chapter.

IAS 21 *The Effects of Changes in Foreign Exchange Rates* deals with two broad areas:
1. where an **individual company** engages in transactions that are denominated in a foreign currency (this area is outside the scope of this text); and
2. where an entity has an interest in a foreign operation, whose financial statements are denominated in a foreign currency (which is the focus of this chapter).

A foreign operation would normally prepare its financial statements in its local currency (its *functional currency* – see definition below). These financial statements must be translated into the functional currency of the reporting entity. This chapter will focus on the principles for the translation of the financial statements of a foreign operation into the functional currency of the reporting entity and the accounting treatment for the resultant exchange differences.

Note: the functional currency of a parent is invariably the same as its presentation currency (see definition of presentation currency below).

Relevant Definitions (IAS 21, para 8)

Presentation Currency This is the currency in which the financial statements are **presented**. Though an entity is allowed to present its financial statements in any currency it chooses, of course, practicalities will tend to determine that the entity will use its functional currency.

Functional Currency This is the currency of the primary economic environment in which the reporting entity operates (see below for the factors that determine a functional currency).

Foreign Currency A currency other than the functional currency of the entity.

Foreign Operation An entity that is a subsidiary, associate, joint venture or branch of a reporting entity, the activities of which are conducted in a country or currency other than those of the reporting entity.

Spot Exchange Rate The exchange rate for immediate delivery.

Closing Rate The spot exchange rate at the end of the reporting period (i.e. the reporting date).

Monetary Items These are units of currency held and assets/liabilities to be received/paid in a fixed or determinable number of units of currency.

Exchange Difference The difference resulting from translating a given number of units of one currency into another currency at different exchange rates.

Functional Currency

IAS 21 *The Effects of Changes in Foreign Exchange Rates*, at paragraph 9, states that:

A reporting entity should consider certain factors when determining its functional currency, i.e.:
- the currency that **mainly influences sales prices** for goods and services, i.e. the currency in which prices are denominated and settled;
- the currency of the country whose **competitive forces and regulations** mainly determine the sales prices of its goods and services;
- the currency that **mainly influences labour, material and other costs** of providing goods/services;

- the currency in which funds from **financing activities are generated**;
- the currency in which **receipts from operating activitie**s are usually retained.

An entity's functional currency reflects the underlying transactions, events and conditions that are relevant to it. In most cases, the functional currency of a reporting entity is the currency of the country in which it is situated and in which it carries out most of its transactions.

Translation of a Foreign Operation

Under IAS 21, a reporting entity must translate the financial statements of a foreign operation into its own functional currency before preparing the consolidated financial statements (as explained above, the functional currency is normally the same as the presentation currency). The financial statements of the foreign operation should be translated into the functional currency of the reporting entity using the presentation currency method. Specifically, this method is used **where a foreign operation has a different functional currency than that of the reporting entity**.

Translation Rules: Presentation Currency Method

The financial statements of a foreign operation should be translated into the functional currency of the reporting entity using the following rules as per IAS 21, paragraph 39:
- **Assets** and **liabilities** should be translated at the **closing rate**.
- **Income** and **expenses** should be translated at the exchange rates at the **dates of the transactions** or at an **average rate** for the period when this is a **reasonable approximation**. (**Note:** the average rate is normally used in examination questions as using the actual rates would be very impractical.)
- All resulting **exchange differences** (see **Example 10.1**) should be **recognised in other comprehensive income**. These differences are not recognised through profit or loss because they have little or no direct effect on the present and future cash flows from operations.

Key Note: the above translation rules apply equally to foreign subsidiaries, associates and joint ventures.

Translation Differences Arising under the Presentation Currency Method

Two exchange differences naturally arise:
1. the difference caused by the retranslation of the opening net assets of the foreign operation (see **Example 10.1**);
2. the difference caused by using the average rate for income and expenses while using the closing rate for assets and liabilities (see **Example 10.1**).

In the absence of such items as revaluations of property, plant and equipment, issues of shares for cash, etc., the following accounting equation is true:

Opening Net Assets + Retained Earnings for a Reporting Period = Closing Net Assets

EXAMPLE 10.1: CALCULATION OF EXCHANGE DIFFERENCES

Assume a foreign operation at a reporting date 31 August 2013. Exchange rates:

1 September 2012	€1 = 5.00 Zicos
Average y/e 31 August 2013	€1 = 4.50 Zicos
31 August 2013	€1 = 4.00 Zicos

Foreign Operation

	Opening Net Assets	+	Retained Earnings	=	Closing Net Assets
(A) Zicos	200		100		300
(B) Exchange rates	5		4.50 Av		4
(C) Euros (A/B)	40	+	22	≠	75

The equation stands up when the figures are expressed in Zicos but does not when translated into Euros, therefore, the two exchange differences must be taken into account.

Exchange difference 1	**Zicos**	**€**	**€**
Opening net assets	200		
At opening rate 5:		40	
At closing rate 4:		50	
Difference			10

Exchange difference 2	**Zicos**		
Retained earnings for year	100		
At average rate 4.50:		22	
At closing rate 4.00:		25	
Difference			3
Total exchange difference			13

The accounting equation now reads:
Opening net assets + retained earnings + net exchange difference = closing net assets or 40 + 22 + 13 = 75.

A **third** difference arises as follows. IAS 21 at paragraph 47 states:

"Any goodwill arising on the acquisition of a foreign operation and any fair value adjustments to the carrying amounts of assets and liabilities arising on the acquisition of that foreign operation shall be treated as assets and liabilities of the foreign operation.

Thus, they shall be expressed in the functional currency of the foreign operation and retranslated at **the closing rate**."

Therefore:

Goodwill in the consolidated statement of financial position should be retranslated at each reporting date using the closing rate, as shown in **Example 10.2.**

EXAMPLE 10.2: PREPARING A CONSOLIDATED SoFP OF A PARENT AND A FOREIGN SUBSIDIARY

The following are the statements of financial position of Munster Ltd and LA Inc. as at 31 August 2013:

	Munster Ltd €	LA Inc. $
Investment in LA	100,000	-
Net assets	-	300,000
	100,000	300,000
Ordinary share capital	100,000	100,000
Retained earnings	-	200,000
	100,000	300,000

Additional information:
1. Munster acquired 75% of the ordinary shares of LA on 1 September 2012 when the retained earnings of LA were $125,000.
2. Non-controlling interests are measured at acquisition date at their share of the net assets of LA.
3. Relevant rates of exchange are:
1 September 2012	€1 = $2.50
31 August 2013	€1 = $2.00
Average y/e 31 August 2013	€1 = $2.2059
4. The functional currency of Munster is the Euro while that of LA is the US Dollar.

Requirement   Prepare the consolidated statement of financial position of Munster Ltd. as at 31 August 2013.

Solution

TRANSLATION OF LA STATEMENT OF FINANCIAL POSITION

	$	Rate	€
Net assets	300,000	2.00	150,000
Ordinary share capital	100,000	2.50	40,000
Pre-acquisition retained earnings	125,000	2.50	50,000
Post-acquisition retained earnings	75,000	Bal. Fig.	60,000 (Note 1)
	300,000		150,000

Note 1: The post-acquisition retained earnings (€60,000) include the exchange differences arising from translation of LA Inc. (see **Example 10.1** and **(W2)** of this solution).

WORKINGS (common to both methods)

(W1) Goodwill		€	€
Investment in LA			100,000
NCI 25% (40,000 + 50,000)			22,500
			122,500
Net assets of LA at acquisition date			
Ordinary shares		40,000	
Retained earnings		50,000	90,000
Goodwill at acquisition date			32,500
Translation difference (W2)			8,125
SoFP			40,625

(W2) Exchange differences from translation of LA		€	€
Exchange difference 1			
Opening net assets (100,000 + 125,000)	$225,000		
At opening rate 2.50		90,000	
At closing rate 2.00		112,500	
Difference			22,500
Exchange difference 2			
Profit for the year	$75,000		
At average rate 2.2059		34,000	
At closing rate 2.00		37,500	
Difference			3,500
Total			26,000
Group's share (75%)			19,500
NCI share (25%)			6,500
Exchange difference 3			
Difference on retranslation of goodwill			
Goodwill			32,500
Equivalent $ at acquisition date	81,250		
Retranslated using closing rate	2.00		40,625
Difference – all attributable to group			8,125
Total differences (26,000 + 8,125)			34,125

JOURNAL ENTRIES (common to both methods)

		€	€
1.	Dr. Goodwill	100,000	
	Cr. Investment in LA		100,000
	Investment in LA		

2. Dr. Goodwill   22,500
    Cr. NCI   22,500
    NCI share of net assets of LA at acquisition date
    25% (40,000 + 50,000)

3. Dr. Ordinary shares   40,000
    Cr. Goodwill   40,000
    Ordinary shares of LA at acquisition date

4. Dr. Retained earnings LA   50,000
    Cr. Goodwill   50,000
    Retained earnings of LA at acquisition date

5. Dr. Retained earnings LA   26,000
    Cr. Foreign currency exchange reserve (75%)   19,500
    Cr. NCI (25%)   6,500
    Exchanges differences (W2)

6. Dr. Retained earnings LA   34,000
    Cr. Retained earnings Munster (75%)   25,500
    Cr. NCI (25%)   8,500
    Post-acquisition retained earnings LA
    (60,000 – 26,000) (see Note 1)

7. Dr. Goodwill   8,125
    Cr. Foreign currency translation reserve   8,125
    Exchange difference on retranslation of goodwill (W2)

WORKINGS (T Account Method)

Investment in LA

Debit		Credit	
M	100,000	Goodwill (Jnl. 1)	80,000

Net Assets

Debit		Credit	
LA	150,000	SoFP	150,000

Ordinary Shares

Debit		Credit	
Goodwill (Jnl. 3)	40,000	M	100,000
SoFP	100,000	LA	40,000
	140,000		140,000

Retained Earnings – Munster

Debit		Credit	
		M at reporting date	nil
SoFP	25,500	Share of LA post-acq. (Jnl. 6)	25,500
	25,500		25,500

Retained Earnings LA

Debit		Credit	
Goodwill (Jnl. 4)	50,000	M – pre-acquisition	50,000
Exchange differences (Jnl. 5)	26,000	M – post-acquisition	60,000
M – post-acq. ret. earns (Jnl. 6)	25,500		
NCI – post-acq. ret. earns (Jnl. 6)	8,500		
	110,000		110,000

Non-controlling interests

Debit		Credit	
		Share of LA net assets (Jnl. 2)	22,500
		Share of exchange diff. (Jnl. 5)	6,500
SoFP	37,500	Share of LA post-acq. (Jnl. 6)	8,500
	37,500		37,500

Foreign Currency Exchange Reserve

Debit		Credit	
		Exchange differences (Jnl. 5)	19,500
SoFP	27,625	Goodwill exch. diff. (Jnl. 7)	8,125
	27,625		27,625

Goodwill

Debit		Credit	
Investment in LA (Jnl. 1)	100,000	Ord. shares LA (Jnl. 3)	40,000
NCI at acq.date (Jnl. 2)	22,500	Retained earnings LA (Jnl. 4)	50,000
Exchange diff. (Jnl. 7)	8,125	SoFP	40,625
	130,625		130,625

WORKINGS (Columnar Method)

	Munster	LA	Adjustments	Consol. SoFP
	€	€	€	€
Investment in LA	100,000		(100,000) Jnl. 1	0
Net assets		150,000		150,000
Goodwill (W1)			40,625	40,625
	100,000	150,000	(59,375)	190,625

Ordinary shares	100,000	40,000	(40,000) Jnl. 3	100,000
Foreign currency exchange reserve (W2)			27,625 Jnl. 5 & 7	27,625
Retained earnings (W3)	0	110,000	(84,500)	25,500
NCI (W4)			37,500	37,500
	100,000	150,000	(59,375)	190,625

(W3) Retained earnings

		€	€
Munster at reporting date			nil
Share of post-acquisition profits of LA (Jnl. 6)			25,500
LA at reporting date	pre-acquisition	50,000	
	post-acquisition	60,000	
		110,000	
Transferred to goodwill (Jnl. 4)		(50,000)	
Exchange differences	Group's share (Jnl. 5)	(19,500)	
	NCI share (Jnl. 5)	(6,500)	
		34,000	
Post-acquisition profits	Group's share (Jnl. 6)	(25,500)	
	NCI share (Jnl. 6)	(8,500)	nil
SoFP			25,500

(W4) NCI

	€
Share of LA's net assets at acquisition date (Jnl. 2)	22,500
Share of exchange differences (Jnl. 5)	6,500
Share of LA's post-acquisition profit (Jnl. 6)	8,500
	37,500

Munster Limited
CONSOLIDATED STATEMENT OF FINANCIAL POSITION
as at 31 August 2013

	€
Net assets	150,000
Goodwill	40,625
	190,625
Ordinary share capital	100,000
Foreign currency exchange reserve	27,625
Retained earnings	25,500
Total shareholders' equity	153,125
Non-controlling interests	37,500
Total equity	190,625

EXAMPLE 10.3: PREPARING A CONSOLIDATED SPLOCI OF A PARENT AND A FOREIGN SUBSIDIARY

The following is the statement of profit or loss of LA Inc. for the year ended 31 August 2013.

	$
Revenue	461,253
Cost of sales	(307,503)
Gross profit	153,750
Distribution costs	(15,000)
Administrative expenses	(37,500)
Finance costs	(7,500)
Profit before taxation	93,750
Income tax expense	(18,750)
Profit for the year	75,000

This example is a continuation of **Example 10.2** and therefore the same rates of exchange apply:

1 September 2012	€1 = $2.50
31 August 2013	€1 = $2.00
Average y/e 31 August 2013	€1 = $2.2059

Requirement   Prepare the consolidated statement of profit or loss and other comprehensive income for the year ended 31 August 2013.

Solution
Translation of LA statement of profit or loss.

	$	Rate	€
Revenue	461,253	2.2059	209,100
Cost of sales	(307,503)	2.2059	(139,400)
Gross profit	153,750		69,700
Distribution costs	(15,000)	2.2059	(6,800)
Administrative expenses	(37,500)	2.2059	(17,000)
Finance costs	(7,500)	2.2059	(3,400)
Profit before taxation	93,750		42,500
Income tax expense	(18,750)	2.2059	(8,500)
Profit for the year	75,000		34,000

Munster Limited
CONSOLIDATED STATEMENT OF PROFIT OR LOSS AND OTHER COMPREHENSIVE INCOME
for the year ended 31 August 2013

	€
Revenue	209,100
Cost of sales	(139,400)

Gross profit	69,700
Distribution costs	(6,800)
Administrative expenses	(17,000)
Finance costs	(3,400)
Profit before taxation	42,500
Income tax expense	(8,500)
Profit for the year	34,000
Other comprehensive income	
Exchange differences on translating foreign operations (Note 1)	34,125
Total comprehensive income for the year	68,125
Profit for the year attributable to:	
Owners of the parent	25,500
Non-controlling interests (W1)	8,500
	34,000
Total comprehensive income for the year attributable to:	
Owners of the parent	53,125
Non-controlling interests (W2)	15,000
	68,125

€

(W1)

LA's profit after tax	34,000
NCI share (25%)	8,500

(W2)

As per *(W1)*	8,500	
Share of exchange differences	6,500	**(Example 10.2** (W2))
	15,000	

Note 1
The exchange differences were calculated in **Example 10.2 (W2)**.

Conclusion

There is only one method recognised in IAS 21 for translating the financial statements of a foreign operation into the functional currency (normally also the presentation currency) of the reporting entity namely: **the presentation currency method**. The need for this method arises when the functional currency of the foreign operation is different from that of the reporting entity. Though a reporting entity can present its financial statements in any currency, in almost all cases its functional currency is the same as its presentation currency.

SUMMARY

1. The presentation currency method is the only method recognised under IAS 21 for translating a foreign operation into the functional currency of the investor. The functional currency is invariably the same as the presentation currency.
2. Assets and liabilities are translated at the closing rate.
3. Share capital and pre-acquisition reserves are translated at the rate at the date of acquisition to facilitate the calculation of goodwill/gain from a bargain purchase.
4. Income and expenses should be translated at the rates at the dates of the transactions but for practical reasons an average rate for the period is often used. However, if exchange rates fluctuate significantly, the use of the average rate for a period is inappropriate.
5. Exchange differences are taken to reserves being shown as 'other comprehensive income' in the statement of profit or loss and other comprehensive income.
6. The group's share of the cumulative exchange differences to the reporting date are shown as a foreign currency exchange reserve in the consolidated SoFP and explained in the notes.

QUESTIONS

Question 10.1

What is the only recognised method for translating the financial statements of a foreign operation into the functional currency of the reporting entity?

Solution

The presentation currency method is the only method recognised under IAS 21 for translating the financial statements of a foreign operation.

Question 10.2

What rate(s) are applied to translate the following:
(a) the assets and liabilities of a foreign operation?
(b) the share capital and pre-acquisition reserves of a foreign operation?
(c) the income and expenses of a foreign operation. Is there any alternative allowed?

Solution

(a) the assets and liabilities are translated using the closing rate;
(b) the capital and pre-acquisition reserves of a foreign operation are translated using the rate at the date of acquisition;

(c) ideally, the income and expenses are translated using the rates at the dates of the transactions but an average rate for the reporting period can be used when this rate approximates to the actual rates.

Question 10.3

Explain the exchange differences that arise:
(a) on translating the financial statements of a foreign operation;
(b) on the preparation of the resultant consolidated financial statements.

Solution

There are two differences that naturally arise on the translation of the financial statements of a foreign operation:
1. The difference caused by the retranslation of the opening net assets of a subsidiary calculated as follows:

		€		€
Opening net assets	at opening rate	X		
	at closing rate	X		
Difference		X	× group's share	Y
2. Profit after tax	at average rate	X		
	at closing rate	X		
Difference		X	× group's share	Y
Total				2Y

A third difference arises on the preparation of the consolidated financial statements which is caused by the requirement of IAS 21 to retranslate the goodwill at each reporting date using the closing rate. The non-controlling interests will be affected by their share of differences **1** and **2**, but not difference number **3** if their interest is measured at their share of the net assets of the subsidiary at the date of acquisition.

However, if the non-controlling interests were measured at fair value at the date of acquisition, then part of the goodwill would be attributable to them. In this circumstance, it would follow that part of the goodwill translation differences that subsequently arise would be attributable to the NCI.

Question 10.4

What is the accounting treatment for exchange differences which arise under the presentation currency method?

Solution

All exchange differences under the presentation currency method are recognised as 'other comprehensive income' in the consolidated SPLOCI.

Note: **Question 10.5** is a longer, review-type question and includes a foreign operation which is a subsidiary. The solution contains:
1. journal adjustments
2. the T account method workings
3. the columnar method workings
4. the consolidated SoFP; and
5 the consolidated SPLOCI and SoCIE.

Question 10.5

From the following information prepare:
1. the consolidated statement of profit or loss and other comprehensive income;
2. the consolidated statement of changes in equity;
3. the consolidated statement of financial position.

STATEMENT OF PROFIT OR LOSS
for the Year Ended 31 July 2013

	Ireland Ltd €000	Joburg Inc. Bingos 000
Revenue	6,400	1,300
Cost of sales	(4,500)	(780)
Gross profit	1,900	520
Distribution costs	(350)	(90)
Administrative expenses	(250)	(120)
Finance costs	(100)	(40)
Profit before taxation	1,200	270
Income tax expense	(130)	(30)
Profit for the year	1,070	240

STATEMENT OF FINANCIAL POSITION
as at 31 July 2013

	Ireland Ltd €000	Joburg Inc. Bingos 000
Assets		
Non-current assets		
Property, plant and equipment	5,050	900
Investment in subsidiary	500	–
	5,550	900

Current assets

Inventory	480	150
Other current assets	1,600	700
	2,080	850
Total assets	**7,630**	**1,750**

Equity and Liabilities

Equity

Capital and reserves

Share capital	2,000	300
Retained earnings	4,650	1,010
	6,650	1,310

Non-current liabilities

Long-term loan	–	120
Current liabilities	980	320
Total equity and liabilities	**7,630**	**1,750**

Exchange Rates

	Bingos
1 August 2011	€1 = 1.60
31 July 2012	1.50
Average 1/8/2011 – 31/7/2013	1.80
31 July 2013	2.00

Ireland Ltd purchased 80% of Joburg Inc on 1 August 2011 when the retained earnings of Joburg Inc were 540,000 Bingos.

Non-controlling interests are valued at acquisition date using the share of net assets method.

SOLUTION NOTES

1. Translate the SPLOCI of Joburg.
2. Prepare the consolidated SPLOCI but be aware that the **total exchange gains/losses for the reporting period** must be included under Other Comprehensive Income, therefore they must be calculated. The NCI's share of the difference (excluding the difference on the retranslation of goodwill) is deducted in arriving at "Total Comprehensive Income" attributable to them.
3. Translate the SoFP of Joburg.
4. Prepare the consolidated SoFP including the cumulative exchange difference on the goodwill from the date of acquisition.
5. Calculate the cumulative exchange differences to both the start and end of the reporting year.
6. Prepare the consolidated SoCIE.

Solution

TRANSLATION OF JOBURG INC SPLOCI AT AVERAGE RATE

	Bingos 000	Rate	Euro €000
Revenue	1,300	1.80	722
Cost of sales	(780)	1.80	(433)
Gross profit	520		289
Distribution costs	(90)	1.80	(50)
Administrative expenses	(120)	1.80	(67)
Finance costs	(40)	1.80	(22)
Profit before tax	270		150
Income tax expense	(30)	1.80	(17)
Profit for year	240		133

Remember: IAS 21 states that under the presentation currency method income and expenses should be translated using the rates at the dates of the transactions but the average rate for the reporting period could be used when this gives a close approximation. If an examination question includes actual rates for:

- opening inventories;
- closing inventories; and
- depreciation;

then those rates should be used, while using the average rate for all other income and expenses.

WORKINGS (Columnar Method)

	Ireland Ltd €000	Joburg Inc €000	Adjustments €000	Consol. SPLOCI €000
Revenue	6,400	722		7,122
Cost of sales	(4,500)	(433)		(4,933)
Gross profit	1,900	289		2,189
Distribution costs	(350)	(50)		(400)
Administrative expenses	(250)	(67)		(317)
Finance costs	(100)	(22)		(122)
Profit before taxation	1,200	150		1,350
Income tax expense	(130)	(17)		(147)
Profit for the year	1,070	133		1,203

CONSOLIDATED STATEMENT OF PROFIT OR LOSS AND OTHER COMPREHENSIVE INCOME
for the Year Ended 31 July 2013

	€000
Revenue	7,122
Cost of sales	(4,933)
Gross profit	2,189

Distribution costs	(400)
Administrative expenses	(317)
Finance costs	(122)
Profit before tax	1,350
Income tax expense	(147)
Profit for the year	1,203

Other comprehensive income

Exchange difference on translating foreign operation (*W5*)	(212)
Total comprehensive income for the year	991

Profit attributable to:	
Owners of the parent	1,176
Non-controlling interests *(W1)*	27
	1,203

Total comprehensive income attributable to:	
Owners of the parent	1,002
Non-controlling interests *(W2)*	(11)
	991

(W1) Non-controlling interest

Profit after tax of Joburg Inc	(133 × 20%) =	27

(W2) Non-controlling interest

NCI in profit for the year		27
Foreign exchange difference *(W5)*	(191 × 20%)	(38)
		(11)

(W3) Goodwill

	€000	€000
Investment in Joburg		500
NCI at acquisition date 20% ×(188 + 337)		105
		605
Net assets of Joburg at acquisition date		
Ordinary shares	188	
Retained earnings	337	525
Goodwill		80
Retranslation difference at period end (W4)		(16)
SoFP		64

(W4) Retranslation of goodwill

	€000		€000
Goodwill at acquisition date	80		
Goodwill at 31 July 2012 (80 × 1.60/1.50)	85	Exchange gain	5
Goodwill at 31 July 2013 (85 × 1.50/2.0)	64	Exchange loss	(21)
			(16)

Note: the exchange differences on goodwill are attributable to the parent only.

(W5) Exchange differences arising y/e 31 July 2013

	Bingos 000	€000	€000

Exchange differences from translation of Joburg

Difference 1

Net assets at 1 August 2012 (1,310 – 240)	1,070		
At opening rate 1.50		713	
At closing rate 2.0		535	
Difference			(178)

Difference 2

Profit after tax	240		
At average rate 1.8		133	
At closing rate 2.0		120	
Difference			(13)

Difference 3

Retranslation of goodwill (W4)		(21)
Total exchange loss taken to other comprehensive income		(212)
Attributable to NCI 20% ×(178 + 13)		(38)
Attributable to the parent		(174)
		(212)

TRANSLATION OF JOBURG INC STATEMENT OF FINANCIAL POSITION USING CLOSING RATE

	Bingos 000	Rate	€000
Property, plant and equipment	900	2.00	450
Inventories	150	2.00	75
Other current assets	700	2.00	350
Long-term loan	(120)	2.00	(60)
Current liabilities	(320)	2.00	(160)
	1,310		655
Capital	300	1.60	188
Pre-acq. retained earnings	540	1.60	337
Post-acq. retained earnings	470	Bal. fig.	130
	1,310		655

Note: the exchange differences arising from the translation of Joburg are included in the post-acquisition retained earnings of €130,000. The calculation of the differences is shown in **W5**.

(W6) Cumulative exchange differences to 31 July 2013

	Bingos 000
Net assets (capital and reserves) at 31 July 2013	1,310
Retained earnings y/e 31 July 2013	(240)

Net assets at 1 August 2012   1,070
Net assets at acquisition date 1 August 2011   (840)
Retained earnings y/e 31 July 2012   230

Exchange differences from translation of Joburg

	Bingos 000	€000	€000
Net assets at acquisition date	840		
At opening rate 1.60		525	
At closing rate 2.00		420	
Difference			(105)
Profit for two years (1,310 – 840)	470		
At average rate 1.80		261	
At closing rate 2.00		235	
Difference			(26)
			(131)

Retranslation of goodwill (W4) attributable to
   Ireland only   (16)
                                                           (147)

Summary

	€000
Attributable to the group (131 × 80%) +16	(121)
Attributable to NCI (131 × 20%)	(26)
	(147)

Journal entries

	€000	€000
1. Dr. Goodwill	500	
Cr. Investment in Joburg		500
Investment in Joburg		
2. Dr. Goodwill	105	
Cr. NCI		105
NCI at acquisition date (W3)		
3. Dr. Ordinary shares	188	
Cr. Goodwill		188
Ordinary shares Joburg at acquisition date		
4. Dr. Retained earnings Joburg	337	
Cr. Goodwill		337
Retained earnings Joburg at acquisition date		

5. Dr. Currency exchange reserve   105
   Dr. NCI   26
   Cr. Retained earnings Joburg   131
   Exchange differences from translation of Joburg (W6)

6. Dr. Retained earnings Joburg (130 + 131)   261
   Cr. Retained earnings Ireland (80%)   209
   Cr. NCI (20%)   52
   Allocation of post-acquisition retained earnings of Joburg (see **Note**)

7. Dr. Currency exchange reserve   16
   Cr. Goodwill   16
   Goodwill retranslation difference (W4)

Note:

Post-acq. retained earnings per translation of Joburg	130
Cumulative exchange losses to 31 July 2013 (W6)	131
	261

Workings (T Account Method)

Property Plant and Equipment

Debit		Credit	
Irl	5,050		
Joburg	450	SoFP	5,500
	5,500		5,500

Investment in Joburg Inc.

Debit		Credit	
Irl	500	Goodwill (Jnl. 1)	500
	500		500

Inventories

Debit		Credit	
Irl	480		
Joburg	75	SoFP	555
	555		555

Other Current Assets

Debit		Credit	
Irl	1,600		
Joburg	350	SoFP	1,950
	1,950		1,950

Long-term Loan

Debit		Credit	
SoFP	60	Joburg	60

Current liabilities

Debit		Credit	
		Irl	980
SoFP	1,140	Joburg	160
	1,140		1,140

Ordinary Share Capital

Debit		Credit	
Goodwill (Jnl. 3)	188	Irl	2,000
SoFP	2,000	Joburg	188
	2,188		2,188

Retained Earnings – Ireland

Debit		Credit	
		Irl at reporting date	4,650
SoFP	4,859	Share of J post-acq. (Jnl. 6)	209
	4,859		4,859

Retained Earnings – Joburg

Debit		Credit	
Goodwill (Jnl. 4)	337	Joburg at reporting date	467
Post-acq. profits (Jnl. 6)	261	Exchange loss (Jnl. 5)	131
	598		598

Foreign Currency Exchange Reserve

Debit		Credit	
Exchange loss (Jnl. 5)	105		
Exchange loss on g/will (Jnl. 7)	16	SoFP	121
	121		121

Goodwill

Debit		Credit	
		Ord. shares Joburg (Jnl. 3)	188
		Ret. earnings Joburg (Jnl. 4)	337
Investment in Joburg (Jnl. 1)	500	Exchange loss (Jnl. 7)	16
NCI (Jnl. 2)	105	SoFP	64
	605		605

Non-controlling Interests

Debit		Credit	
Exchange loss (Jnl. 5)	26	Goodwill (Jnl. 2)	105
SoFP	131	Share of J post-acq. (Jnl. 6)	52
	157		157

WORKINGS (Columnar Method)

Assets	Ireland	Joburg	Adjusts.	Consol. SoFP
	€000	€000	€000	€000
PPE	5,050	450		5,500
Investment in Joburg	500		(500) Jnl. 1	-
Goodwill (W3)			64	64
Inventories	480	75		555
Other current assets	1,600	350		1,950
Total Assets	**7,630**	**875**	**(436)**	**8,069**
Equity and Liabilities				
Ordinary shares	2,000	188	(188) Jnl. 3	2,000
Currency exch. reserve (W7)			(121) Jnl. 5,7	(121)
Retained earnings (W8)	4,650	467	(258)	4,859
NCI (W9)			131 Jnl. 2,5,6	131
Long term loan		60		60
Current liabilities	980	160		1,140
	7,630	**875**	**(436)**	**8,069**

(W7) Currency exchange reserve

	€000	€000
Retranslation of Joburg (W6 and Jnl. 5)	(105)	
Retranslation of goodwill (W6 and Jnl. 7)	(16)	(121)

(W8) Retained earnings

	€000	€000
Ireland at reporting date		4,650
Joburg at reporting date	467	
Joburg at acquisition date	337	
	130	
Exchange loss included (W6 and Jnl. 5)	131	
Post-acquisition profits	261	
Group's share (80%)		209
SoFP		4,859

(W9) NCI

	€000
Value at acquisition date (W3 and Jnl. 2)	105
Exchange difference on translation of Joburg (W6 and Jnl. 5)	(26)
Share of post-acquisition profits of Joburg (Jnl. 6)	52
	131

STATEMENT OF CHANGES IN EQUITY

	Share Capital €000	Foreign Currency Exchange Reserve €000	Retained Earnings €000	NCI €000
At 1 August 2012	2,000	53	3,683 (W10)	142 (W11)
TCI for the year		(174) (W5)	1,176	(11)
At 31 July 2013	2,000	(121) (W6)	4,859	131 (W9)

(W10) Retained earnings b/f at 1 August 2012:

	€000
Ireland: Retained earnings at 31/7/2013	4,650
Retained earnings y/e 31/7/2013	(1,070)
Retained earnings at 1/8/2012	3,580

Joburg:	Capital and reserves:		
	At 1/8/2012 (*See W11*)	713	
	At acquisition date	525	
	Post-acquisition	188	
	Group × 80%		151
Goodwill translation 80 × 1.6/1.5 = 85 (W4)			5
			3,736

Summary:

Retained earnings at 1/8/2012	3,736
Exchange difference	53 *(W12)* – shown as other equity component
Opening balance reserves	3,683

(W11) NCI at 1 August 2012

Joburg	Bingos 000	€000
Net assets at 31 July 2013	1,310	
Retained earnings y/e 31 July 2013	(240)	
Net assets 31 July 2012	1,070	
At the rate of 1.50 at 31 July 2012		
Net assets Joburg 1 August 2012		713
NCI × 20%		142

(W12) Exchange differences as at 31 July 2012

	Bingos 000	€000	€000
Exchange differences from translation of Joburg			
Difference 1			
Net assets at acquisition date (1/8/2011)	840		
At opening rate 1.60		525	
At closing rate 1.50		560	
Difference			35
Difference 2			
Profit for y/e 31 July 2012 (W6)	230		
At average rate 1.80		128	
At closing rate 1.50		153	

Difference $\frac{25}{60}$

Difference 3
Retranslation of goodwill (W4) $\frac{5}{65}$

Summary
Attributable to the group (60 × 80%) +5   53
Attributable to NCI (60 × 20%) $\frac{12}{65}$

Ireland Ltd
CONSOLIDATED STATEMENT OF FINANCIAL POSITION
as at 31 July 2013

	€000
Assets	
Non-current assets	
Property, plant and equipment	5,500
Goodwill	64
	5,564
Current assets	
Inventories	555
Other	1,950
	2,505
Total assets	**8,069**
Equity and Liabilities	
Equity	
Ordinary share capital	2,000
Foreign currency exchange reserve	(121)
Retained earnings	4,859
	6,738
Non-controlling interest	131
	6,869
Non-current liabilities	
Long-term loan	60
Current liabilities	1,140
Total equity and liabilities	**8,069**

Chapter 11

Consolidated Statement of Cash Flows

LEARNING OBJECTIVES

After reading this chapter you should be able to:
- demonstrate an understanding of the issues which are particular to the preparation of a consolidated SoCF;
- explain the effects of non-controlling interests on the consolidated SoCF;
- account for the effects of an associate, a joint venture and a trade investment;
- explain the impact of acquisitions and disposals of subsidiaries, associates and joint ventures on the consolidated SoCF;
- account for a foreign operation; and
- prepare and present a consolidated statement of cash flows.

Introduction

The issues dealt with in this chapter involve a combination of skills namely:
1. using your knowledge of preparing consolidated financial statements; and
2. preparing statements of cash flows.

Before reading this chapter you must
- have prior knowledge and practice of the preparation of statements of cash flows for individual entities in accordance with the provisions of IAS 7 *Statement of Cash Flows*;
- be proficient in the preparation of consolidated financial statements.

IAS 7 requires that all entities prepare a statement of cash flows (SoCF) as an integral part of the entity's financial statements for each financial period. Information about the cash flows of an entity is useful in providing users of financial statements with a basis to assess the ability of the entity to generate cash and cash equivalents, and the needs of the entity to utilise those cash flows. The economic decisions that are taken by users of financial statements require an evaluation of the ability of an entity to generate cash and cash equivalents. IAS 1 *Presentation of Financial Statements* includes a statement of cash flows as one of the components of a complete set of financial statements.

Relevant Definitions

Cash This comprises cash on hand and demand deposits.

Cash equivalents Short-term, highly liquid investments, which are readily convertible to known amounts of cash and that are subject to an insignificant risk of changes in value.

> *Note:* an investment normally qualifies as a cash equivalent only when it has a short maturity of, say, three months or less from the date of acquisition.

Cash flows Inflows and outflows of cash and cash equivalents.

The Statement of Cash Flows

IAS 7 requires that all cash flows are classified by activity, which provides information to users of the financial statements that allows them to assess the impact of those activities on the cash, cash equivalents and the financial position of the entity.

The three types of activity under which IAS 7 classifies cash flows are as follows:
1. **Operating activities**, which are the principal revenue activities of an entity (e.g. cash receipts from sales, cash payments made to suppliers, employees, etc.).

   An entity can report cash flows from operating activities using either:

   (a) **the direct method:**

		€000
Cash received from customers		X
Cash paid to suppliers		(X)
Cash paid to or on behalf of employees		(X)
Other cash payments		(X)
Cash generated from operations	(say)	1,546

   or

   (b) **the indirect method:**

		€000
Profit before tax		X
Adjustments		
Depreciation		X
Interest charge		X
Profit on disposal of PPE		(X)
Increase in inventories		(X)
Increase in receivables		(X)
Increase in payables		X
Cash generated from operations	(say)	1,546

From your studies of the presentation of statements of cash flows for individual entities (which is outside the scope of this text), you should be familiar with both the direct and indirect methods.

> *Key Note:* IAS 7 permits either of the above methods to be used. When answering examination questions you are entitled to use either method, unless one of them is specified. **This text adopts the indirect method as it is the more traditional of the two and, in the author's opinion, the one more familiar to students.**

2. **Investing activities,** which are the acquisition and disposal of long-term assets and other investments which are not cash equivalents. These are expenditures made to acquire resources intended to generate future income and cash flows (e.g. payments to acquire property, plant and equipment).
3. **Financing activities**, which are those that result in changes in the size and composition of the contributed equity and borrowings of an entity (e.g. proceeds from the issue of shares, repayment of long-term loans, etc.).

Issues Peculiar to the Consolidated Statement of Cash Flows

In general, the principles applied in the preparation of a consolidated statement of cash flows are the same as those of an individual entity. However, there are issues that only arise with consolidated statements of cash flows and which need special attention. These are:
- dealing with the non-controlling interests in subsidiaries,
- dealing with associates;
- dealing with joint ventures;
- an acquisition of a subsidiary during an accounting period;
- a disposal of a subsidiary during an accounting period;
- an acquisition or disposal of shares in an associate or a joint venture during an accounting period;
- dealing with a foreign operation.

Before dealing with the above issues, it is important to highlight three principles:
1. A consolidated SoCF should only include inflows and outflows of cash that are **external to the group**. Internal cash flows, such as payment of dividends by a subsidiary to its parent, should be eliminated. This problem should only arise if a consolidated SoCF is being prepared from the individual financial statements of the group entities.
2. If an entity (i.e. an associate or a joint venture) is accounted for under the **equity method** of accounting in the consolidated financial statements, only the cash flows between the group and the entity should be included in the group SoCF.
3. If a subsidiary is acquired or disposed of during an accounting period, the consolidated SoCF should only include the cash flows of that subsidiary for the same period as its results are included in the consolidated statement of profit or loss and other comprehensive income.

Dealing with Non-controlling Interests

A subsidiary is fully consolidated; therefore, all its assets and liabilities, income and expenses are included in the consolidated financial statements, whether or not there is a non-controlling interest. This means that cash flows for subsidiaries, relating to such items as operating activities, taxation, acquisition or disposal of non-current assets, are combined with those of the parent undertaking, However, certain items need special attention i.e.:

1. issue of shares for cash to non-controlling interests (NCI);
2. redemption of shares owned by non-controlling interests; and
3. dividends paid to non-controlling interests.

Cash flows relating to items 1 and 2 would appear in the group statement of cash flows under 'Financing activities'. In the absence of the acquisition or disposal of a subsidiary during the period (part of which is owned by the non-controlling interests), dividends paid to non-controlling interests is the balancing figure between the opening and closing values for non-controlling interests in the statements of financial position plus the NCI share of total comprehensive income (TCI) for the financial period (see **Example 11.1**). The following Pro-forma T account shows the calculation:

Pro Forma: T Account for NCI

Non-controlling Interests			
Debit	**€**	**Credit**	**€**
Cash (dividends) paid **(balancing figure)**	X	Opening balance (opening SoFP)	X
Closing balance (closing SoFP)	X̱ X̲	Share of TCI (see note) (per consolidated SPLOCI)	X̱ X̲

Note: the NCI share of total comprehensive income would include their share of any goodwill impairment.

Example 11.1: Calculation of Dividends paid to NCI

Extracts from Consolidated Statement of Financial Position		
	2013 €000	**2012 €000**
Equity and liabilities		
Equity		
Ordinary share capital		
Retained earnings		
Total shareholders' equity		
Non-controlling interests	860	670

EXTRACTS FROM CONSOLIDATED STATEMENT OF PROFIT OR LOSS AND OTHER
COMPREHENSIVE INCOME

	2013 €000
Profit for the year attributable to:	
Owners of the parent	1,160
Non-controlling interests	280
	1,440
Total comprehensive income for the year attributable to:	
Owners of the parent	1,240
Non-controlling interests	300
	1,540

Non-controlling Interests

Debit		**Credit**	
Dividends paid (bal. fig.)	110	Opening balance	670
Closing balance	860	TCI – Consolidated SPLOCI	300
	970		970

The dividends paid to non-controlling interests, €110,000, can be included under either:
(a) cash flows from **operating** activities; *or*
(b) cash flows from **financing** activities,
    in the statement of cash flows (IAS 7).

(*Note:* this text adopts the option (b) method because dividends paid are a cost of obtaining financial resources and the authors consider this to be a more appropriate presentation.)

If a subsidiary was acquired or disposed during a reporting period, the above T account would be credited with the non-controlling interest in the net assets of the subsidiary at the date of acquisition, or debited with the share of the net assets of the subsidiary at the date of disposal.

Dealing with Associates

Associates are accounted for in the consolidated financial statements using the **equity method of accounting** (see **Chapter 6** (SoFP) and **Chapter 8** (SPLOCI/SoCIE)). This means that the consolidated statement of profit or loss and other comprehensive income includes the group's share of the profit of the associate after tax. This entry does not involve cash flows, but the *group* cash flow is affected by the dividends received from associates. Dividends received from associates can be calculated as follows (see also **Example 11.2**):

PRO FORMA: T ACCOUNT INVESTMENT IN ASSOCIATE

Investment in Associate			
Debit	**€**	**Credit**	**€**
Opening balance		Dividends received from A	
(opening SoFP)	X	(**balancing figure**)	X
Share of profit of A		Closing balance	
(Consol. SPLOCI) (see note)	X	(closing SoFP)	X
	X̄		X̄

Note: the share of profit of A would include any impairment of the investment for the year.

EXAMPLE 11.2: CALCULATION OF DIVIDEND RECEIVED FROM ASSOCIATE

EXTRACTS FROM CONSOLIDATED STATEMENT OF FINANCIAL POSITION

	2013 €000	2012 €000
Non-current assets		
Property, plant and equipment		
Investment in associate	390	240

EXTRACT FROM CONSOLIDATED STATEMENT OF PROFIT OR LOSS AND OTHER COMPREHENSIVE INCOME

	2011 €000
Share of profit of associate	180

Investment in Associate			
Debit		**Credit**	
Balance b/d	240	Dividend received	30
Share of profit	180	Balance c/d	390
	420		420

The dividends received from the associate, €30,000, can be included under either:
(a) cash flows from **investing** activities; *or*
(b) cash flows from **operating** activities,
in the statement of cash flows (IAS 7).

(*Note:* this text adopts the option (a) method only because the authors consider it preferable to show this cash flow as a return on investment.)

If the parent acquired an interest in an associate during a reporting period, the above T account would be debited with the cash outflow.

Dealing with Joint Ventures

As explained in **Chapter 7**, joint ventures are treated in exactly the same manner as associates (i.e. the equity method). See **Example 11.2**.

Acquisition of a Subsidiary during a Reporting Period

The **net cash flow** from the acquisition of a subsidiary must be shown separately and should be dealt with in the group statement of cash flows under 'Investing activities'. Any cash paid as part of the consideration would be included as a cash outflow, while any balances of cash and cash equivalents acquired as part of the combination should be offset against the cash consideration paid.

EXAMPLE 11.3: ACQUISITION OF A SUBSIDIARY

During the period under review, Pat Ltd acquired 90% of the ordinary shares of Sarah Ltd. NCI are measured at their share of the net assets of Sarah Ltd.

Details of the acquisition:

Net assets acquired	€000
Property, plant and equipment	800
Inventories	280
Trade receivables	190
Cash	50
Trade payables	(180)
	1,140
Non-controlling interest @ 10%	(114)
Goodwill (*W1*)	174
	1,200
Discharged by	
Issue of shares	400
Cash paid	800
	1,200

(*W1*) *Goodwill*

	€000
Investment in Sarah	1,200
NCI (10% × 1,140)	114
	1,314
Net assets (capital and reserves) of Sarah at acquisition date	1,140
Goodwill	174

Goodwill			
Debit		**Credit**	
Investment in Sarah	1,200	Net assets Sarah	1,140
NCI	114	Goodwill	174
	1,314		1,314

EXTRACT FROM CONSOLIDATED STATEMENT OF CASH FLOWS

	€000
Investing activities	
Purchase of subsidiary	
(cash paid €800 *less* cash acquired €50)	(750)

It should be noted that property, plant and equipment of €800,000, inventories of €280,000, receivables of €190,000, and payables of €180,000, acquired with Sarah Ltd should be excluded from changes in these items in the cash flow statement (see **Question 11.2**). A note to the cash flow statement should show a summary of the effects of the acquisition, for example:

Acquisition of subsidiary undertaking
During the year under review Pat Ltd acquired 90% of the voting shares of Sarah Ltd. Details of the acquisition were:

	€000
Net assets acquired:	
Property, plant and equipment	800
Inventories	280
Receivables	190
Cash	50
Payables	(180)
	1,140
Non-controlling interest 10%	(114)
Goodwill	174
	1,200
Satisfied by	
Cash paid	800
Issue of shares	400
	1,200

Disposal of a Subsidiary

When a subsidiary is disposed of during an accounting period any cash received from the sale of the investment should be shown separately under 'Investing activities', with any balance of cash and overdrafts transferred as part of the sale being offset against the cash consideration received (see **Example 11.4** and **Question 11.3**).

EXAMPLE 11.4: DISPOSAL OF A SUBSIDIARY

During the accounting period, Driver Plc sold 80% of its holding in Screw Ltd for €140,000 cash. The SoFP of Screw Ltd at the date of disposal was:

	€000
Property, plant and equipment	115
Inventories	55
Receivables	36
Cash	34
Bank overdraft	(20)
Payables	(60)
	160
Ordinary shares €1	50
Reserves	110
	160

EXTRACT FROM CONSOLIDATED STATEMENT OF CASH FLOWS

	€000
Investing Activities	
Sale of subsidiary (cash received 140 less cash transferred 34 plus bank overdraft transferred 20)	126

A note should be given showing the effects of the disposal.

Note: **Disposal of subsidiary undertaking**
During the reporting year Driver Plc sold its entire holding in Screw Ltd. Details of the disposal were:

	€000
Net assets disposed of:	
Property, plant and equipment	115
Inventories	55
Receivables	36
Cash	34
Bank overdraft	(20)
Payables	(60)
	160
Non-controlling interest 20%	(32)
Profit on disposal	12
	140
Satisfied by cash	140

Dealing with Foreign Operations

IAS 7, paragraph 26 states that "the cash flows of a foreign subsidiary shall be translated at the exchange rates between the functional currency and the foreign currency at the dates of the cash flows". However, a weighted average rate for the reporting period can be used (see **Example 11.5**).

EXAMPLE 11.5: ACCOUNTING FOR A FOREIGN SUBSIDIARY

The following are the draft financial statements of Boston Inc. (Boston), a 100%-owned subsidiary of Cork Ltd (Cork), which has other subsidiaries, all of whose functional currency is the Euro. The functional currency of Boston is US Dollars.

STATEMENT OF FINANCIAL POSITION
as at 30 September 2013

	2013 $000	2012 $000
Property, plant and equipment	1,120	960
Inventories	150	130
Receivables	250	220
Cash	50	40
	1,570	1,350
Ordinary shares ($1)	1,000	1,000
Retained earnings	400	200
Payables	170	150
	1,570	1,350

STATEMENT OF PROFIT OR LOSS
for the year ended 30 September 2013

	$000
Operating profit	300
Interest	(50)
Profit before tax	250
Income tax expense	(50)
Profit for the year	200

Relevant information:
1. During the year under review Boston incurred depreciation charges of $140,000 and paid for additions to property, plant and equipment of $300,000.
2. Exchange rates:
1 October 2012	€1 = $1.50
30 September 2013	€1 = $2.50
Average y/e 30 September 2013	€1 = $2.00

If Cork was preparing consolidated financial statements for the year ended 30 September 2013, the financial statements of Boston would be translated from its functional currency (dollars) into the functional currency (and most likely the presentation currency) of Cork using the following translation rules:

- income and expenses at actual rates preferably but most likely at the average rate (as explained in **Chapter 10**);
- assets and liabilities at the closing rate.

However, IAS 7 requires all cash flows of a foreign subsidiary to be translated at the exchange rates between the functional currency and the foreign currency at the dates of the cash flows, or at the average rate if that approximates to actual rates. As a result, it is more practical if the statement of cash flows of the foreign operation is first prepared in its own functional currency and then translated using the average rate before incorporation into the SoCF of the group.

STATEMENT OF CASH FLOWS OF BOSTON
using average rate €1 = $2 for translation

Cash flows from operating activities	€000	€000
Profit before tax (250/2)	125	
Adjustments		
Depreciation (140/2)	70	
Interest charge (50/2)	25	
Increase in inventories (20/2)	(10)	
Increase in receivables (30/2)	(15)	
Increase in payables (20/2)	10	
Cash generated from operations	205	
Interest paid	(25)	
Tax paid (50/2)	(25)	155
Net cash flow from operating activities		
Cash flows from investing activities		
Payments to acquire PPE (300/2)	(150)	
Net cash flow used in investing activities		(150)
Cash flows from financing activities		0
Effects of exchange rates on cash and cash equivalents		(12)
Net decrease in cash and cash equivalents		(7)
Cash and cash equivalents at beginning of year (40/1.50)		27
Cash and cash equivalents at end of year *(50/2.50)		20

* The cash and cash equivalents both at the beginning and the end of the reporting period are included here and in the consolidated SoCF at the respective closing rates, even though the actual cash flows of the foreign subsidiary are included at the average rate, being a close approximation to the actual rates as discussed above.

Calculation: effect of exchange rates on cash and cash equivalents

	€000	€000
Opening balance $40 at opening rate 1.50	= 26.70	
at closing rate 2.50	16.00	
Difference		(10.70)
Increase during year $10 at closing rate 2.50	= 4.00	
at average rate 2.00	5.00	
Difference		(1.00)
Total difference		(11.70)

Note: **the above statement of cash flows of Boston can now be consolidated with the rest of the Cork group and must include the effects of exchange rates on cash and cash equivalents of (€12,000).**

The Treatment of Trade Investments

A trade investment is not part of a group and, consequently, its cash flows would have little impact on the consolidated SoCF. The effects on the consolidated SoCF would be:

- dividends received from a trade investment would be included under 'Investing activities' as a cash inflow;
- any cash paid to acquire a trade investment would be shown as a cash outflow under 'Investing activities';
- if a group sold a trade investment during a reporting period, any cash received as part of the proceeds would be included under 'Investing activities' as a cash inflow.

Note: any increases/decreases in fair values of trade investments during a reporting year shown in the SPLOCI are not "cash movements".

Conclusion

You should now appreciate that it is vital that you must be familiar with the preparation of consolidated financial statements before undertaking the study of the preparation of consolidated statements of cash flows and how important it is to study IAS 7 (the individual entity) beforehand. The treatment of non-controlling interests, associates, joint ventures and trade investments is a logical progression of your previous studies. However, dealing with a foreign operation in the group statement of cash flows is a more complex area. Regular revision of this chapter is advised as the topic is frequently examined.

SUMMARY

Though the preparation of a consolidated statement of cash flows is similar to that of an individual entity, there are specific issues that are particular to the consolidated SoCF namely:

1. Dealing with a non-controlling interest. A **subsidiary** is fully consolidated with a parent, therefore, cash flows relating to such items as operating activities, interest paid, acquisitions of property, plant and machinery and taxation are **automatically included with those of the parent whether or not there is a non-controlling interest**. However, specific items such as the NCI share of a subsidiary acquired or disposed of during a reporting period as well as any dividends paid to them must be accounted for.

2. An **associate** or a **joint venture** is accounted for under the equity method, which means that none of **its assets, liabilities, income and expenses are consolidated.** An associate or a joint venture **has little** effect on the consolidated SoCF, except that dividends paid by either to a group must be included or where an interest in either is acquired or sold during the reporting period.

3. The **acquisition of a subsidiary** during a reporting period should be accounted for under 'Investing activities' as the net of any cash paid as part **of the** consideration and any cash/cash equivalents acquired with the new subsidiary i.e.:
   Purchase of subsidiary   €X

4. The **disposal of a subsidiary** is similarly disclosed except as the net cash inflow of any cash proceeds received and any cash/cash equivalents transferred i.e.:
   Disposal of subsidiary   €X

5. **If an associate or a joint venture is acquired during a reporting year** any cash payment which is part of the purchase price would be included under 'Investing activities' as follows:
   Purchase of associate or joint venture   €X

6. **Any cash proceeds on the disposal of an associate or a joint venture would also be disclosed** under 'Investing activities' as follows:
   Disposal of associate or joint venture   €X

7. The cash flows of a **foreign subsidiary** must be translated at the exchange rates between the functional currency and the foreign currency **at the date of the cash flow**, but a weighted average rate for the reporting period can be used.

QUESTIONS

Question 11.1

The following extracts have been taken from the consolidated financial statements of the Pupil Ltd group for the year ended 30 September 2013 with comparative figures for the previous year:

	2013 €000	2012 €000
SoFP		
Investment in associate	480	390
Non-controlling interests	570	450
SPLOCI		
Share of profit of associate	140	110
Total comprehensive income attributable to non-controlling interests	120	90

During the year ended 30 September 2013, Pupil Ltd acquired an 80% interest in Student Ltd whose net assets at the date of acquisition amounted to €500,000, including a cash balance of €20,000. The purchase consideration comprised:
- An issue of ordinary shares at market value   €300,000
- A deferred cash payment in 2015   €180,000

Pupil Ltd can borrow funds at 8%.

NCI at date of acquisition is measured at their share of net assets of Student Ltd.

Requirements:
(a) Show the extract from the consolidated statement of cash flows for the year ended 30 September 2013 regarding the associate.
(b) Show the extract from the consolidated statement of cash flows for the year ended 30 September 2013, to account for any dividends paid to the non-controlling interests.
(c) Show the entry in the same SoCF to reflect the acquisition of the subsidiary.
(d) Pot Ltd, who has two subsidiaries, acquired an associate Kettle Ltd in October 2012 by making a cash payment of €700,000. How is the acquisition recorded in the consolidated SoCF for the year ended 30 September 2013?

Solution to Question 11.1

(a)

Investment in Associate

Debit		Credit	
Balance b/d	390	Dividend received (bal. fig.)	50
Share of profit	140	Balance c/d	480
	530		530

Investing activities	**€000**
Dividend received from associate	50

(b)

Non-controlling interests

Debit		**Credit**	
Dividends (bal fig.)	100	Balance b/d	450
		TCI for the year	120
Balance c/d	570	Acquisition 20% × 500	100
	670		670

Financing activities	**€000**
Dividends paid to non-controlling interests	100

(c)

Investing activities	**€000**
Purchase of subsidiary	20*

* There was no cash paid during the reporting year as the payment is deferred, but a cash balance of €20,000 was acquired.

(d)

Investing activities	**€000**
Purchase of associate	700

Note: **Questions 11.2** and **11.3** are longer, review-type questions. **Question 11.2** involves non-controlling interests, an associate and the acquisition of a subsidiary during a reporting period. **Question 11.3** involves the disposal of a subsidiary as well as non-controlling interests and an associate.

Each solution contains
1. T account workings where necessary;
2. The consolidated SoCF.

The solution to **Question 11.3** contains the required notes to the consolidated SoCF.

Question 11.2

Based on Institute of Certified Public Accountants in Ireland (CPA), Professional 1 Stage 1 Corporate Reporting Examination, (August 2010) Question 2. The year end has been updated in line with the remainder of the text.

Splash Plc has a number of subsidiaries, one of which, Muck Ltd, was acquired during the year ended 31 December 2012. The draft consolidated financial statements for the year ended 31 December 2012 are as follows:

Splash Plc
CONSOLIDATED STATEMENT OF PROFIT OR LOSS
for the year ended 31 December 2012

	€000
Profit from operations	1,210
Interest	(100)
	1,110
Share of profits of associates	240
Profit before taxation	1,350
Taxation	(482)
Profit for the year	868
Profit for the year attributable to:	
Owners of the parent	764
Non-controlling interest	104
	868

Statements of Financial Position are as follows:

	Splash Plc consolidated		Muck Ltd at acquisition
	2012	2011	
	€000	€000	€000
Assets			
Non-current assets			
Property, plant and equipment	4,730	2,610	610
Intangibles	350	310	–
Investment in associates	520	500	–
	5,600	3,420	610
Current assets			
Inventories	740	610	150
Trade and other receivables	390	350	85
Cash and cash equivalents	40	85	20
Total assets	6,770	4,465	865
Equity and liabilities			
€1 ordinary shares	1,400	1,000	500
Share premium	300	200	100
Retained earnings	1,615	865	80
	3,315	2,065	680

Non-controlling interest	580	610	–
	3,895	2,675	680
Non-current liabilities			
Long-term loans	1,900	1,100	–
Current liabilities			
Trade payables	520	480	75
Taxation	455	210	110
Total Equity and Liabilities	6,770	4,465	865

Additional information:
1. Splash Plc issued 400,000 €1 ordinary shares at a premium of 25 cent and paid a cash consideration of €197,500 to acquire 75% of Muck Ltd. At the date of acquisition, Muck Ltd's assets and liabilities were recorded at their fair value with the exception of some plant which had a fair value of €90,000 in excess of its carrying value. Goodwill on acquisition was €120,000.
2. The property, plant and equipment during the year to 31 December 2012 shows plant with a carrying value of €800,000 which was sold for €680,000. Total depreciation for the year was €782,000.

Requirement Prepare a consolidated statement of cash flows in accordance with IAS 7 *Statement of Cash Flows* for the year ended 31 December 2012.

Solution to Question 11.2

CONSOLIDATED STATEMENT OF CASH FLOWS
for the year ended 31 December 2012

	€000	€000
Net cash flow from operating activities:		
Profit before tax	1,350	
Depreciation	782	
Amortisation/impairment of intangibles	80	
Loss on sale of tangible non-current assets	120	
Interest payable	100	
Share of profit of associates	(240)	
Decrease in inventories (*W6*)	20	
Decrease in trade receivables (*W6*)	45	
Decrease in trade payables (*W6*)	(35)	
Cash generated from operations	2,222	
Interest paid	(100)	
Tax paid (*W5*)	(347)	
Net cash flow from operating activities		1,775.0

Cash flows from investing activities:

Payments to acquire tangible non-current assets (*W1*)	(3,002)
Receipts from sale of tangible non-current assets	680
Purchase of subsidiary company (197.5 – 20)	(177.5)
Dividends received from associate (*W3*)	220
Net cash flow from investing activities	(2,279.5)

Cash flows from financing activities:

Long-term loan received	800
Dividends paid to owners of the parent (*W7*)	(14)
Dividends paid to non-controlling interest (*W4*)	(326.5)
Net cash flow from financing	459.5
Decrease in cash and cash equivalents	(45)
Cash and cash equivalents at 1 January 2012	85
Cash and cash equivalents at 31 December 2012	40

WORKINGS

(*W1*)

Property, Plant and Equipment

Debit		Credit	
Balance b/d 1/1/12	2,610	Disposal	800
Acquisition Muck (fair value)	700	Depreciation	782
Additions (bal. fig.)	3,002	Balance c/d	4,730
	6,312		6,312

(*W2*)

Intangible Assets

Debit		Credit	
Balance b/d	310	Amortisation/impairment (bal. fig.)	80
Goodwill on acq. of Muck	120	Balance c/d	350
	430		430

(*W3*)

Investment in Associates

Debit		Credit	
Balance b/d	500	Dividends received (bal. fig.)	220
Share of profit for year	240	Balance c/d	520
	740		740

(*W4*)

Non-controlling Interests

Debit		Credit	
Dividends paid (Bal. Fig.)	326.5	Balance b/d	610.0
		SPLOCI – share of TCI	104.0
Balance c/d	580.0	Acquisition of Muck*	192.5
	906.5		906.5

*Net assets of Muck at acquisition date   680
 Surplus on property, plant and equipment   90
                                            770 × 25% = 192.50

(*W5*)

Taxation

Debit		Credit	
		Balance b/d	210
Cash (bal. fig.)	347	Acquired with Muck	110
Balance c/d	455	SPLOCI charge for year	482
	802		802

(*W6*)

Net Movement in Inventories, Receivables and Payables:

	Inventories €000	Receivables €000	Payables €000
31 December 2012	740	390	520
31 December 2011	610	350	480
Increase	130	40	40
Less: Acquired with Muck	(150)	(85)	(75)
Consolidated SoCF	20	45	(35)

(*W7*)

Dividends paid to owners of the parent:

	€000
Retained earnings per consolidated SoFP 31/12/2011	865
Total comprehensive income y/e 31/12/2012	764
Profit attributable to the shareholders of Splash	1,629
Retained earnings per consolidated SoFP 31/12/2012	1,615
Difference – dividend paid	14

This dividend was paid as it is not on the consolidated SoFP at 31 December 2012.

Question 11.3

Tango Ltd
CONSOLIDATED STATEMENT OF FINANCIAL POSITION
as at 31 August 2013

	2013 €000	2012 €000
Assets		
Non-current assets		
Property, plant & equipment	3,615	1,970
Goodwill	50	50
Investment in associate	990	860
	4,655	2,880
Current assets		
Inventory	1,570	1,015
Trade receivables	1,110	830
Cash	30	18
	2,710	1,863
Total assets	7,365	4,743
Equity and Liabilities		
Ordinary share capital	2,500	1,800
Share premium	400	100
Revaluation reserve	500	–
Retained earnings	1,680	1,090
Total shareholders' equity	5,080	2,990
Non-controlling interest	124	180
Total equity	5,204	3,170
Non-current liabilities		
Deferred taxation	500	360
Current-liabilities		
Trade payables	747	583
Bank overdraft	84	20
Corporation tax	580	460
Proposed dividends (approved pre-year end)	250	150
	1,661	1,213
Total equity and liabilities	7,365	4,743

CONSOLIDATED STATEMENT OF PROFIT OR LOSS AND OTHER COMPREHENSIVE INCOME
for the year ended 31 August 2013

	€000
Revenue	9,675
Cost of sales	(5,805)

Gross profit	3,870
Operating expenses	(2,550)
	1,320
Profit on disposal of subsidiary	76
Share of profit of associate	160
Profit before tax	1,556
Income tax expense	590
Profit for the year	966
Other comprehensive income	
Property revaluation surplus	500
Total comprehensive income for the year	1,466
Profit for year attributable to:	
Owners of the parent	836
Non-controlling interest	130
	966
Total comprehensive income attributable to:	
Owners of the parent	1,336
Non-controlling interests	130
	1,466

NOTES TO THE FINANCIAL STATEMENTS

1. Profit before tax

	€000
The following have been included:	
Depreciation of property, plant and equipment	220
Interest payable	205

2. Property, plant and equipment
During the year under review plant with a carrying value
of €180,000 was sold at a loss of €30,000.

3. All proposed dividends were approved before the respective reporting dates.
Tango has proposed a dividend of €246,000 for the year under review.

4. Disposal of Subsidiary: Waltz Limited
On 30 April 2013 Tango Ltd disposed of its entire 70% holding in Waltz Ltd
Details of the disposal were:

	€000
Net assets disposed	
Property, plant and equipment	220
Inventories	60
Receivables	80
Cash	30

Payables	(70)
	320
Non-controlling interests (30% × 320)	(96)
Profit on disposal	76
	300

Settled by	
Cash received	300

5. Goodwill on acquisition of Waltz Ltd, €10,000, has been fully impaired.

Requirement Prepare a consolidated statement of cash flows in accordance with IAS 7 *Statement of Cash Flows* for the year ended 31 August 2013.

Solution to Question 11.3

Tango Ltd
CONSOLIDATED STATEMENT OF CASH FLOWS
for the year ended 31 August 2013

	€000	€000
Net cash flow from operating activities		
Profit before tax	1,556	
Depreciation	220	
Loss on sale of tangible non-current assets	30	
Interest payable	205	
Profit on disposal of subsidiary	(76)	
Share of profit of associate	(160)	
Increase in inventories *(W2)*	(615)	
Increase in trade receivables *(W2)*	(360)	
Increase in trade payables *(W2)*	234	
Cash generated from operations	1,034	
Interest paid	(205)	
Tax paid *(W4)*	(330)	
Net cash flow from operating activities		499
Cash flows from investing activities		
Payments to require tangible non-current assets *(W6)*	(1,765)	
Receipts from sale of tangible non-current assets	150	
Disposal of subsidiary company (300 – 30)	270	
Dividends received from associate *(W1)*	30	
Net cash flow from investing activities		(1,315)
Cash flows from financing activities		
Issue of share capital at a premium	1,000	
Dividends paid by Tango Plc *(W5)*	(146)	
Dividends paid to non-controlling interest *(W3)*	(90)	

Net cash flow from financing	764
Decrease in cash and cash equivalents	(52)
Cash and cash equivalents at 1 September 2012	(2)
Cash and cash equivalents at 31 August 2013	(54)

WORKINGS

(W1)

Investment in Associate

Debit		**Credit**	
Bal b/d (opening SoFP)	860	Dividend (bal. fig.)	30
Share of profit (SPLOCI)	160	Bal c/d (closing SoFP)	990
	1,020		1,020

(W2)

	Inventory €000	Receivables €000	Payables €000
At 1 September 2012	1,015	830	583
At 31 August 2013	1,570	1,110	747
Increase	555	280	164
Add: disposed of with subsidiary Waltz Ltd	60	80	70
Consol. SoCF	(615)	(360)	234

(W3)

Non-controlling Interest

Debit		**Credit**	
Cash dividend (bal. fig.)	90	Bal b/d (Opening SoFP)	180
Disposal – Waltz	96	SPLOCI – TCI	130
Bal c/d (CL SoFP)	124		
	310		310

(W4)

Taxation (Current and Deferred)

Debit		**Credit**	
Taxation paid (bal. fig.)	330	Bal b/d (460 + 360)	820
Bal c/d (580 + 500)	1,080	SPLOCI	590
	1,410		1,410

(W5)

Dividends paid by Tango

Debit		Credit	
Cash payment (balance)	146	Balance b/d	150
Balance c/d	250	SoCIE	246
	396		396

(W6)

Property, Plant and Equipment

		Disposals	180
Balance b/d	1,970	Disposal – Waltz	220
Revaluation	500	Depreciation	220
Additions (bal. fig.)	1,765	Balance c/d	3,615
	4,235		4,235

Notes to Consolidated Statement of Cash Flows

Note 1:

During the period the group sold its entire holding (70%) in Waltz Ltd. Details of the disposal were:

	€000
Net assets at date of disposal	220
Property, plant and equipment	60
Inventories	80
Receivables	(70)
Payables	290
Non-controlling interests	(96)
Profit on disposal	76
Net proceeds received in cash	270
Cash balance of subsidiary disposed	30
Cash received on disposal	300

Note 2:

	€000	€000
	2013	2012
Cash and cash equivalents		
Cash on hand and bank overdrafts	(54)	(2)

Chapter 12

Disposal of Shares in Subsidiaries

LEARNING OBJECTIVES

After reading this chapter you should be able to:
- demonstrate an understanding of the importance of **'control'** in determining the method of accounting for disposal of shares in a subsidiary; and
- prepare a set of financial statements *where*, during a reporting year:
  1. a parent disposes of its entire holding in a subsidiary;
  2. a parent sells part of its holding in a subsidiary but does not lose control over that subsidiary;
  3. a parent sells sufficient shares in a subsidiary to lose control but the former subsidiary becomes an associate; and
  4. a parent sells most of its shares in a subsidiary and the remaining investment is a simple/trade investment.

Introduction

This chapter is the final step in your mastering of the principles and techniques of preparing and presenting consolidated financial statements. Though accounting for disposal of shares in a subsidiary is a complex area, the provisions of IFRS 10 *Consolidated Financial Statements* are very specific with regard to the treatment of such disposals. The term **control** (see also **Chapter 2**), i.e. "when the investor is exposed, or has rights, to variable returns from its involvement with the investee and has the ability to affect those returns through its power over the investee" plays a central role in the correct application of accounting principles to each disposal.

Accounting for Disposals

1. Changes to a parent's ownership interest in a subsidiary **that do not result in a loss of control** are accounted for as **equity transactions** (transactions with owners in their capacity as owners). No profit or loss on disposal is reported in the consolidated statement of profit or loss and other comprehensive income.

2. If a parent **loses control** over one of its subsidiaries the following must occur:
   (a) the subsidiary's assets (including goodwill) and liabilities, as well as the non-controlling interests in those net assets, must be derecognised from the consolidated SoFP at their carrying amounts at the date control is lost;

(b) the parent must recognise the fair value of the consideration received, which results in the loss of control in the subsidiary;

(c) the parent must recognise any gain or loss on the disposal, attributable to the parent, in the consolidated SPLOCI; and

(d) the parent must recognise any remaining investment in the former subsidiary at fair value on the date control is lost.

Levels of Disposals

A parent can sell shares in a subsidiary, which can give rise to different structures after the disposal. The following examples are used for illustration purposes:

EXAMPLE 12.1: EXAMPLES OF DIFFERENT LEVELS OF DISPOSAL

Peel Ltd (Peel) acquired 80% of the one million ordinary shares in issue by Skin Ltd (Skin) on 1 September 2010. The reporting date for the group is 31 August. Decision-making by Skin Ltd is dictated by voting rights.

Scenario 1: Disposal of total investment in Skin Ltd
On 1 February 2013, Peel sold its entire holding in Skin for cash. **Control is lost**. Skin is a subsidiary of Peel until 31 January 2013 and its results must be consolidated with the results of Peel until that date. At the reporting date, i.e. 31 August 2013, Skin is no longer a subsidiary and the SoFP as at that date will comprise the assets (excluding the investment but including the sale proceeds and profit on disposal) and liabilities of Peel only.

Scenario 2: Partial disposal of investment in Skin Ltd without loss of control
On 1 June 2013, Peel sells 200,000 of its shares in Skin. In this instance, **control is not lost** as Peel still retains 60% of the share capital of Skin and Skin is, therefore, a subsidiary for the full reporting year ending on 31 August 2013. The non-controlling interests in the profits of Skin change from 20% for the first nine months to 40% for the last three months. Skin Ltd is still a subsidiary at the reporting date so all its assets and liabilities must be consolidated with those of Peel at that date.

Scenario 3: Partial disposal of investment in Skin Ltd with loss of control
On 1 March 2013, Peel sells 400,000 of its shares in Skin. **Control is lost** as Peel now only owns 40% of the share capital of Skin. Skin is a subsidiary for half of the reporting year and an associate for the remainder. In the consolidated SPLOCI for the year ended 31 August 2013, full consolidation is applied to Skin for six months to 28 February 2013 and equity accounting as an **associate** from then until the reporting date. The SoFP as at 31 August 2013 will comprise the assets and liabilities of Peel only (after adjustment for the disposal) and the investment in Skin which is valued as follows:

Fair value as at 1 March 2013   €X
    Plus
40% of the profits of Skin from 1 March 2013 to 31 August 2013   €X

Scenario 4: Partial disposal of investment in Skin Ltd

On 1 March 2013 Peel sells 700,000 of its shares in Skin. **Control is lost** as Peel now only owns 10% of the share capital of Skin. Skin is a subsidiary for half the reporting year and a trade/simple investment for the remainder. In the consolidated SPLOCI for the year ended 31 August 2013, full consolidation is applied to Skin for six months to 28 February 2013 and only dividends received/receivable from then until the reporting date are accounted for. The SoFP as at 31 August 2013 will comprise the assets and liabilities of Peel only (after adjusting for disposal), including the remaining investment in Skin which is valued as follows:

Fair value as at 1 March 2013   €X

The investment (now 10%) would be classified and subsequently measured at each reporting date in accordance with IFRS 9.

The following example (**Example 12.2**) incorporates:

Scenario 1   a parent selling its entire investment in a subsidiary;
Scenario 2   a parent selling part of its investment in a subsidiary but maintaining control over that entity;
Scenario 3   a parent selling part of its investment in a subsidiary whose status changes to an associate;
Scenario 4   a parent selling part of its investment in a subsidiary which subsequently becomes a trade investment.

EXAMPLE 12.2: DIFFERENT LEVELS OF DISPOSAL

The following draft financial statements of Pulp Plc and Shred Ltd for the year ended 31 August 2013 will be used to illustrate the accounting treatment for each of four levels of disposal of shares in a subsidiary by its parent.

STATEMENTS OF PROFIT OR LOSS
for the year ended 31 August 2013

	Pulp Plc €	Shred Ltd €
Revenue	1,015,000	492,000
Cost of sales	(609,000)	(295,000)
Gross profit	406,000	197,000
Distribution costs	(126,000)	(58,000)
Administrative expenses	(180,000)	(81,000)
Finance costs	(40,000)	(18,000)
Profit before tax	60,000	40,000
Income tax expense	(24,000)	(16,000)
Profit for the year	36,000	24,000

STATEMENTS OF FINANCIAL POSITION
as at 31 August 2013

	Pulp Plc €	Shred Ltd €
Investment in Shred	75,000	–
Sundry net assets	265,000	100,000
	340,000	100,000
Ordinary €1 shares	200,000	60,000
Retained earnings	140,000	40,000
	340,000	100,000

Additional information:
1. Pulp Plc acquired 75% of the ordinary shares of Shred Ltd on 1 September 2011 when the retained earnings of Shred Ltd were €10,000.
2. Goodwill impairment for the year ended 31 August 2012 was €4,500.
3. NCI at the date of acquisition was measured using the proportion of net assets method.
4. Decision-making by Skin Ltd is dictated by **voting rights**.

SCENARIO 1: Pulp Plc sells its entire investment for €125,000 on 31 August 2013.

Key point: **Loss of control but Shred Ltd is a subsidiary for the entire reporting year. The sale has not been recorded in the financial statements of Pulp Plc.**

SOLUTION NOTES

1. After the disposal, Shred Ltd is no longer a subsidiary of Pulp Plc.
2. The results of Shred Ltd must be included in the consolidated SPLOCI for the entire year to 31 August 2013 as the investment was sold on the reporting date.
3. The statement of financial position at 31 August 2013 will be that of Pulp Plc only.

IFRS 10 states that, if a parent loses control over a subsidiary, the parent should:
• derecognise the assets (including any goodwill) and liabilities of the former subsidiary at the date when control is lost;
• derecognise the carrying amount of any non-controlling interests at the same date;
• recognise the fair value of any consideration received;
• recognise any investment retained in the former subsidiary at its fair value when control is lost;
• recognise the difference associated with the loss of control attributable to the parent in profit or loss.

Gain on disposal

	€
In the consolidated SPLOCI – P/L:	
Sale proceeds	125,000
Less	
Net assets at disposal date × group's share	
(€100,000 × 75%)	(75,000)

Less
Goodwill (net of impairment) *(W1)* (18,000)
Profit on disposal of investment 32,000

(W1) Goodwill

	€	€
Investment in Shred		75,000
NCI at acquisition date 25% (60,000 + 10,000)		17,500
		92,500
Net assets of Shred at acquisition date		
Ordinary shares	60,000	
Retained earnings	10,000	70,000
Goodwill on acquisition		22,500
Impairment y/e 31 August 2012		4,500
Balance before disposal		18,000

CONSOLIDATED STATEMENT OF PROFIT OR LOSS
for the year ended 31 August 2013

	€
Revenue	1,507,000
Cost of sales	(904,000)
Gross profit	603,000
Distribution costs	(184,000)
Administrative expenses	(261,000)
Finance costs	(58,000)
Profit on disposal of subsidiary	32,000
Profit before tax	132,000
Income tax expense	(40,000)
Profit for the year	92,000

Profit for the year attributable to:	
Owners of the parent	86,000
Non-controlling interest (25% × 24,000)	6,000
	92,000

JOURNAL ENTRIES

	€	€
1. Dr. Goodwill	75,000	
Cr. Investment in Shred		75,000

Investment in Shred

2. Dr. Goodwill   17,500
   Cr. NCI   17,500
   NCI at acquisition date

3. Dr. Ordinary shares   60,000
   Cr. Goodwill   60,000
   Ordinary shares Shred at acquisition date

4. Dr. Retained earnings Shred   10,000
   Cr. Goodwill   10,000
   Retained earnings Shred at acquisition date

5. Dr. Retained earnings Shred   30,000
   Cr. Retained earnings Pulp (75%)   22,500
   Cr. NCI (25%)   7,500
   Post-acquisition retained earnings Shred
      (40,000 – 10,000)

6. Dr. Sundry net assets (cash)   125,000
   Dr. NCI (25% × 100,000)   25,000
   Cr. Sundry net assets Shred   100,000
   Cr. Goodwill   18,000
   Cr. Retained earnings (profit)   32,000
   Disposal of Shred

WORKINGS (T Account Method)

Investment in Shred

Debit		Credit	
Pulp	75,000	Goodwill (Jnl. 1)	75,000

Sundry Net Assets

Debit		Credit	
Pulp	265,000		
Shred	100,000	Disposal Shred (Jnl. 6)	100,000
Cash (Jnl. 6)	125,000	SoFP	390,000
	490,000		490,000

Ordinary Shares

Debit		Credit	
Goodwill (Jnl. 3)	60,000	Pulp	200,000
		Shred	60,000
SoFP	200,000		
	260,000		260,000

Retained Earnings Pulp

Debit		Credit	
Goodwill impairment	4,500	Pulp at reporting date	140,000
		Share of S post-acq. (Jnl. 5)	22,500
SoFP	190,000	Profit on disposal (Jnl. 6)	32,000
	194,500		194,500

Retained Earnings Shred

Debit		Credit	
Goodwill (Jnl. 4)	10,000	Shred at reporting date	40,000
Post-acquisition Pulp (Jnl. 5)	22,500		
Post-acquisition NCI (Jnl. 5)	7,500		
	40,000		40,000

Goodwill

Debit		Credit	
Investment in Shred (Jnl. 1)	75,000	Ordinary shares (Jnl. 3)	60,000
NCI (Jnl. 2)	17,500	Retained earnings (Jnl. 4)	10,000
		Impairment	4,500
		Disposal (Jnl. 6)	18,000
	92,500		92,500

Non-controlling Interests

Debit		Credit	
		Goodwill (Jnl. 1)	17,500
Disposal (Jnl. 6)	25,000	Post-acq. S (Jnl. 5)	7,500
	25,000		25,000

WORKINGS (Columnar Method)

	Pulp €	Shred €	Adjustments €	Consol. SoFP €
Investment in Shred	75,000		(75,000) (Jnl. 1)	
Sundry net assets	265,000	100,000	125,000 (Jnl. 6)	
			(100,000) (Jnl. 6)	390,000

Goodwill (*W1*)				nil
Total assets	**340,000**	**100,000**	**(50,000)**	**390,000**
Ordinary shares	200,000	60,000	(60,000) (Jnl. 3)	200,000
Retained earnings (*W2*)	140,000	40,000	10,000	190,000
Non-controlling interest (*W3*)				nil
Total equity & liabilities	**340,000**	**100,000**	**(50,000)**	**390,000**

(W2) Retained earnings

Pulp at reporting date	140,000
Share of post-acq. of Shred (Jnl. 5)	22,500
75% (40 – 10)	
Impairment of goodwill	(4,500)
Journal 6 – profit on disposal	32,000
	190,000

NCI	€
Goodwill (Jnl. 2)	17,500
Share of S post-acq. (Jnl. 5)	7,500
Disposal (Jnl. 6)	(25,000)
	Nil

Pulp Plc
STATEMENT OF FINANCIAL POSITION
as at 31 August 2013

	€
Sundry net assets	390,000
Ordinary shares	200,000
Retained earnings	190,000
	390,000

STATEMENT OF CHANGES IN EQUITY
for the year ended 31 August 2013

	Ord. shares €	Ret. Earnings €	NCI €
Balance at 1 September 2012	200,000	104,000 (*W4*)	19,000 (*W5*)
Profit for the year		86,000	6,000
Disposal of subsidiary			(25,000)
Balance at 31 August 2013	**200,000**	**190,000**	**nil**

(W4) Retained Earnings at 1 September 2012

Pulp (140 – 36)	104,000
Goodwill impairment	(4,500)

Shred 75% × (40 − 24 − 10)		4,500
		104,000

(W5) Non-controlling Interests
Net assets of Shred at 1/9/2012

(100 − 24)		76,000
× 25%		19,000

Alternative (W5)

At acquisition date (Jnl.2)		17,500
Share of post-acq. of Shred		
25% × (16,000 − 10,000)		1,500
		19,000

Note: the opening retained earnings €104,000 and the opening NCI €19,000 will be the same under all four assumptions as all adjustments affect earnings after that date.

SCENARIO 2: Pulp Plc sold 12,000 of its shares in Shred Ltd on 31 August 2013 for €44,000. Pulp now owns 33,000 shares. The sale has not been recorded in the financial statements of Pulp Plc.

Key point: **Sale of shares in a subsidiary but subsidiary status retained. No loss of control. Shred is a subsidiary for the full year.**

Solution Notes

1. Shred Ltd is a subsidiary for the entire reporting year.
2. Pulp Plc retains control, now owning 55% of Shred Ltd.
3. No profit is recognised in the consolidated SPLOCI on the disposal.

IFRS 10: Changes in a parent's ownership in a subsidiary that do not result in a parent losing control of the subsidiary are equity transactions, i.e. transactions with owners in their capacity as owners.

- The carrying amounts of the controlling and non-controlling interests are adjusted to reflect the changes in their relative interests in the subsidiary.
- Any difference between the amount by which the non-controlling interests are adjusted and the fair value of the consideration paid or received is recognised directly in equity and attributed to the owners of the parent.

Consolidated Statement of Profit or Loss
for the year ended 31 August 2013

	€
Revenue	1,507,000
Cost of sales	(904,000)
Gross profit	603,000
Distribution costs	(184,000)
Administrative expenses	(261,000)
Finance costs	(58,000)

Profit before tax	100,000
Income tax expense	(40,000)
Profit for the year	60,000
Profit for the year attributed to:	
Owners of the parent	54,000
Non-controlling interest (25% × 24,000)	6,000
	60,000

(W1) Goodwill

	€	€
Investment in Shred		75,000
NCI at acquisition date 25% × (60,000 + 10,000)		17,500
		92,500
Net assets of Shred at acquisition date		
Ordinary shares	60,000	
Retained earnings	10,000	70,000
Goodwill on acquisition		22,500
Impairment y/e 31 August 2012		4,500
Balance before disposal		18,000

JOURNAL ENTRIES

		€	€
1.	Dr. Goodwill	75,000	
	Cr. Investment in Shred		75,000
	Investment in Shred		
2.	Dr. Goodwill	17,500	
	Cr. NCI		17,500
	NCI at acquisition date		
3.	Dr. Ordinary shares	60,000	
	Cr. Goodwill		60,000
	Ordinary shares Shred at acquisition date		
4.	Dr. Retained earnings Shred	10,000	
	Cr. Goodwill		10,000
	Retained earnings Shred at acquisition date		
5.	Dr. Retained earnings Shred	30,000	
	Cr. Retained earnings Pulp (75%)		22,500
	Cr. NCI (25%)		7,500
	Post-acquisition retained earnings Shred		
	(40,000 – 10,000)		

6. Dr. Sundry net assets (cash)   44,000
    Cr. NCI (W2)   23,600
    Cr. Parent's equity (SoCIE)   20,400
    Disposal of shares to NCI

(W2) Change in value of carrying value of NCI

	€
Net assets of Shred at date of disposal 31 August 2013	100,000
Goodwill	18,000
	118,000
Transfer to NCI additional 20%	23,600

WORKINGS (T Account Method)

Investment in Shred

Debit		Credit	
Pulp	75,000	Goodwill (Jnl. 1)	75,000

Sundry Net Assets

Debit		Credit	
Pulp	265,000		
Shred	100,000		
Journal 6 (cash)	44,000	SoFP	409,000
	409,000		409,000

Ordinary Shares

Debit		Credit	
Goodwill (Jnl. 3)	60,000	Pulp	200,000
		Shred	60,000
SoFP	200,000		
	260,000		260,000

Retained Earnings Pulp

Debit		Credit	
Goodwill impairment	4,500	Pulp at reporting date	140,000
		Share of S post-acq. (Jnl. 5)	22,500
SoFP	178,400	Journal 6 – disposal	20,400
	182,900		182,900

Retained Earnings Shred

Debit		Credit	
Goodwill (Jnl. 4)	10,000	Shred at reporting date	40,000
Post-acquisition Pulp (Jnl. 5)	22,500		
Post-acquisition NCI (Jnl. 5)	7,500		
	40,000		40,000

Goodwill

Debit		Credit	
Investment in Shred (Jnl. 1)	75,000	Ordinary shares (Jnl. 3)	60,000
NCI (Jnl. 2)	17,500	Retained earnings (Jnl. 4)	10,000
		Impairment of g/will	4,500
		SoFP	18,000
	92,500		92,500

Non-controlling Interests

Debit		Credit	
		Goodwill (Jnl. 2)	17,500
SoFP	48,600	Share of S post-acq. (Jnl. 5)	7,500
		Disposal (Jnl. 6)	23,600
	48,600		48,600

WORKINGS (Columnar Method)

	Pulp €	Shred €	Adjustments €	Consol. SoFP. €
Investment in Shred	75,000		(75,000) (Jnl. 1)	–
Sundry net assets	265,000	100,000	44,000 (Jnl. 6)	409,000
Goodwill *(W1)*			18,000	18,000
Total assets	**340,000**	**100,000**	**(13,000)**	**427,000**
Ordinary shares	200,000	60,000	(60,000) (Jnl. 3)	200,000
Retained earnings *(W3)*	140,000	40,000	(1,600)	178,400
Non-controlling int. *(W4)*			48,600	48,600
Total Equity & Liabilities	**340,000**	**100,000**	**(13,000)**	**427,000**

(W3) Retained earnings

	€	€
Pulp at reporting date		140,000
Journal 6 (disposal)		20,400
Goodwill impairment		(4,500)

Shred at reporting date	40,000	
at acquisition date	(10,000)	
post-acquisition	30,000	
Group's share 75%		22,500
SoFP		178,400

(W4) Non-controlling interests

Goodwill (Jnl. 2)	17,500
Share of S post-acq. (Jnl. 5)	7,500
Additional 20% of S net assets (Jnl. 6)	23,600
	48,600

CONSOLIDATED STATEMENT OF FINANCIAL POSITION
as at 31 August 2013

	€
Goodwill	18,000
Sundry net assets	409,000
	427,000
Ordinary shares	200,000
Retained earnings	178,400
Total shareholders' equity	378,400
Non-controlling interests	48,600
	427,000

CONSOLIDATED STATEMENT OF CHANGES IN EQUITY
for the year ended 31 August 2013

	Ordinary Shares €	Retained Earnings €	NCI €
Balance at 1 Sept 2012	200,000	104,000 *(W4)*	19,000 *(W5)*
Profit for the year		54,000	6,000
Disposal of shares in Shred		20,400	23,600
Balance at 31 August 2013	**200,000**	**178,400**	**48,600**

(W5) Retained earnings 1/9/2012 as in Scenario 1

Pulp (140,000 – 36,000)	104,000
Shred 75% × (16,000 – 10,000)	4,500
Goodwill impairment	(4,500)
	104,000

(W6) Non-controlling interest at 1/9/2012 as in Scenario 1

Shred at 1 September 2012

Ordinary shares	60,000	
Retained earnings (40–24)	16,000	
	76,000 × 25%	19,000

Alternative (W6)

At acquisition date	17,500
Share of post-acq. of Shred	
25% × (16,000 – 10,000)	1,500
	19,000

SCENARIO 3: Pulp Plc sold 24,000 of its shares in Shred Ltd on 28 February 2013 for €80,000. The fair value of the remaining investment in the former subsidiary is €45,000. Pulp now owns 21,000 shares. The sale has not been recorded in the financial statements of Pulp Plc.

Key point: **Sale of shares in subsidiary – loss of control – an associate exists subsequently.**

Solution Notes

1. Shred is a subsidiary for six months of the year under review, therefore, the consolidated SPLOCI will include the full results of Shred for the first six months and Shred will be accounted for under the equity method for the second six months.
2. The SoFP as at 31 August 2013 is of an investing company and an associate.
3. The remaining investment after the disposal is valued at fair value €45,000 (carrying value €35,000) with the surplus going to the consolidated SPLOCI.

IFRS 10 states that, if a parent loses control over a subsidiary, the parent should:
*   derecognise the assets (including any goodwill) and liabilities of the former subsidiary at the date when control is lost;
*   derecognise the carrying amount of any non-controlling interests at the same date;
*   recognise the fair value of any consideration received;
*   recognise any investment retained in the former subsidiary at its fair value when control is lost; and
*   recognise the gain or loss associated with the loss of control attributable to the parent.

Gain on disposal in the individual SPLOCI of Pulp

	€
Proceeds	80,000
Less: Cost of shares sold 75,000 × 24,000/45,000	40,000
	40,000
Net assets at date of disposal	
Net assets of Shred at 31 August 2013	100,000
Less retained earnings y/e 31 August 2013 (24,000 × 6/12)	(12,000)
Net assets at 28 February 2013	88,000
Gain on disposal in consolidated SPLOCI	
Proceeds	80,000
Fair value of 35% retained	45,000
	125,000

Less: net assets disposed of, including goodwill

(88 × 75% + 18)	84,000
Gain	41,000

Note: Revaluation of the remaining investment:

Original cost of investment in Shred	75,000
Cost of shares sold	(40,000)
Remaining cost	35,000
Fair value attributed	45,000
Excess to profit or loss	10,000

Note: in the consolidated SPLOCI each income and expense item of Shred is time apportioned by 6/12 as Shred is a subsidiary for only half of the reporting year.

CONSOLIDATED STATEMENT OF PROFIT OR LOSS
for the year ended 31 August 2013

	€
Revenue (1,015 + (492 × 6/12))	1,261,000
Cost of sales (609 + (295 × 6/12))	(756,500)
Gross profit	504,500
Distribution costs (126 + (58 × 6/12))	(155,000)
Administrative expenses (180 + (81 × 6/12))	(220,500)
Finance costs (40 + (18 × 6/12))	(49,000)
Share of profit of associate (Note)	4,200
Profit on disposal of shares in subsidiary	41,000
Profit before tax	125,200
Income tax expense (24 + (16 × 6/12))	(32,000)
Profit for the year	93,200

Profit for the year attributable to:	
Owners of the parent	90,200
Non-controlling interest (25% × 24,000 × 6/12)	3,000
	93,200

Share of profit of associate: (24,000 × 6/12) × 35%

STATEMENT OF CHANGES IN EQUITY
for the year ended 31 August 2013

	Ord. Shares €	Ret. earnings €	NCI €
Balance at 1 September 2012	200,000	104,000 (*W1*)	19,000 (*W2*)
Profit for the year		90,200	3,000
Disposal of subsidiary			(22,000)
Balance at 31 August 2013	200,000	194,200	nil

(W1) Retained earnings 1/9/12 as before

Pulp (140,000 – 36,000)	104,000
Shred 75% × (16,000 – 10,000)	4,500
Goodwill impairment	(4,500)
	104,000

(W2) Non-controlling interest at 1/9/12 as before

Shred at 1 September 2012

Ordinary shares	60,000	
Retained earnings (40 – 24)	16,000	
	76,000 × 25%	19,000

Alternative (W2)

At acquisition date	17,500
Share of post-acq. of Shred	
25% × (16,000 – 10,000)	1,500
	19,000

Note: the SoFP as at 31 August 2013 consists of Pulp Plc (adjusted by the sale of part of the investment), i.e.

	€	€
Dr. Sundry net assets (cash)	80,000	
Cr. Investment in Shred 24/45 × 75,000		40,000
Cr. Retained earnings (profit)		40,000

plus

The investment in the associate valued as follows:

Fair value at disposal date	45,000
Share of post-acquisition profits 24,000 × 6/12 × 35%	4,200
	49,200

Pulp Plc
STATEMENT OF FINANCIAL POSITION
as at 31 August 2013

	€
Investment in associate	49,200
Sundry net assets (265 + 80) *(W3)*	345,000
	394,200
Ordinary shares	200,000
Retained earnings *(W4)*	194,200
	394,200

(W3) Sundry Net Assets

	€
Per Pulp SoFP 31 August 2013	265,000
Cash proceeds on sale of investment	80,000
	345,000

(W4) Retained Earnings

Retained earnings per Pulp SoFP 31/8/13	140,000
Gain on disposal per individual SPLOCI	40,000
Share of post-acq. profit of associate	4,200
Increase in fair value of investment	10,000
	194,200

SCENARIO 4: Pulp Plc sold 40,500 of its shares in Shred Ltd on 31 May 2013 for €115,000. The fair value of the remaining investment in the former subsidiary is €15,000. There was no change in fair value at the reporting date. The sale has not been recorded in the financial statements of Pulp Plc.

Key Point: **Loss of control. Shred is a subsidiary for nine months. The remaining investment after the disposal is 7.5% – a trade or simple investment.**

Gain on disposal

	€
(a) In the consolidated SPLOCI	
Sale proceeds	115,000
Fair value of remaining 7.5%	15,000
	130,000
Less	
Net assets at disposal date × group's share	
€94,000 × 75% *(W1)*	(70,500)
Less	
Goodwill	(18,000)
Profit on disposal	41,500
(b) In the individual SPLOCI of Pulp	
Sale proceeds	115,000
Cost of shares sold €75,000 × 40,500/45,000	67,500
	47,500

(W1) Net Assets of Shred at disposal date

Net assets at 31 August 2013	100,000
Less profit y/e 31 August 2013 × 3/12	
(24,000 × 3/12)	(6,000)
Net assets at 31 May 2013	94,000
NCI Share 25%	23,500

Note: Consolidated SPLOCI:

1. The results of Shred can only be consolidated for nine months as it ceased to be a subsidiary on 31 May 2013. The figures for revenue, cost of sales, distribution costs, administrative expenses, finance costs and income tax expense include 12 months for Pulp and nine months for Shred.
2. Non-controlling interest in the profits of Shred will be calculated as follows:
Profit after tax of Shred × 9/12 ×25%
24,000 × 9/12 × 25% = €4,500

CONSOLIDATED STATEMENT OF PROFIT OR LOSS
for the year ended 31 August 2013

	€
Revenue (1,015 + (492 × 9/12))	1,384,000
Cost of sales (609 + (295 × 9/12))	(830,250)
Gross profit	553,750
Distribution costs (126 + (58 × 9/12))	(169,500)
Administrative expenses (180 + (81 × 9/12))	(240,750)
Finance costs (40 + (18 × 9/12))	(53,500)
Profit on disposal of subsidiary	41,500
Profit before tax	131,500
Income tax expense (24 + (16 × 9/12))	(36,000)
Profit for the year	95,500
Profit for the year attributable to:	
Owners of the parent	91,000
Non-controlling interest (see Note 2 above)	4,500
	95,500

Note for SoFP:

The SoFP at 31 August 2013 comprises:
The original SoFP of Pulp as at the same date adjusted by Journals 1 and 2.

JOURNALS

1. Adjustment for the sale of the investment.

Dr. Cash	115,000	
Cr. Investment in Shred (90% × 75,000)		67,500
Cr. Retained earnings		47,500

With sale of 90% of its holding.

2. Adjustment for remaining investment 7,500 to be increased to fair value 15,000.

Dr. Investment in Shred	7,500	
Cr. Retained earnings Pulp		7,500

There was no change in the fair value of the investment between 31 May 2013 and 31 August 2013.

STATEMENT OF FINANCIAL POSITION
as at 31 August 2013

	€
Sundry net assets *(W2)*	380,000
Financial asset held for trading	15,000
	395,000

Ordinary shares	200,000
Retained earnings *(W3)*	<u>195,000</u>
	<u>395,000</u>

(W2) Sundry Net Assets

	€
Per original SoFP	265,000
Cash from disposal (Jnl. 1)	<u>115,000</u>
	<u>380,000</u>

(W3) Retained Earnings–Pulp

Per original SoFP	140,000
Profit on disposal (Jnl. 1)	47,500
Increase in investment fair value (Jnl. 2)	<u>7,500</u>
	<u>195,000</u>

CONSOLIDATED STATEMENT OF CHANGES IN EQUITY
for the year ended 31 August 2013

	Ordinary Shares €	Retained Earnings €	NCI €
Balance at 1 Sept 2012	200,000	104,000 *(W4)*	19,000 *(W5)*
Profit for the year		91,000	4,500
Disposal of Shred *(W1)*			(23,500)
Balance at 31 August 2013	<u>200,000</u>	<u>195,000</u>	<u>nil</u>

(W4) Retained earnings 1/9/2012 as before

Pulp (140,000 – 36,000)	104,000
Shred 75% × (16,000 – 10,000)	4,500
Goodwill impairment	<u>(4,500)</u>
	<u>104,000</u>

(W5) Non-controlling interest at 1/9/2012 as before

Shred at 1 September 2012

Ordinary shares	60,000	
Retained earnings (40 – 24)	<u>16,000</u>	
	76,000	× 25% <u>19,000</u>

Alternative (W5)

At acquisition date	17,500
Share of post-acq. of Shred	
25% × (16,000 – 10,000)	<u>1,500</u>
	<u>19,000</u>

Conclusion

This text has taken you on a step-by-step journey from basic principles to:
- preparing and presenting consolidated financial statements (SoFP and SPLOCI/ SoCIE) to include a subsidiary, an associate, a joint venture and a trade investment;
- accounting and calculating goodwill as well as valuing the component parts of the calculation;
- recognising and treating goodwill attributable to non-controlling interests;
- the treatment of a foreign operation in group financial statements;
- preparing and presenting consolidated statements of cash flows; and
- accounting for various levels of disposal of shares in a subsidiary.

'Consolidation' has tended to be a difficult area of accounting for students. We hope that this text has made your journey less daunting and that you will face examination of this topic with confidence.

SUMMARY

1. When a parent sells its entire holding in a subsidiary and loses control over that entity, the results of the former subsidiary should be included in the consolidated SPLOCI until the date on which control is lost. The profit/loss on sale will also be accounted for in the consolidated SPLOCI.
2. When a parent sells part of its holding in a subsidiary but does not lose control over that entity, the transaction should be treated as one between owners in their capacity as owners. No profit/loss is recognised in the consolidated SPLOCI.
3. A parent can sell part of its holding in a subsidiary which results in:
   (a) loss of control over the former subsidiary and
   (b) the status of the former subsidiary changing to an associate.

   If this event occurs during a reporting year, it will result in full consolidation being used in the consolidated SPLOCI up to the date of sale and equity accounting for the remainder of the year.
4. A parent can sell part of its holding in a subsidiary which results in:
   (a) loss of control over the former subsidiary and
   (b) the status of the former subsidiary changing to a trade/simple investment.

   If this event occurs during a reporting year it will result in full consolidation being used in the consolidated SPLOCI up to the date of sale. Any remaining investment after disposal would be accounted for under IFRS 9/IAS 39 and credit would be taken for dividends received/receivable.

QUESTIONS

Question 12.1

Port Ltd (Port) acquired 90% of the ordinary shares of Storm Ltd (Storm) on 1 April 2010. The reporting date for the group is 30 September annually.

Requirement For each of the following disposals of shares in Storm outline the accounting and related effects on the financial statements of the Port group for the year ended 30 September 2013:
(a) Port sells one-half of its holding in Storm on 30 April 2013;
(b) Port sells one-third of its holding in Storm on 31 July 2013;
(c) Port sells its entire holding in Storm on 30 September 2013;
(d) Port sells 90% of its holding in Storm on 31 August 2013.
None of the sales were recorded in the financial statements of Port.

Solution

(a) The first consequence of the disposal is that Port has **lost control** of Storm on 30 April 2013. The results of Storm must be fully consolidated until that date (seven months). The profit/loss on disposal of the subsidiary must be included in the consolidated SPLOCI for the reporting year. The NCI will also be entitled to their share of the profit of Storm to 30 April 2013. On 1 May 2013 the former subsidiary changes status to an associate. The results of Storm from 1 May 2013 to the reporting date 30 September will be accounted for using the equity method. In the statement of financial position as at 30 September 2013 Port will include its investment in Storm at a valuation which would be arrived at as follows:

Fair value of investment at 1 May 2013	€X
Plus	
45% of the profits of Storm 1 May 2013 to 30 September 2013	€X
	€X

(b) **There is no loss of control** over Storm as Port still holds a majority (60%) of the voting rights of Storm after the disposal. The disposal **is accounted for as an equity transaction** and no profit or loss is recorded in the consolidated statement of profit or loss and other comprehensive income for the year ended 30 September 2013. Storm is a subsidiary for the entire reporting year so all its results are fully consolidated. The non-controlling interest in the profits of Storm changes from 10% up to 31 July to 40% for the final two months.

(c) **There is loss of control** over Storm as Port has no interest in Storm after 30 September 2013. The profit or loss on disposal is recorded in the consolidated statement of profit or loss and other comprehensive income for the year ended 30 September 2013. The results of Storm must be fully consolidated for the entire reporting year as the shares were sold on 30 September 2013. The statement of financial position as at 30 September 2013 will comprise the net assets of Port only after adjusting for the sale of the investment. There will be no NCI at the reporting date.

(d) There is loss of control over Storm, as Port has only a 9% interest in Storm after 31 August 2013. The profit or loss on disposal is recorded in the consolidated statement of profit or loss and other comprehensive income for the year ended 30 September 2013. The consolidated statement of profit or loss and other comprehensive income for the year ended 30 September 2013 will include the fully consolidated results of Storm for 11 months. The remaining investment in Storm (9%) is revalued to fair value on 1 September 2013. The statement of financial position as at 30 September 2013 comprises:

 (i) the net assets of Port;
 (ii) the adjustment for the disposal of 81% of the shares in Storm;
 (iii) the remaining investment in Storm now at fair value.
 (iv) the remaining investment in Storm will be accounted for under IFRS 9/IAS 39.

Note: **Question 12.2** deals with a subsidiary which is disposed of at the end of a financial year. The solution consists of:
1. journal adjustments;
2. the T account method workings;
3. the columnar method workings; and
4. the consolidated SoFP, SPLOCI and SoCIE.

Question 12.2

The following are the draft financial statements of Tom Ltd and Harry Ltd for the year ended 31 August 2013:

STATEMENTS OF FINANCIAL POSITION
as at 31 August 2013

	Tom Ltd €000	Harry Ltd €000
Assets		
Non-current assets		
Property, plant and equipment	17, 240	6,380
Investment in Harry Ltd	2,400	–
	19,640	6,380
Current assets	4,670	2,800
Total assets	24,310	9,180
Equity and Liabilities		
Equity		
Ordinary shares €1	10,000	2,000
Retained earnings	10,110	4,660
Total equity	20,110	6,660
Current liabilities	4,200	2,520
Total equity and liabilities	24,310	9,180

STATEMENTS OF PROFIT OR LOSS
for the year ended 31 August 2013

	Tom Ltd €000	Harry Ltd €000
Revenue	9,340	5,200
Cost of sales	(2,300)	(1,300)
Gross profit	7,040	3,900
Operating expenses	(4,720)	(2,700)
Profit before tax	2,320	1,200
Income tax expense	(460)	(200)
Profit for the year	1,860	1,000

1. Tom Ltd acquired 1,200,000 of the ordinary shares of Harry Ltd on 1 December 2011 when the retained earnings of Harry Ltd were €1,800,000.
2. Tom Ltd sold 1,000,000 shares in Harry Ltd on 31 August 2013 for cash proceeds of €5,000,000. The sale has not been recorded by Tom Ltd. The fair value of the remaining investment in the subsidiary at the disposal date amounted to €420,000.
3. Non-controlling interests at the acquisition date are measured using the proportion of net assets method.

Requirement: Prepare for the Tom Ltd group for the year ended 31 August 2013:

(a) The consolidated statement of profit or loss;
(b) The consolidated statement of financial position:
(c) The consolidated statement of changes in equity.

Solution to Question 12.2

IFRS 10 states that, if a parent loses control over a subsidiary, the parent should:

- derecognise the assets (including any goodwill) and liabilities of the former subsidiary at the date when control is lost;
- derecognise the carrying amount of any non-controlling interests at the same date;
- recognise the fair value of any consideration received;
- recognise any investment retained in the former subsidiary at its fair value when control is lost;
- recognise the gain or loss associated with the loss of control attributable to the parent in profit or loss.

SOLUTION NOTES

1. Harry is a subsidiary for the full year, therefore, its results must be fully consolidated for 12 months.
2. The assets, liabilities and non-controlling interests of Harry must be derecognised at 31 August 2013.
3. Net assets (capital and reserves) of Harry at the disposal date per the question are €6,660,000.
4. Non-controlling interests in Harry at the disposal date are €6,660,000 × 40% = €2,664,000.

(W1) Goodwill on acquisition of Harry

	€000	€000
Investment in Harry		2,400
NCI at acquisition date 40% × (2,000 + 1,800)		1,520
		3,920
Net assets of Harry at acquisition date		
Ordinary shares	2,000	
Retained earnings	1,800	3,800
		120

(W2) Consolidated SPLOCI – Gain on disposal

	€000	€000
Sale proceeds		5,000
Fair value of remaining 10%		420
		5,420
Net assets at disposal date	6,660	
× 60%		(3,996)
Goodwill		(120)
Consolidated SPLOCI		1,304

Journal Entries

	€000	€000
1. Dr. Goodwill	2,400	
Cr. Investment in Harry		2,400
Investment transferred for goodwill calculation		
2. Dr. Goodwill	1,520	
Cr. NCI		1,520
NCI measurement at acquisition date		
3. Dr. Ordinary shares	2,000	
Cr. Goodwill		2,000
Ordinary shares of Harry at acquisition date		
4. Dr. Retained earnings Harry	1,800	
Cr. Goodwill		1,800
Retained earnings Harry at acquisition date		
5. Dr. Retained earnings Harry	2,860	
Cr. Retained earnings Tom (60%)		1,716
Cr. NCI (40%)		1,144
Post-acquisition retained earnings of Harry.		

Note:

	€000
Retained earnings Harry at reporting date	4,660
Retained earnings Harry at acquisition date	1,800
Post-acquisition	2,860

6. Dr. NCI (€6,660,000 × 40%)   2,664
    Dr. Current assets (cash proceeds)   5,000
    Dr. Investment in Harry (fair value)   420
    Dr. Current liabilities   2,520
    Cr. PPE   6,380
    Cr. Current assets   2,800
    Cr. Goodwill   120
    Cr. Retained earnings Tom (profit on disposal)   1,304

Disposal of shares in Harry

WORKINGS (T Account Method)

Property, Plant and Equipment

Debit		Credit	
T	17,240	Disposal (Jnl. 6)	6,380
H	6,380	SoFP	17,240
	23,620		23,620

Investment in Harry

Debit		Credit	
T	2,400	Goodwill (Jnl. 1)	2,400
Fair value (Jnl. 6)	420	SoFP	420
	2,820		2,820

Current Assets

Debit		Credit	
T	4,670	Disposal (Jnl. 6)	2,800
H	2,800	SoFP	9,670
Disposal-cash (Jnl. 6)	5,000		12,470
	12,470		

Ordinary Shares

Debit		Credit	
Goodwill (Jnl. 3)	2,000	T	10,000
SoFP	10,000	H	2,000
	12,000		12,000

Retained Earnings Tom

Debit		Credit	
		Tom at reporting date	10,110
		Post. acq. H (Jnl. 5)	1,716
SoFP	13,130	Disposal profit (Jnl. 6)	1,304
	13,130		13,130

Retained Earnings Harry

Debit		Credit	
Goodwill (Jnl. 4)	1,800	H at reporting date	4,660
Post-acq. Tom (Jnl. 5)	1,716		
Post.acq. NCI (Jnl. 5)	1,144		
	4,660		4,660

Current Liabilities

Debit		Credit	
Disposal (Jnl. 6)	2,520	T	4,200
SoFP	4,200	H	2,520
	6,720		6,720

Goodwill

Debit		Credit	
Investment in H (Jnl. 1)	2,400	Ord. shares H (Jnl. 3)	2,000
NCI (Jnl. 2)	1,520	Ret. earnings H (Jnl. 4)	1,800
		Disposal (Jnl. 6)	120
	3,920		3,920

Non-controlling Interests

Debit		Credit	
		Goodwill (Jnl. 2)	1,520
Disposal (Jnl. 6)	2,664	Post-acq. H (Jnl. 5)	1,144
	2,664		2,664

WORKINGS (Columnar Method)

	Tom €000	Harry €000	Adjustments €000	Consol. SoFP €000
Assets				
Non-current assets				
Property, plant and equipment	17,240	6,380	(6,380) (Jnl. 6)	17,240
Investment in Harry Ltd.	2,400	–	(2,400)420 (Jnl. 1,6)	420
Goodwill (W3)			120 (W1) (120) (Jnl. 6)	nil
Current assets	4,670	2,800	(2,800) (Jnl. 6)	9,670
			5,000 (Jnl. 6)	
Total assets	**24,310**	**9,180**	**(6,160)**	**27,330**
Equity and Liabilities				
Equity				
Ordinary shares €1	10,000	2,000	(2,000) (Jnl. 3)	10,000
Retained earnings (W4)	10,110	4,660	(1,640)	13,130

NCI (W5)			1,520 (Jnl. 2)	
			1,144 (Jnl. 5)	
			(2,664) (Jnl. 6)	nil
Current liabilities	4,200	2,520	(2,520) (Jnl. 6)	4,200
Total equity and liabilities	**24,310**	**9,180**	**(6,160)**	**27,330**

(W3) Goodwill

	€000	€000
At acquisition date *(W1)*		120
Disposal (Jnl. 6)		(120)
		Nil

(W4) Retained earnings

		€000
Tom at reporting date		10,110
Profit on disposal of Harry (Jnl. 6)		1,304
Harry at reporting date	4,660	
at acquisition date	(1,800)	
Post-acquisition	2,860	
Tom's share 60%		1,716
		13,130

(W5) NCI

	€000
Goodwill-measurement at acquisition date (Jnl. 1)	1,520
Share of Harry post-acq. ret. earnings (Jnl. 5)	1,144
Disposal (Jnl. 6)	(2,664)
	nil

Tom Limited

CONSOLIDATED STATEMENT OF FINANCIAL POSITION
as at 31 August 2013

Assets	€000
Non-current assets	
Property, plant and equipment	17,240
Investment in Harry Ltd	420
	17,660
Current assets	9,670
Total assets	**27,330**

Equity and Liabilities	
Equity	
Ordinary shares €1	10,000
Retained earnings	13,130
Total equity	23,130

Current liabilities   4,200
Total Equity and Liabilities   **27,330**

SPLOCI Workings

	Tom Ltd.	Harry Ltd.	Adjustments	Consol. SPLOCI
	€000	€000	€000	€000
Revenue	9,340	5,200		14,540
Cost of sales	(2,300)	(1,300)		(3,600)
Gross profit	7,040	3,900		10,940
Operating expenses	(4,720)	(2,700)		(7,420)
Profit on disposal of Harry			1,304	1,304
Profit before tax	2,320	1,200	1,304	4,824
Income tax expense	(460)	(200)		(660)
Profit for the year	1,860	1,000	1,304	4,164

Tom Limited

CONSOLIDATED STATEMENT OF PROFIT OR LOSS
for the year ended 31 August 2013

	€000
Revenue	14,540
Cost of sales	(3,600)
Gross profit	10,940
Operating expenses	(7,420)
Profit on disposal of Harry	1,304
Profit before tax	4,824
Income tax expense	(660)
Profit for the year	4,164
Profit for the year attributable to:	
Owners of the parent	3,764
Non-controlling interests (W6)	400
	4,164

(W6)
Profit after tax: Harry €1,000,000 × 40%

CONSOLIDATED STATEMENT OF CHANGES IN EQUITY
for the year ended 31 August 2013

	Ordinary Shares €000	Retained Earnings €000	NCI €000
At 1 September 2012	10,000	9,366 (W7)	2,264 (W8)
Profit for year		3,764	400
Disposal (Jnl. 6)			(2,664)
At 31 August 2013	10,000	13,130	nil

(W7) Retained earnings 1 September 2012

	€000
Tom (€10,110,000 – €1,860,000)	8,250
Harry 60% × (€4,660,000 – €1,000,000 – €1,800,000)	1,116
	9,366

(W8) NCI at 1 September 2012

	€000
Net assets of Harry at acquisition (Jnl. 2)	1,520
Share of post-acq. ret. earnings to 1 September 2012 40% × (€4,660,000 – €1,000,000 – €1,800,000)	744
	2,264

Appendix 1

Exam-style Questions and Solutions

The revision questions that follow are designed to revise the principles outlined in **Chapters 3–9** inclusive and to gain experience in answering questions from examination papers of professional accountancy institutes.

The following guidance applies to Questions A, B, C and D as well as to questions on the preparation and presentation of consolidated financial statements (or parts thereof) which appear on examination papers:

1. **Requirements** Check what are you being asked to do.
2. **Group structure** Set out clearly the group structure.
3. **Date of acquisition** Was the investment in the subsidiary, associate or joint venture acquired during the reporting year or previously? The answer to this has an effect on the solution.
4. **Complications** What are the 'complications' involved? The question could include such transactions as unrealised profit on inter-company trading, intra-group balances at the reporting date, revaluation of assets at the date of acquisition, the calculation of goodwill including goodwill attributable to the non-controlling interests and treatment of subsequent impairment, etc. **Treat each item as a mini-question and deal with the adjustments using journal entries.**
5. **Dates** Be aware of dates of the various transactions. Do they affect the reporting year or previous years or both?
6. **Associates and joint ventures** Note that both are accounted for, under IAS 28, using the equity method.

OUTLINE OF QUESTIONS

An outline of the questions is as follows:

Question A

Sumo Plc *(Based on Chartered Accountants Ireland, CAP 2, Summer 2010 Question 2)*

Requirement The preparation and presentation of a consolidated:
(a) Statement of financial position;
(b) Statement of changes in equity;
(c) Statement of profit or loss and other comprehensive income,

of a parent, a subsidiary and an associate with 'complications'.

Note: the retained earnings of the subsidiary are not given in the question, they must be calculated.

Question B

Yellow Ltd
Requirement The preparation and presentation of a consolidated:
(a) Statement of financial position,
(b) Statement of profit or loss and other comprehensive income, and
(c) Statement of changes in equity

involving a parent, an subsidiary and a joint venture.

There are many 'complications' in this question, many of which affect years prior to the reporting year. The 'complications' afford an opportunity to link their effect on the consolidated SoFP on one hand and the consolidated SPLOCI and/or SoCIE on the other. The question revises many of the principles covered in **Chapters 3–9**.

Question C

Clock Plc
(Based on Institute of Certified Public Accountants in Ireland (CPA), Professional 1 Stage 1 Corporate Reporting Examination (August 2010))
Requirement
(a) The calculation of goodwill on consolidation when valuing the non-controlling interests at fair value at the date of acquisition.
(b) The preparation and presentation of a statement of profit or loss and other comprehensive income for the Clock Plc group which involves numerous adjustments.

Question D

Patch Plc
Requirement The preparation and presentation of a consolidated:
(a) Statement of financial position;
(b) Statement of profit or loss and other comprehensive income;
(c) Statement of changes in equity;

of a parent and subsidiary **where the subsidiary is purchased with the intention of resale**.

Question A

(Based on Chartered Accountants Ireland, CAP 2 Summer 2010, Question 2. The reporting date has been changed in line with the remainder of the text.)

SUMO Plc ("SUMO"), an Irish company that prepares its financial statements to 31 December each year, is involved in the manufacture of kit cars. On 1 January 2012, SUMO purchased 800,000 of the €1 ordinary shares in COBRA Ltd ("COBRA") for cash, a company that specialises in the manufacture of chassis. The fair value of COBRA's net assets was the same as their book value except for plant and equipment that was understated by €400,000. COBRA has not reflected this in its financial statements at 31 December 2012.

On 1 July 2012, SUMO purchased 300,000 of the €1 ordinary shares in VIPER Ltd ("VIPER") for cash, a company that manufactures customised exhaust systems. On this date, the fair value of VIPER's net assets was the same as their book value.

STATEMENT OF PROFIT OR LOSS
for the year ended 31 December 2012

	SUMO €000	COBRA €000	VIPER €000
Revenue	15,000	2,500	1,000
Cost of sales	(9,000)	(1,250)	(350)
Gross profit	6,000	1,250	650
Operating expenses	(2,200)	(250)	(150)
Operating profit	3,800	1,000	500
Investment income	160	–	–
Profit before tax	3,960	1,000	500
Income tax expense	(1,200)	(300)	(120)
Profit after tax	2,760	700	380

STATEMENT OF FINANCIAL POSITION
as at 31 December 2012

	SUMO €000	COBRA €000	VIPER €000
ASSETS			
Non-current Assets			
Plant and equipment	12,000	2,500	2,000
Investment in COBRA	2,250	–	–
Investment in VIPER	750	–	–
Current Assets			
Inventory	1,800	250	100
Receivables	1,200	150	60
Bank and cash	200	50	30
	18,200	2,950	2,190
EQUITY AND LIABILITIES			
Equity Attributable to Owners			
Ordinary share capital €	10,000	1,000	1,000
Share premium	1,000	200	100
Retained earnings	5,200	1,460	980
Current Liabilities			
Trade payables	1,100	50	60
Dividends payable	500	200	–
Other payables	400	40	50
	18,200	2,950	2,190

Additional information:
1. In October 2012, COBRA sold goods to SUMO with an invoice value of €400,000 on which COBRA made a mark up of 25%. One half of these goods remained in SUMO's inventory at 31 December 2012. There was no other trading between SUMO, COBRA and VIPER during 2012.

2. None of the three companies has issued or cancelled shares since incorporation. Each of the companies depreciates plant and equipment on a straight-line basis at 25% per annum, with depreciation being reflected in operating expenses.
3. With respect to the measurement of non-controlling interests at the date of acquisition of COBRA, the proportionate share method equates to the fair value method. The directors of SUMO are confident that any goodwill arising on the acquisition of COBRA and the carrying value of the investment in VIPER have not been impaired at 31 December 2012.
4. The shareholders of SUMO and COBRA approved the proposed dividends in December 2012. These were paid in 2013.
5. The activities and profits of the three companies accrue evenly throughout the year.

Requirement Prepare the consolidated statements of profit or loss and changes in equity for the year ended 31 December 2012 of SUMO and the consolidated statement of financial position as at that date.

Question B

The following are the financial statements of Yellow Limited (Yellow), Brown Limited (Brown), and Amber Limited (Amber) for the year ended 31 July 2013:

STATEMENTS OF FINANCIAL POSITION
as at 31 July 2013

	Yellow €000	Brown €000	Amber €000
Assets			
Non-current assets			
Property, plant and equipment	24,290	23,030	39,440
Investment in Brown	13,970		
Investment in Amber	19,700		
	57,960	23,030	39,440
Current assets			
Inventories	4,160	2,650	2,020
Trade receivables	3,490	2,200	1,760
Bank	690	–	90
	8,340	4,850	3,870
Total assets	66,300	27,880	43,310
Equity and Liabilities			
Equity			
Ordinary share capital €1	30,000	10,000	18,000
Revaluation reserve	3,000	2,000	1,000
Retained earnings	23,170	6,180	21,220
Total equity	56,170	18,180	40,220

Non-current liabilities

10% debentures	5,000	3,000	–

Current liabilities

Trade payables	4,640	4,060	3,090
Bank overdraft	–	2,400	–
Taxation	490	240	–
	5,130	6,700	3,090
Total equity and liabilities	**66,300**	**27,880**	**43,310**

STATEMENTS OF PROFIT OR LOSS AND OTHER COMPREHENSIVE INCOME
for the year ended 31 july 2013

	Yellow	Brown	Amber
	€000	€000	€000
Revenue	44,760	33,200	21,900
Cost of sales	(33,570)	(24,900)	(16,420)
Gross profit	11,190	8,300	5,480
Distribution costs	(3,100)	(2,520)	(2,300)
Administrative expenses	(5,170)	(4,180)	(3,520)
Finance costs	(470)	(380)	(160)
Profit/Loss before taxation	2,450	1,220	(500)
Income tax expense	(490)	(240)	–
Profit/Loss for the year	1,960	980	(500)
Other Comprehensive Income			
Property revaluation surplus	2,000	1,000	1,000
Total comprehensive income for the year.	3,960	1,980	500

The following information is relevant:
1. Yellow purchased 90% of the ordinary shares of Brown on 1 August 2010 when Brown had the following reserves:

	€000
Revaluation reserve	1,000
Retained earnings	3,800

2. Yellow acquired 50% of the ordinary shares of Amber on 1 July 2012 when the retained earnings of Amber amounted to €21,000. Yellow Ltd and Sky Ltd have joint control of the arrangement and have rights to its net assets.
3. In arriving at the consideration for the shares in Brown, its property, plant and equipment was revalued by €500,000. No entries were made in the financial statements of Brown to reflect the revaluation. The average remaining useful life of the revalued assets was five years at 1 August 2010.

4. The fair value of the non-controlling interests in Brown at the date of acquisition was €1,730,000.
5. During the year under review Brown sold goods to Yellow to the value of €600,000 on which Brown made a gross profit of 25%. At the reporting date, Yellow had €200,000 of these goods in its inventory and still owed Brown €300,000.
6. On 1 August 2011, Brown sold an item of plant to Yellow for €360,000. The asset had cost €400,000 two years earlier. It is group policy to depreciate plant over 10 years on a straight line basis. Yellow depreciated the plant purchased from Brown over its remaining life of eight years.
7. Goodwill on acquisition of Brown was impaired as follows:
   y/e 31 July 2012   €40,000
   y/e 31 July 2013   €20,000
8. The carrying value of the investment in Amber was impaired by €10,000 during the reporting year.

Requirement Prepare the consolidated statements of:
(a) Financial position as at 31 July 2013;
(b) Profit or loss and other comprehensive income for the year ended 31 July 2013;
(c) Changes in equity for the year ended 31 July 2013.

Question C

(Based on Institute of Certified Public Accountants in Ireland, Autumn 2010. The reporting date has been changed in line with the remainder of the text.)

Clock Plc prepares its financial statements to 30 June each year. On 1 July 2012, Clock Plc purchased 75% of the issued share capital of Mouse Ltd by issuing two shares in Clock Plc for every four shares in Mouse Ltd. The market value of Clock Plc's shares at 1 July 2012 was €4 per share. At the date of acquisition, Mouse Ltd had 10 million €1 ordinary shares and retained earnings of €9 million.

On 1 January 2013, Clock Plc acquired 30% of the shares of Tick Ltd for €3 each. Tick Ltd's issued share capital at 1 January 2013 was four million €1 ordinary shares.

The draft Statements of Profit or Loss for the three companies for the year ended 30 June 2013 are as follows:

	Clock Plc €000	Mouse Ltd €000	Tick Ltd €000
Revenue	32,600	18,200	6,000
Cost of sales	(18,400)	(11,400)	(2,800)
Gross profit	14,200	6,800	3,200
Other income	3,100	1,800	200
Operating expenses	(6,400)	(2,100)	(1,400)
Operating profit	10,900	6,500	2,000
Finance costs	(1,800)	(1,400)	(600)
Profit before tax	9,100	5,100	1,400
Taxation	(2,100)	(1,800)	(300)
Profit for the year	7,000	3,300	1,100

Additional information:
1. The fair value of the net assets of Mouse Ltd at the date of acquisition was equal to their carrying value with the exception of land. The land had a fair value of €1million below its carrying value and this has not changed since the date of acquisition.
2. At 30 June 2013, the fair value of Mouse Ltd's specialist plant and equipment was €600,000 in excess of its carrying value. The remaining useful life of these assets is four years and Mouse Ltd has not reflected this fair value in its financial statements.
3. Sales by Clock Plc to Mouse Ltd, in the year to 30 June 2013, amounted to €3.2 million. Clock Plc made a profit of cost plus a third on all sales. Mouse Ltd's year-end inventory includes €1.2 million in relation to purchases from Clock Plc.
4. Included in Mouse Ltd's operating expenses is an amount of €500,000 in respect of management charges invoiced and included in revenue by Clock Plc.
5. Clock Plc's policy is to value the non-controlling interest at fair value at the date of acquisition. At the date of acquisition, the goodwill attributable to the non-controlling interest was €200,000.
6. All profits and losses are deemed to accrue evenly throughout the year.

Requirement
(a) Calculate the goodwill arising on the acquisition of Mouse Ltd.
(b) Prepare a consolidated Statement of Profit or Loss and Other Comprehensive Income for the Clock group for the year ended 30 June 2013.

Question D

Patch Plc (Patch) acquired 80% of the ordinary share capital of Stitch Ltd (Stitch) for €160,000 on 1 August 2012, with the intention of resale. There have been no changes in the issued share capital of Stitch since that date. The following balances are extracted from the books of the two companies at 31 July 2013:

	Patch €000	Stitch €000
Assets		
Non-current assets		
Property, plant and equipment	218	160
Investment in Stitch	160	–
	378	160
Current assets		
Inventories	111	65
Trade receivables	30	15
Cash	19	2
	160	82
Total assets	**538**	**242**
Equity and liabilities		
Equity		
Ordinary shares (€1)	300	100
Share premium	20	10
General reserve	68	10
Retained earnings	50	60
	438	180

Current Liabilities		
Trade payables	50	32
Taxation	50	30
	100	62
Total equity and liabilities	**538**	**242**

Additional information:

1. At 1 August 2012 the balances on the reserves of Stitch were as follows:

	€000
Share premium	10
General reserve	10
Retained profits	30

2. At the date of acquisition of Stitch the fair values of the net assets were the same as their carrying values with the exception of property, plant and equipment:

	€000
Carrying value	140
Fair value (less cost to sell)	120

3. At 31 July 2013 the carrying value of the inventory of Stitch exceeded the fair value (less cost to sell) by €10,000.

4. Statements of profit of loss year ended 31 July 2013

	Patch	Stitch
	€000	€000
Revenue	600	500
Cost of sales	(420)	(350)
Gross profit	180	150
Operating expenses	(90)	(80)
Profit before tax	90	70
Income tax expense	(60)	(40)
Profit for the year	30	30

5. Non-controlling interests are measured at acquisition date using the proportion of net assets method.

Requirement Prepare the consolidated statements of profit or loss and other comprehensive income and changes in equity for the year ended 31 July 2013 of Patch Plc and the consolidated statement of financial position as at that date.

SOLUTIONS

SOLUTION TO QUESTION A

SOLUTION NOTES

1. The subsidiary was acquired on the first day of the reporting year. When a subsidiary is acquired during the year under review, the retained earnings at the date of acquisition are rarely provided in the question, therefore, they must be calculated.

2. The investment in Viper (30%) was made during the year and its profits must be time-apportioned for inclusion in the consolidated SPLOCI.
3. The 'complications' will affect the reporting year only.
4. The opening consolidated retained earnings in the consolidated SoCIE will consist of Sumo only because, as already stated, the investments in the other two entities were made during the year under review.
5. The investment income in the SPLOCI of Sumo cannot be consolidated as it represents a dividend receivable from Cobra.

Group structure

	Cobra		**Viper**
Group 800/1,000	80%	300/1,000	30%
Non-controlling interests	20%		

(W1) Goodwill

	€000	€000
Investment in Cobra		2,250
NCI at acquisition date (2,560 × 20%)		512
		2,762
Net assets at date of acquisition		
Ordinary shares	1,000	
Share premium	200	
Revaluation surplus	400	
Retained earnings (Note 1)	960	2,560
SoFP		202

Note 1:

Retained earnings at 31/12/2012		1,460
Profit y/e 31/12/2012	700	
Proposed dividend	(200)	
Retained earnings y/e 31/12/2012		(500)
Retained earnings at 1/1/2012		960

JOURNAL ENTRIES SoFP (common to both methods)

	€000	€000
1. Dr. Goodwill	2,250	
Cr. Investment in Cobra		2,250
Transfer of investment for goodwill calculation		
2. Dr. Goodwill	512	
Cr. NCI		512
NCI measurement at acquisition date		
3. Dr. Ordinary shares	1,000	
Cr. Goodwill		1,000
Ordinary shares Cobra at acquisition date		

4. Dr. Share premium   200
    Cr. Goodwill   200
    Share premium Cobra at acquisition date
5. Dr. Retained earnings   960
    Cr. Goodwill   960
    Retained earnings Cobra at acquisition date
    (See (W1) Note1 above)
6. Dr. Plant and equipment   400
    Cr. Goodwill   400
    Revaluation surplus at acquisition date
7. Dr. Retained earnings (Cobra)   100
    Cr. Plant & equipment   100
    Depreciation on surplus for 1 year
8. Dr. Retained earnings (Cobra)   40
    Cr. Inventory   40
    Unrealised profit $400 \times \frac{1}{5} \times \frac{1}{2}$
9. Dr. Dividends payable   160
    Cr. Receivables   160
    Cancellation of intragroup dividend
10. Dr. Investment in Viper   57
    Cr. Retained earnings (Sumo)   57
    Share of post-acquisition profit of Viper
    $380 \times \frac{6}{12} \times 30\%$
11. Dr. Retained earnings Cobra (**Note 2**)   360
    Cr. Retained earnings Sumo (80%)   288
    Cr. NCI (20%)   72
    Post-acquisition retained earnings Cobra

Note 2:

Retained earnings 31/12/2012	1,460
Retained earnings at acquisition date **(Note 1)**	(960)
Post-acquisition	500
Less extra depreciation (Jnl. 7)	(100)
Less unrealised inventory profit (Jnl. 8)	(40)
Revised post-acquisition retained earnings	360

WORKINGS (T Account Method)

Plant and Equipment

S	12,000	Extra depreciation (Jnl. 7)	100
C	2,500		
Revaluation (Jnl. 6)	400	SoFP	14,800
	14,900		14,900

Investment in Cobra

S	2,250	Goodwill (Jnl. 1)	2,250

Investment in Viper

S	750		
Post-acq. ret. earning (Jnl. 10)	57	SoFP	807
	807		807

Inventories

S	1,800	Unrealised profit (Jnl. 8)	40
C	250	SoFP	2,010
	2,050		2,050

Receivables

S	1,200	Group dividend (Jnl. 9)	160
C	150	SoFP	1,190
	1,350		1,350

Bank and Cash

S	200		
C	50	SoFP	250
	250		250

Ordinary Shares

Goodwill (Jnl. 3)	1,000	S	10,000
SoFP	10,000	C	1,000
	11,000		11,000

Share Premium

Goodwill (Jnl. 4)	200	S	1,000
SoFP	1,000	C	200
	1,200		1,200

Retained Earnings Sumo

Debit		Credit	
		Sumo at reporting date	5,200
		Share of V's post-acq. retained earnings (Jnl. 10)	57
SoFP	5,545	Share of C's post-acq. retained earnings (Jnl. 11)	288
	5,545		5,545

Retained Earnings Cobra

Debit		Credit	
Goodwill (Jnl. 5)	960	Cobra at reporting date	1,460
Extra depreciation (Jnl. 7)	100		
Unrealised profit (Jnl. 8)	40		
Sumo – share of post-acq. (Jnl. 11)	288		
NCI – share of post-acq. ret. earns (Jnl. 11)	72		
	1,460		1,460

Trade Payables

		S	1,100
SoFP	1,150	C	50
	1,150		1,150

Dividends Payable

Intra group (Jnl. 9)	160	S	500
SoFP – non-controlling interest	40	C	200
SoFP – owners of parent	500		
	700		700

Other Payables

		S	400
SoFP	440	C	40
	440		440

Goodwill

Investment in C (Jnl. 1)	2,250	Ord. shares (Jnl. 3)	1,000
NCI (Jnl. 2)	512	Share premium (Jnl. 4)	200
		Retained earnings (Jnl. 5)	960
		Revaluation (Jnl. 6)	400
		SoFP – goodwill	202
	2,762		2,762

Non-controlling Interests

Debit		**Credit**	
		Goodwill (Jnl. 2)	512
		Share of C's post-acq. retained	
SoFP	584	earnings (Jnl. 11)	72
	584		584

WORKINGS (Columnar Method)

	Sumo	Cobra	Adjustments	Consol. SoFP
	€000	€000	€000	€000
Plant and equipment	12,000	2,500	400 (100) (Jnl. 6 and 7)	14,800
Investment in Cobra	2,250		(2,250) (Jnl. 1)	
Goodwill *(W1)*			202	202
Investment in Viper	750		57 (Jnl. 10)	807
Inventory	1,800	250	(40) (Jnl. 8)	2,010
Receivables	1,200	150	(160) (Jnl. 9)	1,190
Bank and cash	200	50		250
Total Assets	**18,200**	**2,950**	**(1,891)**	**19,259**
Ordinary shares	10,000	1,000	(1,000) (Jnl. 3)	10,000
Share premium *(W2)*	1,000	200	(200) (Jnl. 4)	1,000
Retained earnings *(W3)*	5,200	1,460	(1,115)	5,545
Non-controlling interests *(W4)*			584	584
Trade payables	1,100	50		1,150
Dividends payable	500	200	(160) (Jnl. 9)	540
Other payables	400	40		440
Total Equity and Liabilities	**18,200**	**2,950**	**(1,891)**	**19,259**

(W2)
Share premium

	€000	€000
Sumo at reporting date		1,000
Cobra at reporting date	200	
acquisition date	(200)	
post-acquisition	nil	
Group's share 80%		nil
SoFP		1,000

(W3)
Retained earnings

	€000	€000
Sumo at reporting date		5,200
Journal 10 – share of Viper post-acq. retained earnings		57
Cobra at reporting date	1,460	
Journal 7 – additional depreciation	(100)	
Journal 8 – unrealised inventory profit	(40)	
	1,320	
Cobra at acquisition date *(W1)* (Note 1)	(960)	
Post-acquisition	360	
Group's share 80%		288
SoFP		5,545

(W4)
NCI

	€000
Measurement at acquisition date (Jnl. 2)	512
Share of Cobra post-acquisition retained earnings (Jnl. 11)	72
SoFP	584

Sumo Plc
CONSOLIDATED STATEMENT OF FINANCIAL POSITION
as at 31 December 2012

	€000
Assets	
Non-current assets	
Plant and equipment	14,800
Goodwill	202
Investment in associate	807
	15,809
Current assets	
Inventory	2,010
Receivables	1,190
Bank and cash	250
	3,450
Total assets	**19,259**

Equity and liabilities

Equity

Ordinary share capital	10,000
Share premium	1,000
Retained earnings	5,545
Total shareholders' equity	16,545
Non-controlling interests	584
Total equity	17,129
Current liabilities	
Trade payables	1,150
Dividends payable	540
Other payables	440
	2,130
Total equity and liabilities	**19,259**

JOURNAL ENTRIES (SPLOCI/SoCIE)

Note: only the elements of the following journal entries which affect the SPLOCI and the SoCIE are taken into account in the preparation of the consolidated SPLOCI and the consolidated SoCIE.

		€000	€000
(a)	Dr. Operating expenses Cobra (SPLOCI – P/L)	100	
	Cr. PPE (SoFP)		100
	Additional depreciation on revaluation surplus		
(b)	Dr. Investment in Viper (SoFP)	57	
	Cr. SPLOCI – P/L		57
	Share of profit of associate for reporting year		
	(30% × €380,000 × 6/12)		
(c)	Dr. Group revenue (SPLOCI – P/L)	400	
	Cr. Group cost of sales (SPLOCI – P/L)		400
	Intragroup sales for reporting year		
(d)	Dr. Cost of sales: Cobra (SPLOCI – P/L)	40	
	Cr. Inventory (SoFP)		40
	Unrealised inventory profit in reporting year		

SPLOCI WORKINGS (Columnar Method)

	Sumo	Cobra	Adjustments		Consol. SPLOCI
	€000	€000	€000		€000
Revenue	15,000	2,500	(400)	(Jnl. c)	17,100
Cost of sales	(9,000)	(1,250)	400 (40)	(Jnl. c/d)	(9,890)
Gross profit	6,000	1,250	(40)		7,210
Operating expenses	(2,200)	(250)	(100)	(Jnl. a)	(2,550)
Share of profit of associate			57	(Jnl. b)	57
Profit before tax	3,800	1,000	(83)		4,717
Income tax expense	(1,200)	(300)			(1,500)
Profit for the year	2,600	700	(83)		3,217

Sumo Plc
CONSOLIDATED STATEMENT OF PROFIT OR LOSS
for the year ended 31 December 2012

	€000
Revenue	17,100
Cost of sales	(9,890)
Gross profit	7,210
Operating expenses	(2,550)
Share of profit of associate	57
Profit before tax	4,717
Income tax expense	(1,500)
Profit for the year	3,217

Profit for the year attributable to:

Owners of the parent	3,105
Non-controlling interests *(W5)*	112
	3,217

(W5) Non-controlling interests

	€000
Cobra – profit after tax	700
Additional depreciation (Jnl. a)	(100)
Unrealised profit (Jnl. d)	(40)
	560 × 20% = 112

Sumo Plc
CONSOLIDATED STATEMENT OF CHANGES IN EQUITY
for the year ended 31 December 2012

	Ord. Shares €000	Share Premium €000	Retained Earnings €000	NCI €000	Total €000
Balance at 1 January 2012	10,000	1,000	2,940 *(W6)*	–	13,940
Acquisitions				512	472
Proposed dividend			(500)	(40)	(500)
Profit for the year			3,105	112	3,217
Balance at 31 December 2012	10,000	1,000	5,545	584	17,129

(W6) Retained earnings 1/1/2012

	€000
Sumo (5,200 – 2,260)	2,940
Cobra	nil
Viper	nil
	2,940

Cobra and Viper cannot be included in the group retained earnings at the start of the year as both were acquired during the reporting year. There was no NCI balance at 1 January 2012.

Solution to Question B

SOLUTION NOTES

1. This question involves a parent, a subsidiary and a joint venture.
2. The subsidiary was acquired before the year under review, therefore, the reserves at the date of acquisition are given in the question.
3. The investment in the joint venture was made before the reporting year.
4. The question involves goodwill attributable to both the parent and the non-controlling interests and impairment thereof.
5. Some of the adjustments for the "complications" affect previous years and will therefore have to be taken into account when calculating both the group retained earnings and the non-controlling interests at the start of the year in the consolidated statement of changes in equity.

Group structure.   Brown   Amber
Group   90%   50%
NCI   10%

(W1) Goodwill

	€000	€000
Investment in Brown (Jnl. 1)		13,970
Fair value of non-controlling interest (Jnl. 2)		1,730
		15,700
Net assets Brown at acquisition date		
Ordinary shares (Jnl. 3)	10,000	
Revaluation surplus (Jnl. 4)	500	
Revaluation reserve (Jnl. 5)	1,000	
Retained earnings (Jnl. 6)	3,800	15,300
Goodwill on acquisition		400
Impairment (Jnl. 12)		(60)
SoFP		340

JOURNAL ENTRIES SoFP (common to both methods)

	€000	€000
1. Dr. Goodwill	13,970	
Cr. Investment in Brown		13,970
Transfer of investment for goodwill calculation		
2. Dr. Goodwill	1,730	
Cr. NCI		1,730
Fair value of NCI at acquisition date		
3. Dr. Ordinary shares	10,000	
Cr. Goodwill		10,000
Ordinary shares Brown at acquisition date		
4. Dr. PPE	500	
Cr. Goodwill		500
Revaluation surplus on PPE at acquisition date		
5. Dr. Revaluation reserve	1,000	
Cr. Goodwill		1,000
Revaluation reserve Brown at acquisition date		

6. Dr. Retained earnings Brown   3,800
      Cr. Goodwill   3,800
   Retained earnings Brown at acquisition date

7. Dr. Retained earnings Brown   300
      Cr. PPE   300
   Three years' additional depreciation on revaluation of PPE
       at acquisition date (500 × 3/5)

8. Dr. Retained earnings Brown   50
      Cr. Inventory   50
   Unrealised profit (200,000 × 25%)

9. Dr. Trade payables   300
      Cr. Trade receivables   300
   Cancellation of intragroup balance.

10. Dr. Retained earnings Brown   40
       Cr. PPE   40
    Unrealised profit on sale of PPE

	€000
Proceeds	*360*
Carrying value (400,000 × 80%)	*320*

11. Dr. PPE   10
       Cr. Retained earnings Yellow   10
    Write back of surplus depreciation

	€000
Depreciation by Yellow (360/8)	*45*
Depreciation on original cost (400/10)	*40*
	5
× 2 years	*10*

12. Dr. Retained earnings Yellow (90%)   54
       Dr. NCI (10%)   6
       Cr. Goodwill   60
    Cumulative impairment of goodwill

13. Dr. Retained earnings Yellow   10
       Cr. Investment in Amber   10
    Impairment of carrying value of investment.

14. Dr. Investment in Amber   610
       Cr. Revaluation reserve Yellow (50% × 1,000)   500
       Cr. Retained earnings Yellow 50% (21,220 – 21,000)   110
    Share of Amber post-acq. reval. reserve and retained earnings

15. Dr. Retained earnings Brown   1,990
       Cr. Retained earnings Yellow (90%)   1,791
       Cr. NCI (10%)   199
    Post-acquisition retained earnings of Brown

	€000
Retained earnings Brown at reporting date	*6,180*
Pre-acquisition (Jnl. 6)	*(3,800)*
	2,380
Additional depreciation (Jnl. 7)	*(300)*

Unrealised inventory profit (Jnl. 8)		*(50)*
Unrealised profit on PPE (Jnl. 10)		*(40)*
Adjusted post-acquisition		*1,990*

16. Dr. Revaluation reserve Brown   100
     Cr. NCI   100
     NCI share of post-acq. revaluation reserve 10% (2,000 – 1,000)

WORKINGS (T Account Method)

Property, plant and equipment

Debit		Credit	
Yellow	24,290	Additional depreciation (Jnl. 7)	300
Brown	23,030	Unrealised profit (Jnl. 10)	40
Reval. surplus (Jnl. 4)	500		
Surplus depr. (Jnl. 11)	10	SoFP	47,490
	47,830		47,830

Investment in Brown

Debit		Credit	
Yellow	13,970	Goodwill (Jnl. 1)	13,970

Investment in Amber

Debit		Credit	
Yellow	19,700	Impairment (Jnl. 13)	10
Share of post-acq. (Jnl. 14)	610	SoFP	20,300
	20,310		20,310

Inventories

Debit		Credit	
Yellow	4,160	Unrealised profit (Jnl. 8)	50
Brown	2,650	SoFP	6,760
	6,810		6,810

Trade Receivables

Debit		Credit	
Yellow	3,490	Intragroup (Jnl. 9)	300
Brown	2,200	SoFP	5,390
	5,690		5,690

Bank

Debit		Credit	
Yellow	690	SoFP	690

Ordinary Shares

Debit		Credit	
Goodwill (Jnl. 3)	10,000	Yellow	30,000
SoFP	30,000	Brown	10,000
	40,000		40,000

Revaluation Reserve

Debit		Credit	
Goodwill (Jnl. 5)	1,000	Yellow	3,000
NCI (Jnl. 16)	100	Brown	2,000
SoFP	4,400	Share of Amber post-acq. (Jnl. 14)	500
	5,500		5,500

Retained Earnings Yellow

Debit		Credit	
G/will impairment (Jnl. 12)	54	Yellow at reporting date	23,170
Impairment invest. in A (Jnl. 13)	10	Surplus depr. (Jnl. 11)	10
		Share of post-acq. A (Jnl. 14)	110
SoFP	25,017	Share of post acq. B (Jnl. 15)	1,791
	25,081		25,081

Retained Earnings Brown

Debit		Credit	
Goodwill (Jnl. 6)	3,800	Brown at reporting date	6,180
Extra depr. (Jnl. 7)	300		
Unrealised profit invent.(Jnl. 8)	50		
Unrealised profit PPE (Jnl. 10)	40		
Share of post-acq. Y (Jnl. 15)	1,791		
Share of post-acq. NCI (Jnl. 15)	199		
	6,180		6,180

Non-controlling Interests

Debit		Credit	
G/will impairment (Jnl. 12)	6	Goodwill (Jnl. 2)	1,730
		Post-acq. reval. reserve B (Jnl. 16)	100
SoFP	2,023	Post-acq. ret. earnings B (Jnl. 15)	199
	2,029		2,029

Debentures

Debit		Credit	
		Yellow	5,000
SoFP	8,000	Brown	3,000
	8,000		8,000

Trade Payables

Debit		Credit	
Intra group (Jnl. 9)	300	Yellow	4,640
SoFP	8,400	Brown	4,060
	8,700		8,700

Bank Overdraft

Debit		Credit	
SoFP	2,400	Brown	2,400

Taxation

Debit		Credit	
		Yellow	490
SoFP	730	Brown	240
	730		730

Goodwill

Debit		Credit	
Investment in B (Jnl. 1)	13,970	Ord. shares B (Jnl. 3)	10,000
NCI (Jnl. 2)	1,730	PPE revaluation B (Jnl. 4)	500
		Reval. reserve B (Jnl. 5)	1,000
		Retained earnings B (Jnl. 6)	3,800
		Goodwill impairment (Jnl. 12)	60
		SoFP	340
	15,700		15,700

WORKINGS (Columnar Method)

Assets	Yellow €000	Brown €000	Adjustments €000	Consol. SoFP €000
PPE (W2)	24,290	23,030	500; (300) (Jnl. 4/7) (40); 10 (Jnl. 10/11)	47,490
Goodwill (W1)			340	340
Investment in Brown	13,970		(13,970) (Jnl. 1)	–
Investment in Amber (W3)	19,700		(10); 610; (Jnl. 13/14)	20,300
Inventories	4,160	2,650	(50) (Jnl. 8)	6,760
Trade receivables	3,490	2,200	(300) (Jnl. 9)	5,390
Bank	690	–		690
Total assets	66,300	27,880	(13,210)	80,970
Equity and Liabilities				
Ordinary share capital	30,000	10,000	10,000) (Jnl. 3)	30,000
Revaluation reserve (W4)	3,000	2,000	(1,000); (100) (Jnl. 5/16) 500 (Jnl. 14)	4,400
Retained earnings (W5)	23,170	6,180	(4,333)	25,017
NCI (W6)			2,023	2,023
10% debentures	5,000	3,000		8,000
Trade payables	4,640	4,060	(300) (Jnl. 9)	8,400

Bank overdraft	–	2,400		2,400
Taxation	490	240		730
Total equity and liabilities	**66,300**	**27,880**	**(13,210)**	**80,970**

(W2) PPE

		€000
Yellow		24,290
Brown		23,030
Revaluation surplus at acquisition date	(Jnl. 4)	500
Additional depreciation on revaluation surplus	(Jnl. 7)	(300)
Unrealised profit on disposal to Yellow	(Jnl. 10)	(40)
Depreciation reduction on unrealised profit	(Jnl. 11)	10
SoFP		47,490

(W3) Investment in Amber

	€000
Yellow	19,700
Impairment of carrying value (Jnl. 13)	(10)
Share of post-acquisition revaluation reserve and profits (Jnl. 14)	610
SoFP	20,300

(W4) Revaluation reserve

	€000	€000
Yellow at reporting date		3,000
Share of Amber post-acquisition (Jnl. 14)		500
Brown at reporting date	2,000	
at acquisition date	(1,000)	
Post-acquisition	1,000	
Group's share 90%		900
SoFP		4,400

(W5) Retained earnings

	€000	€000
Yellow at reporting date		23,170
Surplus depreciation (Jnl. 11)		10
Share of Amber post-acquisition (Jnl. 14)		110
Goodwill impairment (Jnl. 12)		(54)
Impairment of investment in Amber (Jnl. 13)		(10)
Brown at reporting date	6,180	
at acquisition date	(3,800)	
	2,380	
Additional depreciation (Jnl. 7)	(300)	
Unrealised inventory profit (Jnl. 8)	(50)	
Unrealised profit on PPE (Jnl. 10)	(40)	
Adjusted post-acquisition	1,990	
Group's share 90% (Jnl. 15)		1,791
		25,017

(W6) NCI

	€000
Fair value at date of acquisition (Jnl. 2)	1,730
Goodwill impairment (Jnl. 12)	(6)
Share of Brown post-acquisition retained earnings (Jnl. 15)	199
Share of Brown post-acquisition revaluation reserve (Jnl. 16)	100
SoFP	2,023

JOURNAL ENTRIES (SPLOCI/SoCIE)

Note: only the elements of the following journal entries which affect the SPLOCI and the SoCIE are taken into account in the preparation of the consolidated SPLOCI and the consolidated SoCIE.

		€000	€000
(a)	Dr. SPLOCI – P/L	260	
	Cr. Investment in Amber (SoFP)		260
	Share of loss of joint venture for reporting year		

		€000
	Share of loss (€500,000 × 50%)	(250)
	Impairment of investment	(10)
		(260)

		€000	€000
(b)	Dr. Admin. expenses Brown (SPLOCI – P/L)	100	
	Cr. PPE (SoFP)		100
	Additional depreciation on revaluation surplus for the reporting year		
(c)	Dr. Group retained earnings 1/8/2012 (SoCIE)	180	
	Dr. NCI at 1/8/2012 (SoCIE)	20	
	Cr. PPE (SoFP)		200
	Additional depreciation for two years on revaluation surplus of PPE		
(d)	Dr. Group revenue (SPLOCI – P/L)	600	
	Cr. Group cost of sales (SPLOCI – P/L)		600
	Intragroup sales for the reporting year		
(e)	Dr. Cost of sales: Brown (SPLOCI – P/L)	50	
	Cr. Inventory (SoFP)		50
	Unrealised inventory profit		
(f)	Dr. Group retained earnings 1/8/2012 (SoCIE)	36	
	Dr. NCI at 1/8/2012 (SoCIE)	4	
	Cr. PPE (SoFP)		40
	Unrealised profit on sale of PPE to Yellow on 1/9/2011		
(g)	Dr. PPE (SoFP)	5	
	Cr. Admin. expenses: Yellow (SPLOCI – P/L)		5
	Reduction of depreciation for the reporting year on unrealised profit on sale of PPE		
(h)	Dr. PPE (SoFP)	5	
	Cr. Group retained earnings 1/8/2012 (SoCIE)		5
	Reduction of depreciation for the year ended 31/7/2012 on unrealised profit on sale of PPE		

(i)   Dr. SPLOCI – P/L   20
      Cr. Goodwill (SoFP)   20
      Current year's impairment of goodwill

(j)   Dr. Group retained earnings 1/8/2012 (SoCIE)   36
      Dr. NCI at 1/8/2012 (SoCIE)   4
      Cr. Goodwill (SoFP)   40
      Impairment of goodwill y/e 31/7/2012 attributed
      to group (90%) and non-controlling interests (10%)

(k)   Dr. PPE (SoFP)   3,000
      Dr. Investment in Amber   500
      Cr. SPLOCI – OCI   3,500
      Property revaluation surplus

Note: Yellow will be credited with €3,400,000 and non-controlling interest will be credited with €100,000 through total comprehensive income for the year.

WORKINGS – SPLOCI (Columnar Method)

	Yellow	Brown	Adjustments	Consol. SPLOCI
	€000	€000	€000	€000
Revenue *(W7)*	44,760	33,200	(600) (Jnl. d)	77,360
Cost of sales *(W8)*	(33,570)	(24,900)	600; (50) (Jnl. d/e)	(57,920)
Gross profit	11,190	8,300	(50)	19,440
Distribution costs	(3,100)	(2,520)		(5,620)
Administrative expenses *(W9)*	(5,170)	(4,180)	(100); 5 (Jnl. b/g)	(9,445)
Finance costs	(470)	(380)		(850)
Impairment of goodwill			(20) (Jnl. i)	(20)
Share of loss of Amber *(W10)*			(260) (Jnl. a)	(260)
Profit/Loss before taxation	2,450	1,220	(425)	3,245
Income tax expense	(490)	(240)		(730)
Profit/Loss for the year	1,960	980	(425)	2,515

(W7) Revenue

	€000
Yellow	44,760
Brown	33,200
Intragroup sales (Jnl. d)	(600)
	77,360

(W8) Cost of sales

	€000
Yellow	33,570
Brown	24,900
Intragroup (Jnl. d)	(600)
Unrealised inventory profit (Jnl. e)	50
	57,920

(W9) Administrative expenses.

	€000
Yellow	5,170
Brown	4,180
Current year's additional depreciation on revaluation surplus (Jnl. b)	100
Current year's depreciation reduction on sale of PPE (Jnl. g)	(5)
	9,445

(W10) Share of loss of Amber (joint venture)

	€000
Amber loss for the year (500 × 50%)	(250)
Current year's impairment of investment (Jnl. a)	(10)
	(260)

Yellow Limited
CONSOLIDATED STATEMENT OF PROFIT OR LOSS AND OTHER COMPREHENSIVE INCOME
for the year ended 31 July 2013

	€000
Revenue	77,360
Cost of sales	(57,920)
Gross profit	19,440
Distribution costs	(5,620)
Administrative expenses	(9,445)
Finance costs	(850)
Impairment of goodwill	(20)
Share of loss of joint venture	(260)
Profit before taxation	3,245
Income tax expense	(730)
Profit for the year	2,515
Other comprehensive income	
Property revaluation surplus *(W11)*	3,500
Total comprehensive income for the year	6,015

	€000
Profit for the year attributable to:	
Owners of the parent	2,434
Non-controlling interests *(W12)*	81
	2,515

	€000
Total comprehensive income for the year attributable to:	
Owners of the parent	5,834
Non-controlling interests *(W13)*	181
	6,015

(W11) Property revaluation surplus

	€000
Yellow	2,000
Brown 1,000 × 100%	1,000
Amber 1,000 × 50%	500
	3,500

(W12) NCI

	€000
Profit for the year Brown	980
Additional depreciation for current year (Jnl. b)	(100)
Unrealised inventory profit (Jnl. e)	(50)
	830
NCI share 10%	83
Share of current year's goodwill impairment (20 × 10%)	(2)
	81

(W13) NCI

	€000
As per (W2)	81
Share of Brown other comprehensive income (1,000 × 10%)	100
	181

STATEMENT OF CHANGES IN EQUITY
for the year ended 31 July 2013

	Ordinary Shares €000	Revaluation Reserve €000	Retained Earnings €000	NCI €000
At 1/8/2012	30,000	1,000 *(W14)*	22,583 *(W15)*	1,842 *(W16)*
TCI for the year		3,400	2,434	181
At 31/7/2013	30,000	4,400	25,017	2,023

(W14) Revaluation reserve 1/8/2012

	€000
Yellow (3,000 – 2,000)	1,000
Brown 90% (1,000 – 1,000)	nil
Amber	nil
	1,000

(W15) Retained earnings 1/8/2012

	€000
Yellow (23,170 – 1,960)	21,210
Impairment of goodwill y/e 31/7/2012 (40 × 90%) (Jnl. j)	(36)
Depreciation surplus y/e 31/7/2012 (Jnl. h)	5
Brown (6,180 – 980 – 3,800) × 90%	1,260
Additional depreciation (group's share) 200 × 90% (Jnl. c)	(180)
Unrealised profit on sale of PPE (group's share) 40 × 90% (Jnl. f)	(36)
Amber 50% (21,220 + 500 – 21,000)	360
	22,583

(W16) NCI at 1/8/2012

	€000	€000
Fair value at date of acquisition (Jnl. 2)		1,730
Retained earnings increase to 1/8/2012		
Retained earnings per question at 31/7/2013	6,180	
Less profit y/e 31/7/2013	(980)	
	5,200	
Less retained earnings at acquisition date	(3,800)	
Increase to 1/8/2012	1,400	
Additional depreciation (2 years) (Jnl. c)	(200)	
Unrealised profit on sale of PPE (Jnl. f)	(40)	
	1,160	
NCI share 10%		116
Share of goodwill impairment y/e 31/7/2012 (Jnl. j)		(4)
NCI at 1/8/2012		1,842

Yellow Limited
CONSOLIDATED STATEMENT OF FINANCIAL POSITION
as at 31 July 2013

	€000
Assets	
Non-current assets	
Property, plant and equipment	47,490
Goodwill	340
Investment in Amber	20,300
	68,130
Current assets	
Inventories	6,760
Trade receivables	5,390
Bank	690
	12,840
Total assets	**80,970**
Equity and Liabilities	
Equity	
Ordinary share capital	30,000
Revaluation reserve	4,400
Retained earnings	25,017
Total shareholders' equity	59,417
Non-controlling interests	2,023
Total equity	61,440
Non-current liabilities	
10% debentures	8,000
Current liabilities	
Trade payables	8,400
Bank overdraft	2,400
Taxation	730
	11,530
Total equity and liabilities	**80,970**

Solution to Question C

SOLUTION NOTES

1. Mouse Ltd is a 75% owned subsidiary of Clock Plc which was acquired on the opening day of the reporting year. The results of Mouse for the full year can be consolidated.
2. Tick Ltd is a 30% owned associate which was acquired halfway through the reporting year. The amount to be consolidated using the equity method is:
   Profit after tax €1,100,000 × $^6/_{12}$ × 30% = €165,000

3. Cost of investment in Mouse
   10,000,000 × $^2/_4$ × 75% × €4   = €15,000,000

(a) Goodwill

	€000	€000
Investment in Mouse		15,000
NCI at fair value (Note 1)		4,700
		19,700
Net assets Mouse at acquisition date		
Ordinary shares	10,000	
Retained earnings	9,000	
Decrease in value of land to fair value	(1,000)	
		18,000
SoFP		1,700

Note1

NCI proportion of Mouse net assets (18,000 × 25%)	4,500
Attributable goodwill per question	200
Fair value at the date of acquisition	4,700

Goodwill

Debit		Credit	
Investment in Mouse	15,000	Ord. shares Mouse	10,000
NCI at fair value (Note 1)	4,700	Ret. earnings Mouse	9,000
Decrease in land	1,000	SoFP	1,700
	20,700		20,700

(b) Adjustments for consolidated SPLOCI:
1. Land revaluation: no adjustment is necessary as land is not depreciated.
2. Other comprehensive income of €600,000 must be shown in the consolidated SPLOCI of which 25% (€150,000) is attributable to the non-controlling interests.
3. Reduce revenue and cost of sales by intragroup sales €3,200,000.
   Increase Clock's cost of sales by unrealised inventory profit €1,200,000 × $^1/_4$ = €300,000.
4. Reduce revenue (Clock) and operating expenses (Mouse) by management fees €500,000.

JOURNAL ENTRIES

Note: only the elements of the following journal entries which affect the SPLOCI and are taken into account in the preparation of the solution.

	€000	€000
1. Dr. PPE (SoFP)	600	
Cr. SPLOCI – OCI		600

Revaluation gain on PPE

Note: Clock will be credited with €450,000 and non-controlling interests will be credited with €150,000 through total comprehensive income for the year.

	€000	€000
2. Dr. Group revenue (SPLOCI – P/L)	3,200	
Cr. Group cost of sales (SPLOCI – P/L)		3,200

Intragroup sales for the reporting year

	€000	€000
3. Dr. Cost of sales: Clock (SPLOCI – P/L)	300	
Cr. Inventory (SoFP)		300

Unrealised inventory profit

	€000	€000
4. Dr. Revenue: Clock (SPLOCI – P/L)	500	
Cr. Operating expenses Mouse (SPLOCI – P/L)		500

Cancellation of intragroup management charges

	€000	€000
5. Dr. Investment in Tick (SoFP)	165	
Cr. SPLOCI – P/L		165

Share of profit of associate for the reporting year
(30% × €1,100,000 × 6/12)

CONSOLIDATED SPLOCI WORKINGS

	Clock €000	Mouse €000	Adjustments €000	Consol. SPLOCI €000
Revenue	32,600	18,200	(3,200) (500) (Jnl. 2/4)	47,100
Cost of sales	(18,400)	(11,400)	3,200 (300) (Jnl. 2/3)	(26,900)
Gross profit	14,200	6,800	(800)	20,200
Other income	3,100	1,800		4,900
Operating expenses	(6,400)	(2,100)	500 (Jnl. 4)	(8,000)
Finance costs	(1,800)	(1,400)		(3,200)
Share of profit of associate			165 (Jnl. 5)	165
Profit before tax	9,100	5,100	(135)	14,065
Income tax expense	(2,100)	(1,800)		(3,900)
Profit for the year	7,000	3,300	(135)	10,165

CONSOLIDATED STATEMENT OF PROFIT OR LOSS AND OTHER COMPREHENSIVE INCOME
for the year ended 30 June 2013

	€000
Revenue	47,100
Cost of sales	(26,900)

Gross profit	20,200
Other income	4,900
Operating expenses	(8,000)
Finance costs	(3,200)
Share of profit of associate	165
Profit before tax	14,065
Income tax expense	(3,900)
Profit for the year	10,165
Other comprehensive income	
Revaluation gain on property, plant and equipment	600
Total comprehensive income for the year	10,765

Profit for the year attributable to:	
Owners of the parent	9,340
Non-controlling interests *(W1)*	825
	10,165
Total comprehensive income for the year attributable to:	
Owners of the parent	9,790
Non-controlling interests *(W2)*	975
	10,765

(W1)

	€000	€000
Profit after tax Mouse	3,300 × 25%	825

(W2)

As per *(W1)*	825
Revaluation gain (600 × 25%)	150
	975

Solution to Question D

SOLUTION NOTES

When a subsidiary is acquired with the intention of resale, the consolidation procedures are the same as usual but the presentation in the consolidated financial statements is significantly different in accordance with IFRS 5 *Non-current Assets Held for Sale and Discontinued Operations* thus:
1. In the consolidated SPLOCI the results of the subsidiary are shown as a single line item as follows:
   Profit/Loss on discontinued operation   €X
2. In the consolidated SoFP the total assets and liabilities of the subsidiary are each reported as single line items as follows:
   Assets held for sale   €X
   Liabilities held for sale   (€X)

(W1) Goodwill

	€000	€000
Investment in Stitch		160
NCI at acquisition date (20% × 130)		26
		186

Net assets of Stitch at acquisition date.

Ordinary shares	100	
Share premium	10	
General reserve	10	
Retained earnings	30	
Decrease in value of PPE	(20)	130
SoFP		56

JOURNAL ENTRIES (common to both methods)

	€000	€000
1. Dr. Goodwill	160	
Cr. Investment in Stitch		160
Transfer of investment for goodwill calculation		
2. Dr. Goodwill	26	
Cr. NCI		26
NCI measurement at acquisition date		
3. Dr. Ordinary shares	100	
Cr. Goodwill		100
Ordinary shares Stitch at acquisition date		
4. Dr. Share premium	10	
Dr. General reserve	10	
Dr. Retained earnings	30	
Cr. Goodwill		50
Reserves of Stitch at acquisition date		
5. Dr. Goodwill	20	
Cr. PPE		20
Decrease in value of PPE at acquisition date		
6. Dr. Retained earnings Stitch	10	
Cr. Inventory		10
Decrease to fair value (less cost to sell) of inventory at reporting date		
7. Dr. Retained earnings Stitch (60 – 30 – 10 Jnl. 6)	20	
Cr. Retained earnings Patch (80%)		16
Cr. NCI (20%)		4
Post-acquisition retained earnings of Stitch		

WORKINGS (T Account Method)

Property, Plant and Equipment

P	218	Decrease in value (Jnl. 5)	20
S	160	SoFP	218
		SoFP held for sale	140
	378		378

Investment in Stitch

P	160	Goodwill (Jnl. 1)	160

Inventories

P	111	Decrease at year end (Jnl. 6)	10
S	65	SoFP	111
		SoFP held for sale	55
	176		176

Receivables

P	30	SoFP	30
S	15	SoFP held for sale	15
	45		45

Cash

P	19	SoFP	19
S	2	SoFP held for sale	2
	21		21

Ordinary Shares

Goodwill (Jnl. 3)	100	P	300
SoFP	300	S	100
	400		400

Share Premium

Goodwill (Jnl. 4)	10	P	20
SoFP	20	S	10
	30		30

General Reseves

Goodwill (Jnl. 4)	10	P	68
SoFP	68	S	10
	78		78

Retained Earnings Patch

Debit		Credit	
		Patch at reporting date	50
SoFP	66	Share of S post-acq. (Jnl. 7)	16
	66		66

Retained Earnings Stitch

Debit		Credit	
Goodwill (Jnl. 4)	30	Stitch at reporting date	60
Inventory reduction (Jnl. 6)	10		
Post-acquisition (Jnl. 7) Patch	16		
Post-acquisition (Jnl. 7) NCI	4		
	60		60

Goodwill

Debit		Credit	
Investment in S (Jnl. 1)	160	Ord. shares S (Jnl. 3)	100
NCI (Jnl. 2)	26	Sh. premium S (Jnl. 4)	10
PPE increase (Jnl. 5)	20	Gen. reserves S (Jnl. 4)	10
		Ret. earnings S (Jnl. 4)	30
		SoFP – held for sale	56
	206		206

Non-controlling Interests

Debit		Credit	
		Goodwill (Jnl. 2)	26
SoFP	30	Post-acq. ret. earns S (Jnl. 7)	4
	30		30

Payables

SoFP	50	P	50
SoFP held for sale	32	S	32
	82		82

Taxation

SoFP	50	P	50
SoFP held for sale	30	S	30
	80		80

WORKINGS (Columnar Method)

	Patch €000	Stitch €000	Adjustments €000	Consol. SoFP €000	Consol. SoFP Held for sale €000
PPE	218	160	(20) (Jnl. 5)	218	140
Investment in S	160		(160) (Jnl. 1)		
Goodwill *(W1)*			56		56
Inventories	111	65	(10) (Jnl. 6)	111	55
Receivables	30	15		30	15
Cash	19	2		19	2
Total assets	**538**	**242**	**(134)**	**378**	**268**
Ordinary shares	300	100	(100) (Jnl. 3)	300	
Share premium *(W2)*	20	10	(10) (Jnl. 4)	20	
General reserve *(W3)*	68	10	(10) (Jnl. 4)	68	
Retained earnings *(W4)*	50	60	(44)	66	
Non-controlling interests *(W4)*			30	30	
Payables	50	32		50	32
Taxation	50	30		50	30
Total equity and liabilities	**538**	**242**	**(134)**	**584**	**62**

(W2) Share premium

	€000	€000
Patch at reporting date		20
Stitch at reporting date	10	
at acquisition date	(10)	
post-acquisition	nil × 80%	nil
SoFP		20

(W3) General reserve

	€000	€000
Patch at reporting date		68
Stitch at reporting date	10	
at acquisition date	(10)	
post-acquisition	nil × 80%	nil
SoFP		68

(W4) Retained earnings

	€000	€000
Patch at reporting date		50
Stitch at reporting date	60	
Decrease in value of inventory (Jnl. 6)	(10)	
Adjusted balance at reporting date	50	
Stitch at acquisition date	(30)	
Post-acquisition	20	
Group's share 80%		16
SoFP		66

(W5) NCI

	€000
Measurement at acquisition date (Jnl. 2)	26
Share of post-acquisition of S (Jnl. 7)	4
SoFP	30

CONSOLIDATED STATEMENT OF FINANCIAL POSITION
as at 31 July 2013

Assets	€000
Non-Current Assets	
Property, plant and equipment	218
	218
Current Assets	
Inventory	111
Receivables	30
Cash	19
	160
Assets held for sale	268
Total assets	**646**

Equity and liabilities	
Equity	
Ordinary share capital	300
Share premium	20
General reserve	68

Retained earnings	66
Total shareholders' equity	454
Non-controlling interests	30
Total equity	484
Current liabilities	100
Liabilities held for sale	62
Total equity and liabilities	**646**

Note: in the consolidated SPLOCI:
- the profit after tax is derived from the income and expenses of Patch; and
- the profit on discontinued operation is based on the profit after tax of Stitch (30) less the write down (10) of the inventory from carrying value to fair value less cost to sell.

CONSOLIDATED STATEMENT OF PROFIT OR LOSS
for the year ended 31 July 2013

	€000
Revenue	600
Cost of sales	(420)
Gross profit	180
Operating expenses	(90)
Profit before tax	90
Income tax expense	(60)
Profit after tax	30
Profit on discontinued operation (30 – 10)	20
Profit for the year	50
Profit for the year attributable to	
Owners of the parent – from continuing operations	30
– from discontinued operations	16
Non-controlling interests – from continuing operations	–
– from discontinued operations	4
	50

CONSOLIDATED STATEMENT OF CHANGES IN EQUITY
for the year ended 31 July 2013

	Share Capital €000	Share Premium €000	General Reserve €000	Retained Earnings €000	NCI €000
Balance at 1 August 2012	300	20	68	20 (Note 1)	– (Note 2)
Acquisition					26
Profit for the year				46	4
Balance at 1 July 2013	300	20	68	66	30

Note 1: stitch was acquired during the reporting period, therefore there were no post-acquisition profits at 1 August 2012. Stitch cannot be included in the opening retained earnings.
Note 2: there was no NCI balance at 1 August 2012 as Stitch was acquired during the year under review.